FRITZ

FRITZ

Martin Shepard

SECOND CHANCE PRESS

Sagaponack, NY

First published in 1975 by Saturday Review Press

Library of Congress Catalog Card Number 80:50243
International Standard Book Numbers:
0-933256-14-0 (Cloth)
0-933256-15-9 (Paper)

SECOND CHANCE PRESS, INC.
Sagaponack, New York 11962

to Paul Frey

Acknowledgments

All quotations from Fritz Perls, unless otherwise noted, are taken from *In and Out the Garbage Pail* or *Gestalt Therapy Verbatim*, and are reprinted with permission of Real People Press.

I am grateful to the following people for having shared their experiences of Fritz with me. Without their help, this book could not have been written:

Lloyd Aleksandr, Julian Beck, John Brinley, Arthur Ceppos, Al Drucker, Paul Frey, Marty Fromm, Ren and Art Gold, Bernie Gunther, Ann Halprin, Ralph Hefferline, Elaine Kempner, Janet Lederman, Jane Levenberg, Abe Levitsky, Teddy Lyon, Judith Malina, Natalie Mann, Dwight McDonald, J. L. Moreno, Michael Murphy, Vince O'Connell, Laura Perls, Rae and Steve Perls, Dick Price, Diane Berghoff Reifler, Stella Resnick, Janie Rhyne, Ilana Rubenfeld, Gene and Juanita Sagan, Will Schutz, Bob Shapiro, Elliot Shapiro, Irma Lee Shepherd, Julian Silverman, Jim Simkin, John Stevens, Ed Taylor, Marjorie, Cathy, and Wilson Van Dusen, Alan Watts, and Sue Williamson.

Thanks, as well, are due to Grace Bechtold, Knox Burger, Craig Braun, Marc Jaffe, Bob Kriegel, and my wife, Judy, for their support, encouragement, and suggestions.

Contents

Prologue

My occupation is psychiatry and my formal training has in-cluded psychoanalysis. I had always assumed that analytic treatment was the last word in therapy: the point beyond which advancement was impossible. It was untenable to continue holding that belief after my training, however, when I began to witness the casualties of the "cure" as well as the successes. These casualties included therapists as well as patients—people who were capable of articula-ting intricate conceptualizations of their own and others' behavior, yet seemed pale imitations of human beings. Passion, drama, courage, wit, and audacity seemed lacking in healer and sufferer alike.

It was both a surprise and a delight to meet Fritz Perls in the winter of 1968 and to become familiar with his work. His approach (which was then untaught at the uni-versities, hospitals, or analytic training center I attended) toward curing people of their preoccupations was both brilliant and yet phenomenally simple, since it worked, primarily, by focusing attention on the present moment. When one can fully tune in to the here and now, the mind has no room to record yesterday's recriminations or tomor-row's potential travails. Moreover, Fritz dared to display emotions I had felt—feelings that seemed to be denied among many other professionals I trained with.

I saw Fritz demonstrate his Gestalt Therapy on a number of occasions before he died and witnessed the burgeoning interest in his work. The more I saw of him, the more fascination he held for me. I appreciated, among other things, his ability to laugh at life's adversities. He was, for example, tired and ill during the last full workshop that he ever gave. Nonetheless, he summoned up enough energy to be with those who occupied his "hot seat." After working with some idealistic young woman who entertained ideas of living happily-ever-after with her husband, he commented, dryly, that: "Life is a rose garden. The petals wilt and the thorns remain."

Intrigued with both the man and his formulations, I began—in the fall of 1972—to discover whatever I could about him. The task took a year and a half. I read all his published works and many of those that referred to him. I cross-indexed names, dates, and places. Finally, armed with a bulky tape recorder, I traveled about the country visiting people he had known and places he had been.

In New York, I saw his wife, Laura, and his elder sister, Grete. In New Jersey, I interviewed Ren, his daughter. There was a flight to Miami and the home of his former lover, Marty Fromm, followed by long distance phone calls to her in Mill Valley as she divided her Gestalt practice between Florida and California. I went to New Mexico to talk with his son, Steve, and then to California to speak with those who knew him at the height of his career. Finally, there was a journey to Chicago to visit some friends who were with him when he died.

Whatever historical shortcomings this biography has result from Fritz's personality plus the traumas of the Second World War. Although Fritz's professional transition from Freudian analyst (with its emphasis on childhood development) to the here and now Gestalt approach represented a slowly evolving process, in his personal life he rarely seemed to share past events with other people. Impressions of this continually changing man could only be gathered by speaking with people who knew him during particular time segments. But who was there to tell me about Fritz before he turned thirty-three?

His only surviving sister, Grete, suffered a stroke some years ago and was unable to present any coherent story of those early years. Other friends and family members were decimated by the Nazis. Fritz's school and university records were also unobtainable, another result of the holocaust. Nor have any of the psychoanalysts Fritz saw survived him.

The picture of these formative years that I present is thus based largely upon fragmentary recollections Fritz wrote about in *In and Out the Garbage Pail,* some few anecdotes he related to those I spoke with, and personal extrapolations and interpretations to fill in the gaps as best I could. My task became simpler after Fritz arrived in the United States.

I remember the late Alan Watts, the philosopher, recalling Fritz as being "quite a marvel. His presence made people in awe and yet there was this fundamentally twinkly attitude. Because he did something that the paternalistic tradition has never done. The paternalistic tradition in the Catholic Church, in the Jewish tradition, has always been somewhat antisexual. And Fritz was different. He was paternalistic, yes. Patriarchal, yes. But very sexy. And this I appreciated because it accorded with my own views.

"What I learned from Fritz was the courage to be me. I felt I had a brother. We saw things the same way. There are times when the most loving thing you could do for other people is to be honestly selfish and say what you want. Because if you don't do that you will deceive them by making promises to do things which you are not going to come through with. So if you say, quite frankly, 'Sorry. I can't be bothered with this. It's too much,' they are not deceived. And I think that's one of the most important things Fritz had to say. To be honestly selfish is sometimes much kinder than being formally loving."

That made sense to me, for Fritz, in many ways, felt like my spiritual brother as well. I could empathize with his bravery in being perpetually open to new approaches in both his life and his work. I, too, knew that—to use Fritz's words—"to die and be reborn is not easy."

I was struck, in my conversations about the man, by the contradictions within him, by the discrepancy between his message of *be here now* and his perpetual restlessness. I am particularly indebted to Julian Beck, the actor and director, for his comments, which eloquently addressed themselves to this issue.

"A visionary like Fritz," said Julian, "is always going to be discontent with the present. Because he's always going to be seeing beyond. That discontent or bitterness that you talk about his having at the end is because he was still yearning for something that was going to go beyond everything that he had yet experienced. And that comes out of a certain Divine Discontent. Which he had."

All told, I taped and talked and phoned and visited with over fifty people who encountered Fritz, and compiled over six hundred pages of typed interviews. What follows is, in large part, their story.

MS
September 1974

Man is timid and apologetic; he is no longer upright; he dares not say "I think," "I am," but quotes some saint or sage. He is ashamed before the blade of grass or the blowing rose. These roses under my window make no reference to former roses or to better ones; they are for what they are; they exist with God to-day. There is no time to them. There is simply the rose; it is perfect in every moment of its existence. Before a leaf-bud has burst, its whole life acts; in the full-blown flower there is no more; in the leafless root there is no less. Its nature is satisfied, and it satisfies nature, in all moments alike. But man postpones or remembers; he does not live in the present, but with reverted eye laments the past, or, heedless of the riches that surround him, stands on tiptoe to foresee the future. He cannot be happy and strong until he too lives with nature in the present, above time.

Ralph Waldo Emerson

FRITZ

1

The Finder of Gestalt

Friedrich Salomon Perls was admitted to the Weiss Memorial Hospital of Chicago on March 8, 1970. He was seventy-six years old at the time. His friends had asked that the news of his hospitalization not be given to the papers because they feared the place would be overrun by hippies, eager to pay respects to their psychological mentor. A police guard was put up so that no one would disturb him during his illness. But the grapevine, being what it was, the young and the hip would assemble and sit on the grass in front of the hospital until March 14, the day he died.

The only other person to have warranted police protection at Weiss Memorial was Sammy Davis, Jr. That an aged and gruff psychiatrist inspired a public loyalty similar to that accorded a nationally recognized song and dance man was quite impressive. Particularly for a man who rose, in his own words, "from an obscure lower-middle-class Jewish boy to a mediocre psychoanalyst to the possible creator of a 'new' method of treatment and the exponent of a viable philosophy which could do something for mankind."

Ten years earlier, "fed up with the whole psychiatric racket," doubting his own significance, and despairing over his lack of professional recognition, he dropped out for fifteen months and traveled about the world. Yet, by the time of his death, it was clear that Fritz Perls might have as significant an impact on psychotherapy as did another German Jew. For thirty years Fritz had radically challenged the assumptions and directions of Sigmund Freud and the psychoanalysts. And in his final years, many people began to listen. For the culture had begun to catch up with the man.

The long-haired, bearded, unwashed dropout could readily identify with him because Fritz had traveled the same road. When he arrived in New York in 1946, he was Central Casting's prototype of a European psychoanalyst—pin-striped suits, spats, a cane, and an occasional beret which sat upon a stern, trimly mustachioed face. By 1966, firmly established as a fixture at The Esalen Institute of Big Sur, California, Fritz had donned the uniform of the West Coast Mountain hippies. A roly-poly five foot nine inch chain-smoking bald-pated long hair, with a full-flowing beard, sparkling eyes, and a gruff no-nonsense voice, given to wearing jump suits, Cossack shirts, and beaded necklaces, he looked like a combination of Santa Claus, Rasputin, elf, primordial Father Earth, sage, guru, perhaps Jehovah himself. By his own description a "gypsy" and a seeker of new experiences, he had been through the drug scene, the Zen scene, and was still going strong within the sex scene.

Older intellectuals had much in common with him too, for Frederick (his anglicized first name) Perls, M.D., Ph.D., could hold his own with the best of them. He had the benefit (and the curse) of a classical German education. A lover of opera, of Mozart and Mahler, he could quote Heine and Rilke to his ladies and Goethe, Schopenhauer, and Nietzsche to his colleagues. During his lifetime he authored four books,* directed some theater, tried his hand at movie making, and debated with such esoteric

---

* *Ego, Hunger and Aggression, Gestalt Therapy, In and Out the Garbage Pail*, and *Gestalt Therapy Verbatim. The Gestalt Approach and Eyewitness to Therapy* was published posthumously.

luminaries as Baba Ram Dass and the Maharishi Mahesh Yogi.

His friends and acquaintances in the field of psychology included such classicists as Paul Schilder, Kurt Goldstein, and Kurt Lewin. Among the psychoanalysts he encountered and was affected by were Paul Federn, Helene Deutsch, Otto Fenichel, Karen Horney, Ernest Jones, Erich Fromm, Clara Thompson, and, above all, Wilhelm Reich. His theatrical contacts extended back to the great German directors Max Reinhardt and Fritz Lang, through writers Christopher Isherwood and James Agee, actors Julian Beck and Judith Malina, and dancer Ann Halprin. From the world of philosophy and ideas he had more than a passing acquaintance with Sigmund Friedlander, Jan Smuts, Paul Goodman, Alan Watts, and Michael Murphy.

Fritz's niche in history rests not on the shoulders of his friends, however, but upon his own tireless efforts to revolutionize the practice of psychotherapy. Often alone, often scorned, often ridiculed, he nonetheless persisted until his message was heard. Given to wisdom and wit, passion and paranoia, he injected a new vitality into psychology. He called his school *Gestalt,* and he preached it with the same sense of drama and paradox as he lived.

Fritz's basic message was *be here now* and *be truly yourself*. This he taught by example as well as in therapeutic sessions. Laura Perls, his estranged wife, once referred to him as half prophet and half bum. Fritz felt the description accurate and used it himself, proudly. The prophet in him was fond of leading his psychological workshops in a reading of his *Gestalt Prayer:*

> I do my thing, and you do your thing.
> I am not in this world to live up to your
>   expectations
> And you are not in this world to live up to
>   mine.
> You are you, and I am I,
> And if by chance we find each other, it's
>   beautiful.
> If not, it can't be helped.

Many people, from Esalen psychologist William Schutz to Laura, a fellow Gestalt therapist, have been quite critical of the Prayer.

"I'm disappointed that it's so influential," said Schutz. "I think it's had a negative effect as well as positive— a kind of 'Fuck you' attitude."

Laura finds herself "rather unhappy about it. Particularly the last sentence, for it abdicates all responsibility to work on anything."

Such charges have a certain validity. People do hear what they wish to hear and are prone to justify their actions by pointing to authoritative sources. If I wish to be rude and uncooperative, I can always claim that I am doing so because I am simply "doing my thing" and quote the Gestalt Prayer as others would the Bible. And certainly, Fritz did insist upon only doing what interested *him*.

Fritz was aware not only of his selfishness, but aware, as well, that the same trait exists in everyone. Admonitions to "stop being selfish" are usually little more than moralistically couched manipulations that have, at their heart, the message "satisfy *my*-self, not *your*-self." He would be the last person in the world to deny his self-indulgence. Indeed, he asserted it unapologetically: "I believe that I do what I do for myself," he wrote in his free-floating autobiography, *In and Out the Garbage Pail*, "for my own interest in solving problems, and most of all for my vanity."

A century ago, a Yankee from Boston expressed sentiments indistinguishable from the German Jew's Gestalt Prayer. "Trust thyself; every heart vibrates to that iron string," wrote Emerson, in his essay, *Self-Reliance*. "I will not hurt you and myself by hypocritical attentions. If you are true, but not in the same truth with me, cleave to your companions; I will seek my own."

Like Emerson, Fritz believed that the only thing that made sense, in the end, was to follow your own intuition and interests, as arbitrary or rough edged as society might judge them. It is only by following that path that you can appreciate your authentic self. Each man, in his own way, believed that the intuitive wisdom of the soul was the best instructor. "Trust your inner self," they both argued, "and not the culturally acquired inner doubter."

"I have often been called the founder of Gestalt Therapy," Fritz said. "That's crap. If you call me the finder or refinder of Gestalt Therapy, okay. For Gestalt is as ancient and old as the world itself."

Gestalt is a German word that implies "wholeness." It is akin, in many ways, to the Eastern concept of Tao. It recognizes that foreground and background form a complete whole and cannot be separated from one another without either losing their individual meanings or destroying the wholeness that was. Fish make no sense without oceans. Night is meaningless without day. Water may consist of two parts of hydrogen and one part of oxygen, but if you break it down for the purpose of analysis, you are left with two gases and nothing to drink. Gestalt, in this sense, is as old as the appreciation of the ancient Chinese symbol of Yin and Yang—where one shape defines the other, and both are required to complete the whole.

Fritz saw his new/"old" therapy as a natural outgrowth of his own philosophical existentialism. He was aware of the fact that life—indeed, all of existence—occurs in a perpetual present moment, that all things are transient and ever-changing, and that past and future are concepts that we think of in some *present* time.

He was cognizant of the fact that emotional suffering is related to the degree to which people are not sufficiently aware of what is occurring in the ever-present *Now;* that unmet needs and undischarged tensions cause stress and, in sufficient quantity, are responsible for mental illness. He recognized that some people live perpetually in the past, ruminating about "what I should have done . . . what I should have said," or blame history (their parents, friends, spouses, or society) for their lack of present-day fulfillment. Others miss out on life's riches by being future oriented—always preparing and daydreaming for a tomorrow that never occurs—like the donkey who walks toward a carrot that always remains dangling two feet in front of his head. Anxiety was similarly described by Fritz as "stage-fright," wherein an anxious, fearful person is speculating about some future challenge instead of savoring the moment.

In his work, Fritz tried to teach people what *is*, for he knew that without full awareness of ourselves, we cannot lead fulfilled lives. No person can attend to his wounds unless he is aware of his hurt. No man can discharge his tensions if he is oblivious of his anger. No woman can satisfy the needs of the flesh if she is unaware of her sexual appetites.

Fritz's *Gestalt Therapy* focused upon the never-ending moment to moment interaction between man and his environment. Whereas Freud, with his concept of *libidinous energy,* postulated that sex was the main motivating factor behind most of life's activities, Fritz simply assumed that the organism is always striving for homeostasis—seeking to take in things from the world that it needs in order to be in balance and seeking to discharge things when it is overloaded.

To appreciate the challenge such self-evident concepts posed to his psychoanalytic colleagues, one need only cite the remark of Maria Bonaparte, one of Freud's disciples, upon reading the manuscript of Fritz's first book, *Ego, Hunger and Aggression,* in 1940.

"If you don't believe in the libido theory anymore," she said, "you'd better hand in your resignation."

Gestalt thinking led Fritz to realize that there was more to existence than Freud's twin motivating forces of Eros (sex) and Thanatos (destructiveness, the anti-life force). As he wrote in *Ego, Hunger and Aggression:*

> Attempts have been made to enumerate and classify instincts. Any classification which does not consider the organismic balance, however, must needs be arbitrary, a product of the specific interest of the classifying scientist.

To be entirely exact, one has to recognize hundreds of instincts and to realize that instincts are not absolute, but relative, depending on the requirements of the respective organism.

Fritz referred to "incomplete Gestalts" instead of "instincts," need systems that required satisfaction. He also recognized that completing a Gestalt was no end in itself, but merely allowed the next Gestalt to emerge. Thus a thirsty man desires a drink before he wants a woman. And after his woman he feels driven to make an important telephone call that he has thought about all day.

For people to be in balance, to discharge tensions, to meet their needs requires, firstly, that they recognize their bodily yearnings. Too many of us, in the course of growing up, have lost touch with our own myriad impulses. We are taught, through our parents or our subculture, that certain urges make us unlovable. Yet the impulses don't go away. Instead, we develop tics to hide our aggression, ulcers to mask our competitiveness, indifference to disguise our longing for love, propriety to avoid our sexual lusts, or phobias to deny our desire for independence. Rather than recognize our needs and tensions as our own—the better to fulfill or discharge them—we have learned *how not to accept them.* What we do, instead, is project our needs onto others, attributing to them what we ourselves lack.

Thus, timid people who always fear verbal or physical attack have usually disowned part of their aggressiveness. The *other* person becomes the angry one and *not me.* The "he-man" who accuses gentler people of being "sissies" invariably denies his own softness and tenderness. The "professional" old maid who spies on young girls and their beaus and condemns their "immorality" disowns and projects onto others her own sexuality. As does the bully who beats up young men with long hair for being "faggots" after projecting his own untolerated homosexuality onto them.

Gestalt Therapy offered people a chance to recognize and accept their projections as their own feelings, so as to be able to fulfill themselves, discharge their tensions, and thus be ready for subsequent challenges and responses. Adopting some simple techniques from Psychodrama, Fritz had his patients play act at being those people or things that they complained about. In the process, they often came to appreciate that "I am you," expand their acceptance of self/other, and lead a richer and less troubled existence.

Like other existentialists, Fritz tried his best to minimize concepts and maximize phenomenology. He knew that concepts were nothing more than *interpretations* of events. Phenomenology, on the other hand, restricted itself to a *description* of things you could touch, feel, taste, see, or hear. "Lose your mind and come to your senses" was a phrase that he liked to use.

In his work, Fritz paid attention to the obvious, as a good phenomenologist might. He read the language of the body with an uncanny accuracy. He attended to the sound of your voice as much as to your words. If you said "I love you" in the same tone that you order cheesecake in a restaurant, he might confront you with that, have you play act your voice—describe yourself as your voice—so that you might recognize how bereft of feelings you were.

His therapy aimed at synthesis, not analysis. It was immediate and dealt with what was occurring in the *Here and Now*—not with events that had occurred in a distant childhood. It offered passion, drama, and confrontation in place of psychoanalytic detachment. It was a psychology of *experiences*, not *words*.

"If you write a book about Fritz," said Wilson Van Dusen, a West Coast phenomenologist who brought Fritz to California in 1959, "you must emphasize what things were like when he turned up on the scene. We were all imbued with psychoanalysis; we *must* get an extensive history of the person. We were all basically retrospective, strongly retrospective in both our analysis and therapies. We couldn't conceive of understanding a patient without an extensive history. And for a man just to walk into a room and describe people's behavior so accurately added a whole new dimension. This is where I considered Fritz very great. His incomparable capacity to observe. He could see all that he needed to see in the present. He often said, 'I'm only trying to see the obvious. You're sitting in this way and the implications of this are . . .' It was dealing right here on the surface, the skin, the obvious. Yet *all you needed to know was there.* The patient's history would only elaborate—repeat again—*what you are seeing now.*

"This was illuminating. At the time I was well into existential analysis. I was drifting in the general direction of the *Here and Now.* We had gobs of existential psychological theory from Binswanger, Minkowski, Heidegger. But here was a man who could put into practice a rather tortured theory. So naturally I studied and learned as much as I could from him."

Fritz was strongly committed to the idea that all external controls, "even *internalized* external control—'you should'—interfere with the healthy working of the organism." Freud called this internalized external control the Superego. Fritz referred to it more colloquially as the "Topdog."

"Many people," he wrote, "dedicate their lives to actualize a concept of what they *should* be like rather than to actualize *themselves.* This difference between *self*-actualizing and self-*image* actualizing is *very* important. Many people only live for their image."

One thing that can certainly be said about Fritz was that he did not live up to any conventional or predictable image. Whereas psychiatrists are expected to be kind and helpful listeners, Fritz was often curt and rude. Although notorious for being a tightwad, he could also turn unexpectedly generous. He felt that social conventions were "phony" and refused to abide by the rules of "niceties." Thus, while he could be charming when meeting someone who captured his attention, he could also turn you off with an icy "I never asked to be introduced to you" remark. He

refused to be predictable, refused to be pigeonholed, refused to be "in character," preferring to let the situation
govern his response:

> Once you have a *character*, you have developed a rigid sys-
> tem. Your behavior becomes petrified, predictable, and you
> lose your ability to cope freely with the world with all your
> resources. You are predetermined just to cope with events
> one way, namely, as your character prescribes it to be. So it
> seems a paradox when I say that the richest person, the most
> creative person, is a person who has *no* character.

Fritz's commitment to integrity, self-discovery, authenticity, and liberation through "doing your own thing"—doing what you want to do and stop topdogging yourself—
was matched by his commitment to living in the present.
Just as "shouldisms" were damned by him, so were
"aboutisms." He would not suffer listening to gossip nor
would he gossip *about* others. *When* he was with you, he
was with *you*. People who knew him in New York knew
little of his life in Europe or South Africa. Those who met
him in Florida or California knew nothing of his days in
New York.

For example, while Fritz lived with Wilson and Marjorie Van Dusen when he came to California in 1959, they
had children of their own running about the house. Yet
they never knew that Fritz had children. And many people, particularly women, were so taken with his "I-Thou"
encounter, that they fancied themselves as having a "special relationship with Fritz," not realizing that what was
special was not their relationship but, rather, Fritz's way of
relating to them in that eternal, timeless, *present* of his.

This fierce determination on his part to *BE* his message—to live what he preached (or preach what he
lived)—required both courage and conviction. In saying
what he felt and refusing to abide by convention, he
aroused the enmity of many former friends and fellow professionals. Thus, his attempt to be true to himself and
allow himself to act spontaneously required, along the

way, a discipline far harsher than any momentary observer would guess.

Judith Malina, who, with her husband, Julian Beck, are the cofounders of The Living Theater, offers this view: "He was a revolutionary in that he enacted in his own life's behavior what his furthest thinking and the furthest spirit of the times led him to. He enacted it fully and he gave himself over to it. He was as close to his own image of a total person as he could see it. He took all the risks—unafraid and unashamed and unabashed—and went very far, all the way in terms of what he would see as ideal for himself. And that's the most revolutionary thing one can do."

Through his way of life, his work with others, and his writings, Fritz continually encouraged the emotions to find satisfaction. He directed awareness to needs that haven't been met. Until he came along, the standard therapeutic position was one that favored *analysis* of attitudes as opposed to *acting* upon them. Many patients were cautioned, in the course of their analyses, not to make any major decisions affecting their lives until their treatment was over. Divorces, marriages, moves to other cities, changes of jobs, were either to be postponed indefinitely or acted upon only after lengthy discussions with the therapist. Pejorative diagnostic labels such as "acting-out" were applied to those patients who dared act upon their feelings without prior approval from their analysts.

The average analyst, acting somewhat like a Superparent, assumed an attitude of "Wait a minute. Before you go around satisfying these impulses, let's get a sense of what they mean and how acting upon them is going to affect things in your life right now and in the future. Your actions might be dangerous." Restated, the line is, "Stay in the path you're used to so far and don't yearn for completion of something that's open and waiting and unknown, because it might somehow harm you." Fritz, of course, denied that any psychotherapist had the gift of prophecy.

Crystal ball gazing might work for fortunetellers, but not for psychiatrists.

The standard precautionary approach did, though, justify the typical therapist's distrust of his own impulsiveness. The unfortunate fallout of such an attitude was that many patients never learned to have faith in their own intuition, their own uniqueness, and their own spontaneity. Most therapy was thus geared to promote temperance, caution, and an adjustment to the conventional way.

Fritz, with his simple insistence upon acting in accord with one's feelings, threw down the gauntlet to his more conventional colleagues. For taking his stand, saying his piece, and daring to live his own unique life, Fritz was treated with contempt by the traditionalists. Fond of teaching, he was never invited to teach his psychology at any of our prestigious institutions. Neither Columbia nor Yale extended him a faculty appointment. Nor would any of our leading psychiatric hospitals dare to let him work and instruct within their confines. The orthodox analysts and their neo-Freudian friends who ran such places considered Fritz to be a *bête noire*. He was alternately ignored, criticized as being "simplistic," or damned for his personal excesses—for his brazen sexuality, his slovenly ways, his arrogance and egomania.

But Fritz persisted in spite of the critics. Like Johnny Appleseed, he sowed the seeds of Gestalt Therapy across the United States and Canada. From New York to Detroit, Cleveland to Toronto, Miami to Columbus, Atlanta to Los Angeles, San Francisco, Chicago, Big Sur, and Vancouver, he saw, he taught, and he eventually conquered.

America in the forties and fifties was the land of logical positivism. We had licked the Great Depression, won the Second World War, and presumed that all human problems could be overcome by intelligent planning, good will, and technological progress. Psychoanalysis, whose influence in Europe was aborted by Hitler's legions, came into its own upon our shores. Its nineteenth-century mechanistic scientific precepts (postulating *root* instincts which then have a cause and effect result on all future development) permeated our universities and became the major influence upon clinical psychology.

In such a cultural sea, Fritz and Gestalt made odd-looking fish.

But by the mid 1960s, things had obviously changed. Vietnam and environmental pollution, violence and social unrest, revealed as a lie the proposition that principles, intelligence, and science might be mankind's salvation. An evening spent among New York's East Side intellectuals—all discussing their analyses, their Oedipal troubles, and their transferences—made it clear that Freud was not the final solution to the neurotic problem. There were countless numbers of people, by now, who had passed through the psychoanalytic mill, "understood" all the causes of their neuroses, and yet were just as neurotic as ever.

A great number of people had come of age exposed to existential concepts. They had grown up reading Sartre and Camus instead of Plato and the Classicists, Kerouac instead of Hawthorne, practicing mantras and meditation instead of matins. The simple *here and now* Gestalt approach no longer seemed simple-minded to a generation familiar with Zen and Tao and other ancient Eastern wisdoms. If the forties and fifties were concerned with being "cool," the sixties advocated "letting it all hang out." Fritz led a very open life and let his feelings "hang out" before others better than any other psychiatrist in history. And the paradox of the restless/calmly flowing, searching/knowledgeable person that Fritz Perls was made it easy for people to identify with him.

This, then, was Fritz Perls's legacy: more than any other man in his time, he helped change the direction of psychotherapy. He led many of us away from a preoccupation with the past to a concentration on the present, away from blaming parents to accepting responsibility for oneself, away from the narrow confines of the libido theory into the broad awareness of myriad numbers of needs, away from an *analysis* of one's condition and toward a *satisfaction of one's desires*. And he did this while struggling to break away from his own conditioning and into ever-greater authenticity.

2

Berlin: The Early Years

Fritz was born in a Jewish ghetto on the outskirts of Berlin on July 8, 1893, the third child of Amelia Rund and Nathan Perls. It was a uniquely interesting and challenging world that the infant discovered himself in.

It was a time of the Kaiser, of a Germany built upon respect for culture, education, authority, and discipline. It was a land of burghers and aristocrats with traditions of courtly manners, state service, public austerity, and personal dignity. The industrial revolution had not yet despoiled the landscape nor cluttered and gutted the cities. Craftsmanship was still admired in this insular, traditional society.

The roots of Fritz's "searchingness" and openmindedness arose in the very circumstances of his birth, for he and his family exemplified the "modern" German Jew. Such people wished to consider themselves German, but still observed limited religious customs. Unfortunately, neither German nor Jewish society would accept them.

In their attempts to break out of the narrow confines of the Jewish ghetto, they antagonized their more orthodox brethren who chose to remain. Often, these "modern" Jews felt uncomfortable with, ashamed of, and alienated from their own Jewishness, from the clanish rituals that tended to exclude the non-Hebraic world. Still, their attempts to enter the larger community of the German Aryan were equally ungratifying, as the same Jewish birthright made them unwelcome. Accepting of and acceptable to neither camp, these Jews were essentially rootless persons who would search for and remain open to new ideas, new people, and, hopefully, a more accepting and acceptable subculture in which to live.

Fritz, for example, has written about his father's involvement with the Freemasons, setting up lodges across Germany as any secular Christian might. What he never mentioned was that his father was also active in a Jewish cultural organization, the B'nai Brith, and performed functions for their lodges across the Fatherland as well.

It is possible that Nathan Perls, Fritz's father, was never as proud of his work among the Jews as he was of his functions in the nonsectarian world. Or, he may have kept it relatively secret from the rest of the family because of his sexual liaisons with the B'nai Brith ladies. If so, Fritz may simply not have known or if he did know was not impressed with this aspect of Nathan's activities, as opposed to being embarrassed by his father's "Jewishness."

But Fritz also was unclear about the label "Jew." Although he could joke, in later years, of being a Zen Judaist, he was also capable of denying his birthright, as he did, initially, with his first American publisher, Arthur Ceppos. Ceppos, who became close to Fritz in later years, recalls how astonished he was when he casually inquired whether Fritz was Jewish only to have Fritz deny it.

Amelia Rund Perls came from an orthodox Jewish family. An attractive daughter of a lower-middle-class tailor, she lacked much formal education. Nonetheless, she developed an interest in the world outside the ghetto because of her youthful passion for art, theater, and opera. In meeting and marrying Nathan Perls, she was to go further away from Jewish tradition, as Nathan was far ahead of Amelia on the path toward becoming "assimilated."

Nathan was an impressive figure of a man. A wine

salesman, he was witty, charming, entertaining, exceptionally handsome, and sported a magnificent beard. He was a popular companion for most men and irresistible to innumerable women. Amelia, when they first met, was no exception. Yet once married and after suffering through several of Nathan's affairs, his charm and appeal waned for her.

Marriage, in the late 1800s in Germany, whether for ghetto dwellers, "modern" Jews, or even Aryans, was a sacred institution. Separations were rare, divorces unheard of, and most disillusioned couples struggled through life, chained to one another, as best they could. Amelia and Nathan were no different, in this regard, from countless others. Already alienated from one another at the time of Fritz's birth, the gulf between them widened steadily for the rest of their lives.

Amelia had trouble delivering Fritz, so that his entry into the world required the assistance of a physician's forceps. In the earliest weeks of his life, he fell gravely ill with a near fatal bout of vomiting, diarrhea, and dehydration, the result of nursing problems that arose when Amelia developed a nipple infection. He recovered, however, with no apparent residual effects and, for his first nine years, thrived both physically and psychologically.

Else, his eldest sister, was three years old at the time of his birth. Legally blind (actually half blind) and particularly unattractive, she clung a great deal to her mother. Undoubtedly resenting the extra attention and partiality that Amelia, of necessity, offered Else and fearing, as they grew older, the possible burden of his filial obligation to eventually care and provide for her, Fritz never liked Else. He would eventually write, with great candor, that "when I heard of her death in a concentration camp, I did not mourn much."

He did enjoy and was close to Grete, his second sister, who was one and one-half years his senior. Grete, described by Fritz as a "tomboy, a wildcat with stubborn, curly hair," must have viewed him as a live doll—someone not only to play with but to play mother *toward*, just as her mother was involved in the extra special mothering of Else. Fritz's chief references to Grete in *Garbage Pail* concern those mothering qualities of affection through sustenance: how they loved one another and how Grete "was always sending me the most expensive and delicious European candies," or how she sent him some marzipan—one of his favorite treats. Also, during the decade Fritz lived in New York, Grete lived with him and Laura, where she cooked, served, and waited upon the family.

When Fritz was three, the Perls family moved from their Jewish neighborhood to the fashionable center of Berlin, occupying an apartment at Ansbacher Strasse 53. The city, in 1896, afforded more space for a growing child than it does today. The age of electricity had not yet dawned. Horse-drawn trolleys provided transportation, and small apartment houses, with courtyards and gardens, provided respect and opportunity for outdoor living.

Fritz called his childhood a happy one. There was the camaraderie that existed between himself and Grete as they romped and played through the city's streets. In the winter there was ice skating, and in the summertime, swimming. His early remembrances of school were happy ones, as were those of his mother's parents. "He is made from such stuff as gathers praise from God and Man," his grandparents would say, as young Fritz poured through the books in his grandfather's library. There were visits, with his mother, to the theater, the opera, and the art museums. An older neighbor boy, Theo Freiberg, would invite Fritz to take part in plays that were staged in the alcoves of their living rooms. There were Hebrew lessons in the temple, in preparation for his *bar mitzvah*, and the excitement of watching the first halting flights of the Wright brothers on the Tempelhof Field.

During these same years, while the family was achieving middle-class respectability and financial security, he became acutely aware of his parents' ever-increasing alienation from one another. Nathan, away from Berlin quite often, peddling Palestinian wines as "a *'Chief Repre-sentative'* of the Rothschild Company," when home was unavailable to his children. His attitude was that of an honored guest, who was to be waited upon and treated with respect. Amelia, hurt by his peccadillos and outraged by his stinginess with money, was apparently unwilling to pay him the homage he desired. Arguments would frequently lead to bitter fighting, with Nathan beating Amelia and cursing at her while she, in turn, yanked his impressive beard.

Fritz came to hate his father "and his pompous righ-teousness. . . . How much my attitude was influenced by my mother's hatred of him, how much she poisoned us children with it, I could not say." Beginning with young adulthood, he even began to doubt his paternity, suspect-ing that his actual father might be Herman Staub, an uncle, the pride of the family and Germany's leading legal authority. Whether this idea, first offered to him by psy-choanalyst Wilhelm Reich, reflected an actuality, appealed to Fritz's vanity, or represented his dismissal of Nathan's person, it remained an open question for Fritz until his death and resisted all his attempts to answer it.

The origins of his rebelliousness can be traced to his being conceived by parents who did not love one another and by a father who was stern, autocratic, and most uncar-ing, a man who frequently referred to young Friedrich as a *stück scheisse*—"a piece of shit." But his father was also away a lot, selling merchandise in the provinces. This gave his son plenty of opportunity to express his dissatis-factions toward Nathan free from discipline—dissatisfac-tions that mirrored those of his mother, who tacitly ac-cepted and very likely encouraged Fritz's growing contentiousness.

Fritz's parents began to think of him as "bad" at age ten after he broke into his father's secret room (an incredi-bly messy place where Nathan secreted his Freemason material), stole a gold coin that was being saved for Else, and spent it on stamps for a Christian boy whose friendship he hoped to buy. After this "crime" he ran away from home for several days in an unsuccessful attempt to avoid punishment. On returning he was shunned for his "terrible" conduct.

The conditions of his adolescence insured his belligerence. "I am a very bad boy and cause my parents plenty of trouble," he wrote concerning his thirteenth year. Rebelling against the rigid discipline and anti-Semitism of the hated *Mommsen gymnasium*, as well as the rote memory work it required, Fritz, who had graduated from elementary school at the top of his class, became unmanageable. He was tolerated at the gymnasium for three years, until he was finally expelled for failing grades. The same youth who had been eager to please his parents was now untameable.

Amelia, believing that her ambitions for her son would never be realized, was driven to great despair. Fritz would steal from her purse, fail to prepare his school work, truant, and, in terror of his parents' scoldings, intercept the school's notification of his poor work and forge his parents' signatures on these notices. He was, of course, caught at this.

The carpet beaters that an exasperated mother came to use on him broke, rather than breaking him. He cut the thongs of her cat-o-seven tails. Resenting her punishments and taking pleasure "in my bad years, playing and imagining myself Mephistopheles," he once ran from her wrath, "locked the door, smashed the glass window of that door and made faces at her, enjoying her impotence to get at me."

After his expulsion from school, Fritz worked as an apprentice for a soft goods merchant. His unruliness resulted in his dismissal from that job also. Another dropout from the *Mommsen gymnasium* was Ferdinand Knopf, a close friend, who initiated Fritz into the rites of sex. Years earlier, capable of erections but not quite old enough to achieve orgasms, the boys would sit about and simultaneously masturbate to Ferdinand's stories of his elder sister's escapades. Not long afterward, at age thirteen, Ferdinand, with the aid of candy bars, induced a prostitute to accompany them to Greenforest, a wooded area away from the city. When Fritz's turn came, the girl, impatient with his tardiness in reaching orgasm, pushed him away. When Fritz caught Ferdinand looking at him, he felt betrayed, turning his first sexual experience into a humiliating one.

Fritz's rebelliousness extended to his religion as well. Although Nathan might have felt his Jewishness to be progressive, to Fritz it represented hypocrisy. He saw his family's attendance at temple on High Holidays not as a desire to preserve some ancient and cherished tradition, but as an undignified insurance policy lest there was some vengeful God lurking about. He declared himself an atheist and remained one until the end.

By age fourteen, Ferdinand found another school for them to enroll in, the *Askanische gymnasium*. Quite liberal in outlook, the school employed teachers who were more concerned with children than programs. Fritz came to love quite a few of these people, who accepted his independent ways, welcomed and supported his burgeoning interest in the theater, and offered him the positive feedback he had been so sorely lacking.

From childhood on, the theater, theatricality, and dramatic tension held much fascination for Fritz. The shows staged for parents in the living room during prepubescent years were not abandoned with the coming of adolescence. Instead, Fritz trouped along to neighboring communities as part of a "company" that his older friend, Theo, directed. By mid-adolescence, Fritz began to serve as an extra at the Royal Theater. While only a silent member of a milling crowd or chorus, he nonetheless relished the costumes, the glitter, and the chance to be onstage. So enchanted was he with his walk-ons that he willingly refused the half-mark (twelve and a half cent) salary that such "extras" were offered.

By his late adolescence, he discovered the fabled director and teacher Max Reinhardt. "The first creative genius I ever met," Reinhardt was to make a lasting impression upon his young student through his mastery of nuance, his use of dramatic silences, and for creating moving images. Reinhardt, a harsh disciplinarian, insisted that his actors abandon the stagey bravura style and project pain or laughter that was free of the melodramatic clichés then in vogue. Fritz, admiring the director's passion, his dedication and commitment to his vision, and his artistry, spent many hours a week at the *Deutsche Theater* studying and working for him.

Words, for Reinhardt, had to be consonant with gesture and action. He was alert to subtlety, to the music in voices, and was quick to point out tone or motion that didn't ring true. Painted props and other artifices were sacrificed for an interactional reality that stressed building a tension between the characters and between the actors and the audience.

Although admittedly not much of an actor himself, Fritz was undeniably impressed with the director's role. His own great genius in being able to realize and read the importance of body language stemmed from this early apprenticeship with Reinhardt.

No longer dipping into his mother's purse, he earned enough money from his evening performances to not only pay for acting lessons but to purchase a motorbike. He fell in love with Lotte Cielinsky, a fellow thespian who beamed when she saw Fritz backstage, costumed as a French nobleman. Learning from compassionate schoolteachers during the day and Max Reinhardt at night, Fritz redeemed himself scholastically. His improvement at school and positive theatrical involvement served to bring Fritz and his mother closer to one another, although the distance between his father and himself remained.

In his sixteenth year, the family moved from Ansbacher Strasse. Fritz was able to continue attending his gymnasium, however, and upon graduation he entered the University of Berlin and began the study of medicine. At the ripe old age of twenty-one, he found his studies interrupted by the First World War.

If this is all we know of Fritz's early years, what are we to make of it? What light might it shed upon his later development?

Fritz's *Gestalt Therapy* would come to focus on the present moment and avoid the psychoanalyst's intrigue with early history. It is possible that Fritz's disinterest in the past was related to his not wanting to rekindle many painful memories of childhood. His constant hunger for affirmation may have stemmed from his early feeding problems at his mother's breast, from his getting less "nourishment" than his eldest sister, and from his father's denigrations of him. "I am sure," he wrote, "that most of my showing off is overcompensation . . . for my unsureness, . . . to hypnotize you into the belief that I am something extra special."

Fritz as an adult was always sexually preoccupied, having a "compulsion to look at female genitals, to touch them, to manipulate them." One might attribute this to an identification with a lecherous father, to an unsettling initial sexual experience, and to his doubts concerning his paternity—doubts that left an abiding curiosity regarding the twin mysteries of conception and birth.

Throughout his life Fritz had a penchant for the short-term relationship as opposed to more sustained and longer-term involvements. This could have sprung from his lack of belief in himself and his need to prove himself, again and again, to countless others. His never experiencing a trusting, loving, enduring relationship with any woman might have resulted, as well, from his fear and mistrust of females, beginning with a mother who punished him with whips and carpet beaters.

There is, finally, the fact of Fritz's belligerent outspokenness. It emerged as a clear response to the hypocrisies that existed at home, against the rejection of an unloving father, and as a challenge to the authoritarianism he encountered both at home and in school.

And yet, was Fritz's background so very different from that of many others? Was his mother any more ambitious for her son than most? Was corporeal punishment uncommon at that time? Was his parents' unhappy marriage so peculiarly unique? Was it unusual, in Germany, to have an authoritarian, remote father? Or a father who had numerous affairs? Did Fritz see any more hypocrisy in his own home than any other intelligent youngsters might see in theirs? I doubt that any of these questions can be answered affirmatively.

Certainly, the tree grows as the twig is bent. The environment of childhood of necessity helps shape and influence a man's later life. Yet it is never clear *why* we are affected by certain things. Psychological explanations, be they glib or profound, often miss the mark. Some children, raised in adversity, develop into loving and affectionate people. Others—even siblings raised under similar circumstances—become aloof, cruel, or heartless adults. To state, as some interpreters would, that one child imprinted the parents' attitudes and the other rebelled against them might be an accurate *description*. Still, such descriptions *explain* nothing, for they are not predictive. The fact of the adult's attitude might just as well speak for itself.

Part of the desire for *historical* explanations stems from our having grown up in the age of Freud. It is, though, just as likely that the reason for Fritz's special development lies hidden, forever, within the chemistry of his genes, or, perhaps, in the position of the stars at the time of his birth. In 1968, while working on *Garbage Pail*, he opened an astrology book, looked up his sign—Cancer—and read: "The moon gives desire to touch, to collect, it encourages curiosity and affects emotions strongly. It indicates ability to draw people toward you."

"How amazingly that fits," he wrote. "Add a 'strong

stubborn intellect' and you have covered much of my identity. Astrology, another mystery."

To best understand Fritz requires that we dispense with the explanations offered by analysts and mystics alike. Pure description of what occurred is sufficient. Such phenomenology is not only closer to what Fritz taught, but is more attuned to late-twentieth-century science. If we simply follow events, Fritz's life and development make sense. What we then see occurring is a natural and logical unfolding of given traits within a given context.

3

From the Kaiser to the Führer

When World War I erupted, Fritz was studying medicine. Becoming a physician seemed a reasonable enough occupation considering his gifted interest in mathematics and the sciences and family pressures to choose a profession that afforded a decent livelihood. Although the theater remained his first love, it was clearly not a suitable occupation for a middle-class Jewish youth seeking to make his way in the world.

Fritz had no taste for killing. His army physical had already classified him as "fit for landstorm," which was even below "fit for reserve" status, due to a bad stoop and an elongated heart which resulted in a lack of stamina. Yet, with the general mobilization, he chose, in 1915, to volunteer for Red Cross work. Most of the time he remained in Berlin and continued his studies.

On one occasion he was sent to Mons, on the Belgian border, and was assigned to pass out coffee and refreshments to the trainloads of wounded returning from the front. He was shocked and dismayed to find that the wounded Germans would not let him comfort the wounded English. After four weeks there, bored and disheartened, he left his post without permission, returning to Berlin and his studies.

In 1916, with the front lines frozen, both Germans and Allies were being slaughtered by the tens of thousands. As replacements were needed for front line troops, standards for fitness declined. Fritz and his long-time friend, Ferdinand Knopf, decided to enlist in the army before they would be called up. Ferdinand enlisted in the supply brigade. Fritz chose the *Luftschiffer* batallion, whose work with Zeppelins played a minor part in the war.

His survival was more a matter of luck than wise choice. Being a medical student, he was made a medic and was shortly transferred to the Thirty-sixth Pioneer Battalion, a unit trained for gas attacks. He was appalled by the lead truncheons carried by some of the soldiers— volunteer "specialists" whose job it was to enter opposing trenches and club gassed Englishmen to death.

Fritz received an exceptionally strong dose of anti-Semitism during the war. Not considering himself Jewish by virtue of religious belief, yet considered that by the officers he served under, he often wondered who his enemies were—the English Tommies he was fighting against or his countrymen who gave him more hazardous assignments in the hope, perhaps, of having one less Hebe around. He was to describe those years as the hardest period of his life. He witnessed death and destruction on a colossal scale and found himself, at times, anguished by having so many injured to attend to that he did not know where to turn or who to choose to help.

Fritz spent nine months in the trenches before his first furlough. At the front, he was wounded, suffered lung damage from being gassed, and on a third occasion was hospitalized due to the high fever of influenza brought on by the cold and the filth of living in the trenches.

He narrowly escaped death one day in Flanders when his orders were changed from staying with the medical officer in the third trench to joining an attack group in the more dangerous front line. At three in the morning the gas attack was made. For two hours his company endured a barrage of British fire. It was then that he received his wound, when an exploding shell fragment caught him in the middle of his forehead. On returning to the lines, he discovered that the third trench took a direct hit, killing the doctor in charge and both medics.

Perhaps his grimmest experience occurred when the wind shifted during one gas attack. Many of the gas masks his compatriots used failed. Equipped with only four small oxygen tanks and with soldiers clinging to him and pleading for air, he had to rip the tanks away again and again from one man in order to offer air to another. He wrote, in *In and Out the Garbage Pail*, of a powerful temptation to tear off his own mask and surrender to the inevitable agony.

Once, on furlough to Berlin, he bought a ticket at The Royal Opera House to see *Figaro*. The contrast between the sufferings in the trenches and the beauty and elegance on stage affected him so greatly that he ran from the theater before the performance ended and broke into heart-wrenching tears.

Numbness was one result of his life as a soldier. He underwent periods of great detachment, depersonalization, and for years lost the capacity for inner imagery and fantasy. He went about his tasks as if in a trance, without apparent concern for his own survival. In 1917, he calmly walked into a railroad station to attend to casualties after the station and two nearby ammunition trains had been hit. On another occasion, under Allied bombing, he helped unload cases of ammunition, winning a medal while simultaneously manifesting his loss of emotional responsiveness.

By 1917, Fritz was promoted from private to officer and served as a medical sublieutenant. The horrors were in large part over for him. As an officer, he fared much better than the enlisted men, with frequent furloughs, decent food, and more adequate quarters. Upon the German defeat in 1918, his batallion was ordered to return to its home base immediately. Forced to march twenty hours a day with little to eat, the hardships returned. It was then that he began his lifelong habit of smoking.

The war had cost him the closest male friend he would ever have when Ferdinand Knopf was killed. His own suffering and the suffering he witnessed destroyed whatever personal stability he had achieved prior to his military service. The barbarity, contemptuous authoritarianism, racial indecencies, and pain he experienced would have a most profound effect on shaping his future existence—accounting, in large part, for his tremendous humanitarianism coupled with a deep cynicism about human nature. With no friends or ties to keep him in one place too long, he would develop, from this point on, into a wanderer and would spend the next thirty years of his life searching for direction, authenticity, and inner peace.

Returning to his studies, he chose, in 1919, to go to Freiburg for a semester. He qualified as an M.D. in Berlin on April 3, 1920.

During the postwar period, Fritz coped, as best he could, with the disastrous economic situation that existed in Germany. Food was scarce and there was a galloping inflation. He lived with his mother and Else (Grete having married and left home), renting two rooms from Amelia to help her maintain financial solvency. By this time, Fritz and his father had ceased to have any effective contact. Nathan isolated himself more and more from the rest of the family as they moved from apartment to apartment, living, finally, in a room shut off from the rest of the house. The two men rarely found themselves together, and from the mid 1920s on, Fritz had ceased speaking to him. When Nathan died, some years later, Fritz neglected to attend the funeral.

Establishing a practice as a neuropsychiatrist, Fritz concentrated on prescribing medical cures for a variety of psychological and neurological complaints. Along with some M.D. friends, he became a member of Berlin's bohemian class, hanging out, at first, in the Cafe of the West

and later the Romanische Cafe. This began his clear identification with the counterculture, an identification that
continued throughout his life.

Along with many young people on both continents who
had fought in the Great War, Fritz began to realize how
they had been duped—that the war had served no end
other than profiting a number of industrialists. Revolting
against the hypocrisy and narrow nationalism of the day,
he associated himself with the *Bauhaus* group—with dissident artists, poets, architects, writers, and political radi-
cals, people who were challenging the established order of
things on all fronts in the hope of establishing a less authoritarian and more creative society. Whereas other psychiatrists might get so deeply involved in their own
work that they become insular and academic, Fritz was
seriously interested in the activities of the larger world.

Mary Wigman was revolutionizing dance in Germany
in the same way that Isadora Duncan was in the United
States. Each woman was seeking to replace the highly styl-
ized form of dance that existed with a more personal form,
a form that flowed from the artist's spirit. They sought
spontaneity in movement that was natural and individ-
ualistic, that was flowing and continuously creative rather
than routine and ritualized. One of her students, Palucca,
was associated with the Bauhaus. Through her, Fritz came
to know and respect Wigman's teachings as a natural extension of his earlier apprenticeship with Max Reinhardt.

Among the crowd of artists, rebels, and writers was the
philosopher Sigmund Friedlander, who was to have a profound effect on Fritz's future development. Fritz found
that Friedlander's message offered a possible "antidote to
my existential confusion and bewilderment."

By the time they met, Fritz had despaired of finding
answers through the teachings of the traditional philoso-
phers—whether the moralistic preachings invoked by his
father or the works of Plato—who set up ideal schemes for
existence which they themselves could not adhere to. He
was tired, as well, of the Germanic tradition of explaining

things by offering hundreds of different Rules, Categories or Truths that purported to answer the riddle of life but only left the student more confused than ever.

Friedlander, in his work *Creative Indifference,* introduced Fritz to simplicity—to the German equivalent of Taoism: that opposites define each other and that there is a resting point, in the center, embracing both polarities. Friedlander felt that it was only through staying in this indifferent center point and accepting the bivalent attitudes that man could become well balanced. Many of Fritz's later Gestalt formulations stemmed from this early encounter—such as the notions that the organism strives to maintain the *zero point* for optimal functioning; that when one element is lacking or overdefined (whether it is love or hate, thirst or overhydration) an attempt is made to achieve closure (*zero*—neither surplus nor shortage) by incorporating what is lacked or discharging what exists in excess; and that *this,* not elaborate instinct theories, can best be used to explain most human behavior.

In 1922, he began making weekly overnight trips to Bremerhaven, acting as a consultant to an expatient of his—a butcher—and his friends. It was a marvelous opportunity for him. Not only was he supplied with food for himself and his family during those terribly lean postwar years, but he was paid his fees in the dollars that came in with the great transatlantic ships, a bonanza during the raging inflation then rocking the Fatherland. He accumulated $500, enough at that time to have purchased several apartment houses in Berlin. Instead, the wanderer used this money to come to New York.

Fritz was encouraged to come to America by a distant relative who persuaded him that economic conditions in the United States offered him a far better opportunity. He left his family and arrived in New York in October 1923. He worked in the Department of Neurology in The Hospital for Joint Diseases, where he continued his work in neuropsychiatry as he simultaneously studied to prepare for certification as a physician in this country.

He was not to find the fulfillment he sought. Hampered by language difficulties, put off by what he felt to be infantile and adolescent conduct in those he met and worked with, and missing the play of ideas and creative ferment of his Bauhaus associates in the lofts and cafes of Berlin, he suffered only increased isolation, alienation and loneliness. An illness to Else provided him an excuse to return to Germany in April 1924.

Nineteen twenty-five was a significant year for Fritz. Thirty-two years old at the time, still living in his mother's home, unsure of himself physically, sexually, socially, professionally, he became involved with a woman who not only stimulated him tremendously but also challenged all his sexual assumptions. The richness, grief, pain, confusion, and pleasure of this relationship provided the vehicle that eventually transported Fritz from his medically oriented practice into that of psychotherapy.

Consider, if you will, Fritz's mental state at the time. He wanted to make some mark in the world, but had no unique point to make. He suffered from a pervasive feeling of not being worth anything (Nathan's "You're a piece of shit" feedback). Stooped, round-shouldered, short, and balding, he considered himself quite ugly. Emotionally benumbed by his war experiences, he went through his days like a robot, as if in a cloud, lacking inner imagery or emotional sparkle. His numbness and lack of faith in his worth extended to his sexual capacities. He doubted his potency, his ability as a lover, the size and adequacy of his penis. His sexual views and attitudes were ultraconventional and wrought with guilt. He even believed that he had damaged his memory through excessive masturbation when younger.

Enter Lucy, a distant relative whose mother was a good friend of Amelia Perls. Fritz was asked to visit Lucy in the hospital where she awaited an operation for the removal of a kidney. Upon entering her room he was overwhelmed by her blonde-haired beauty. She represented the type of woman he worshiped from afar. His previous sexual experiences were apparently perfunctory, noninvolving, infrequent, and with undesirable partners. He had never known a woman of such radiant appeal. Imagine his shock when after ten minutes of polite conversation the Princess turned to the awkward Frog and said, "You are beautiful. Come kiss me." That this should happen to him! And from a married woman! . . . With children! This was truly inconceivable.

The passion of those kisses in her hospital room, which she gave to render herself oblivious to her impending surgery, marked the beginning of an erotically rich and stormy relationship. Lucy became Fritz's guide on the road to sexual affirmation or, as it then seemed to Fritz, to wickedly satisfying perversity. Possessive, passionate, reckless, experimental, Lucy would be considered "far, far out" even in today's psychedelic generation.

After her recovery, Fritz saw Lucy frequently. One day she dropped by his office with a friend. Standing in the physiotherapy room, Fritz, through a crack in his sliding door, spied Lucy and her girlfriend making love in the consulting room. When the friend began to lick Lucy's genitals, "I explode, jump into the room, push the girl aside and have a short and strong orgasm with Lucy."

Later the girls arranged a foursome which afforded Fritz his first homosexual encounter with the girlfriend's husband. Although no physical gratification followed from his experience with this man, the combined aspects of breaking through another taboo and watching the women make love filled Fritz with excitement.

Fritz was particularly astonished and dumbfounded to hear from Lucy that his uncle, the eminent, moralistic, famed attorney, Herman Staub—the man he later believed might be his actual father—had had sexual relations with her when she was thirteen.

These experiences, coming after years of emotional deadness were at times overwhelming. Love, lust, guilt,

surprise, shame, jealously, and desire would clash, rever-
berate, encourage and destroy one another within his
sunken chest. In an attempt to come to terms with these
forces, Fritz entered psychoanalytic treatment in 1926. His
fascination with the process soon led to his training to be a
psychoanalyst himself.

Psychoanalysis, an upstart, controversial, radical approach at the time, was entirely consistent with Fritz's
search for new ways. But it was the anguish and excitement of his love affair with Lucy that led him to Karen
Horney, his first analyst. This, in turn, slowly transformed
his medically oriented practice and led, eventually, to his
own contribution: Gestalt Therapy.

Horney, the therapist he chose, had already established
a reputation as one of the early, innovative psychoanalytic
pioneers. She, too, would later break from orthodox analytic doctrine and found her own, more liberally oriented
school. Worried about his memory, preoccupied with matters sexual, confused as to his goals, employing a cynicism
and an arrogance to hide his feelings of inner worthless-
ness, Fritz believed that analytic insight, dealing as it did
with just such matters, might lead him from the valley of
confusion to the mountain of enlightenment. In the same
measure it would fill the spiritual void that existed in his
life by supplying answers to questions that science, nature, Marxism, and philosophy had not.

Based in large part on the turmoil Fritz was undergoing
with Lucy, Horney's advice was to separate himself from
her and leave Berlin once more. Frankfurt seemed like the
place to go, as Fritz, at that time, was intrigued by the
work of Kurt Goldstein, who was seeing brain injuries
through the lenses of Gestalt *psychology*—seeing how
people *perceived* things differently. He was also attracted
by the Existentialists—Buber, Tillich, and others—who
met and wrote and taught there. Frankfurt was, as well, a
beautiful and cultivated city. And he might stay, at first,
with his mother's brother, Julius Rund, a warm and unas-

suming man. Horney recommended that Fritz continue his analysis with Clara Happel, a student of hers in Frankfurt.

He arrived there in October after painfully wrenching himself free of Lucy and secured an assistantship to Goldstein at his Institute for Brain Damaged Soldiers. At one of Goldstein's seminars he met Lore Posner, twenty-one years old and a graduate student of Gestalt psychology.

Gestalt psychology had little in common with what Fritz was later to call *Gestalt Therapy*. The Gestalt psychology that Lore studied and Fritz was marginally exposed to was of academic interest only. It described perception: how individuals saw things. It dealt with foreground/background and helped students to appreciate the concept of relativity. Depending on one's interest while viewing a fish tank, one can notice either the fish or the water. These Gestaltists had no idea of using their research in any psychotherapeutic way. Their interest was an experimental one, not one of helping people overcome emotional difficulties. Had Fritz not borrowed the term in 1951 for his therapeutic system, *Gestalt* would have faded to the dusty back bookshelves of graduate school libraries, a mere footnote in the history of academic psychology.

Lore (who later anglicized her name to Laura) was much younger than Fritz. Attractive, wide-eyed, and eager to nurture this "lively, spontaneous, witty . . . cynical and kind of desperate man," her quiet attentions helped fill the emptiness that Lucy's absence had caused. Fritz had a commonality of interests with her. They shared a love of the arts. Laura was an accomplished pianist, wrote poetry, and enjoyed classical music, theater, and opera. Indeed, her knowledge in these areas far surpassed Fritz's.

The oldest of three children, Laura was born into a family where appearances mattered. Her father, of whom she was fond, was a successful jewelry manufacturer who obviously returned his daughter's affection. He provided her with the sort of education that was usually only given to male children. Considered to be the brightest of the

Posner children, Laura displayed an independent intelligence that gained the respect of family and teachers alike.

"I received much recognition from early childhood on," she told me. "I was a musician when I was five, wrote poetry when I was six and seven, and I went to a classical *gymnasium*, which girls at that time didn't do. I was the only girl in my class at first."

Laura's mother was brought up to be a lady. Her passion was gardening, her concern was for the household, and she deferred to her husband continually. Laura felt her mother was too passive and lacked a point of view, qualities that caused Laura to lose respect for her.

When Laura met Fritz she was immediately attracted to him. The fact that her father and her brother Robert felt antagonistic toward him did not faze her one iota. As the family's leading intellectual she could readily counter their arguments. The entire family opposed her romance with this bohemian black sheep. "They imagined I should marry a businessman who made a lot of money."

Robert asked their father to investigate Fritz, to show him up, to find something out so that he could get rid of him. But their father said, "No. I don't like him. But if I do anything against him I lose my daughter. And I don't want to do that."

Beyond Laura's physical attractiveness, Fritz was undoubtedly drawn to her intellectuality, her degree of acculturation, and her academic involvement. She represented the refined lady, the counterpart to his bohemian tramp.

For Laura, Fritz was most probably a powerful father figure. Twelve years her senior and more experienced, he had certain conventional trappings that were not to be denied, being a decorated war veteran and a doctor as well. Over and above that she must have found his bohemian Bauhaus life style appealing, as it stood in sharp contrast to the upper-middle-class preoccupations of her family. One can see Laura's attraction to Fritz as a way of differentiating herself from her family and their values—as an act of "mature youth in rebellion." Thus, the two of them saw and admired in one another desires and attitudes that they couldn't openly and fully live out in their own lives.

Laura soon saw Fritz as a man whose cynicism hid a basic insecurity, who never received proper affirmation in the course of growing up, and, though he was too proud to ask, who sorely needed love and respect. She had faith that her compassion, wisdom, and love might cure what ailed him. Not long after their meeting they became lovers.

Fritz remained in Frankfurt for a year. At the exact moment his money ran out, Clara Happel, his second analyst, abruptly informed him that his analysis was finished and that, being free of complexes, he could now go on to do *control work*—to train as a practicing psychoanalyst under supervision. Fritz was surprised. He felt, if anything, more at loose ends now than before. Much of his previous accomplishments had come about by virtue of his forcing himself to do those things he was conditioned to feel were important: to study, to earn his degree, to secure decent appointments. Part of his analysis with Happel had concentrated on finding his own values, not those that his parents or society subtly trained him to want. He was questioning, in his therapy, what he later termed "shouldisms," or his "Topdog." The day this "should" system temporarily collapsed, his guideposts disappeared. Lost, confused, uncertain, he spent that night wandering aimlessly through the streets of Frankfurt until dawn.

Feeling no inner push urging him to take a contradictory stand, he followed Happel's suggestion and went on to Vienna, the center of psychoanalytic learning. No longer in psychoanalytic treatment himself, he began to receive supervision of his own cases from Helene Deutsch and Edward Hitschmann, two therapists with excellent reputations as teachers. But again, the search for salvation led him into a blind alley. On a personal level he missed the sexual release and physical affection his relationship with Laura had afforded, for the prudery of the Viennese maidens prevented him from having a single casual affair in the year he spent there. Nor did he find psychoanalytic illumination. Helene Deutsch impressed him most with her analytic coldness. Once, upon giving her a gift, he received an interpretation of his motivations instead of a "thank you" from her.

What he did get out of his training work was not intentional. It was an appreciation of easiness, warmth, and common sense. He especially recalled the time Paul Federn, a dignified, fatherly psychoanalyst, during one of his lectures, commented, "Man kann gar nicht genug vöeglin" ("You just can't fuck enough"). Or Hitschmann's droll comment, when Fritz asked him about the neo-Freudian schools, that "They all make money."

There was another incident with Hitschmann which, in retrospect, pointed the way to Fritz's Gestalt Therapy formulations. Hitschmann, an affable, easy-going man, allowed for more casual give and take in supervisory hours than the icy Helene Deutsch. Fritz began to share his doubts about his own capacities as a man and about the adequacy of his penis. Finally, Hitschmann said, "Well, take out your penis. Let's have a look at the thing." This he did. They talked about its size and decided it was certainly adequate. This put to rest Fritz's fantasies about it. This ability to deal with the present, to explore the actuality and not the fantasy, was to lead, eventually, to Fritz's work in the *here and now*.

In 1928, after spending a depressing year in Vienna, he completed his supervisory work, left a clinical assistantship at the mental hospital under the direction of Paul Schilder, another of the early psychoanalysts, and returned to Berlin where he established his own analytic practice. Laura was still about, waiting patiently in the wings. And so was the analyst's couch, since Fritz knew that he was still unsettled. His delving into the past to find peace of mind had not brought contentment. Perhaps he had not analyzed its effects fully, had not worked through his Oe-

dipal conflict—his hatred for his father and his possessiveness about his mother? His feeling that he had not
done those things caused him to seek his third analyst. It
was a catastrophic experience with a man named Eugen J.
Harnik.

"I wish that I could, in some way, describe the state of
stupidity and moral cowardice to which his so-called treatment reduced me," Fritz wrote. Harnik, who reportedly
later died in an asylum, believed in passive analysis. For
one hour a day, five days a week, for a year and a half,
Fritz trooped to the couch, lay down, and talked. He was
greeted neither by "Hello" nor "Goodbye." A few minutes
before the end of each hour, Harnik shuffled one foot upon
the floor, indicating that Fritz should shortly leave. He offered, perhaps, one sentence a week as feedback. Fritz,
getting no cues as to what path to follow, filled the air with
words. Once, getting a rare comment that Fritz seemed to
be a ladies' man, Fritz proceeded to labor on, week after
week, with tales of amatory activities that he undertook, in
large measure, to do the right thing by his therapist. He
lacked the confidence to break off treatment. Could he,
after all, rightfully become an analyst if his analysis with
both Happel and Harnik were unsuccessful?

Laura, by then, was pressing for marriage. They had
been keeping company for four years. Fritz was now
thirty-seven years old. When he mentioned the possibility
to Harnik, his response was, "You are not allowed to make
an important decision during your analysis. If you marry
I'll break off your analysis."

"Being too cowardly to discontinue my couch life on
my own responsibility," he wrote, "I put the responsibility
on him and exchanged psychoanalysis for marriage."

And why not? He liked Laura, although not madly in
love with her. They had their common interests. Perhaps
he would find greater purpose through becoming a husband and a father. Besides which, his sense of morality
told him that it was the right thing to do. He had, after all,
deflowered her four years ago. ("She deceived me," he

later told a colleague, "pretending to be experienced when she was a virgin.") There seemed nothing better to do, given the circumstances.

The wedding took place on August 23, 1929, over the objections of the Posner family, who thought that Laura was marrying beneath herself.

Whatever ill effects Fritz suffered in his various psychoanalysis, in an affirmative sense he experienced first hand Freud's insights into hidden motivations—into forces directing a person to act in a particular way that were out of that person's awareness. He also came to recognize the importance of sex and aggression as two of these motivating forces. His analysts taught him, as well, that dreams were "the Royal Road to the Unconscious," the importance of careful listening, and the awareness of how earlier life experiences affect current behavior. Fritz's first six years of analytic practice in Frankfurt, Vienna, and finally Berlin—from 1926 through 1932—were passed as a bona fide, trained, certified Freudian psychoanalyst. He was more openminded than most, perhaps, but almost as orthodox in practice.

Still not ready to give up on his own psychoanalysis, Fritz turned again to Karen Horney for advice, as the two of them had a mutual respect for one another.

"See Wilhelm Reich," she suggested. "He's the only one who might get through to you."

A brilliant, outspoken, radical psychoanalyst, Reich was causing much ferment among his fellow Freudians by questioning the importance of working with childhood memories. With him, Fritz's search began to bear its first fruits, as he left the confusion of retrospective ruminations. Reich's focus on "body armor" (posture, gesture, muscular tension) not only lessened the importance of historical data, but Reich himself offered Fritz *involvement*.

After Freud, the major influence on Fritz's developing psychological style had to be Wilhelm Reich. Fritz was impressed with Reich's vitality, his sense of aliveness, his rebelliousness, and his willingness to enter into a discussion of any situation, particularly sexual and political ones. Reich, through his book, *Character Analysis*, was also the first analyst to state that more can be achieved therapeutically by being aware of the patient's present attitude than can be accomplished by verbal searchings for historical facts. Reich's awareness of bodily attitudes reinforced Fritz's earlier appreciation of the importance of posture and movement which he had learned in a different setting from Max Reinhardt and Palucca. Further, Reich's techniques allowed for direct body contact, where the therapist would lay hands on tensed muscles, muscles that withheld hatred or hurt, terror or tears. This would eventually help free Fritz from the analytic taboo against touching patients.

Fritz soon felt energized and stimulated rather than preoccupied and withdrawn. He became a proud father when Renate, his daughter, was born on July 23, 1931. Becoming involved in the anti-Fascist movement, he taught at the Workers College and tried, along with others, to bring about a conciliation between communists and socialists to stop Hitler.

The burning of the Reichstag signified the failure of the anti-Nazi opposition. Political opponents were being rounded up in Berlin in large numbers. Fritz, Laura, and Ren had to sleep separately, in the homes of different friends, to avoid arrest. Reich, an avowed Marxist, fled to Norway. In April 1933, Fritz crossed the border into Holland with 100 marks, the equivalent of $25, smuggled out in his cigarette lighter. Laura and Ren left for the safer South of Germany and stayed with her family.

His analysis with Reich was severed. His flourishing practice gone. The most handsome apartment imaginable—filled with furniture carved from rare woods and ultramodern accessories all fashioned by Bauhaus masters— a wedding gift from the Posner family that was photographed in Germany's leading architectural magazine, stood empty.

The situation in Holland was equally grim. Fritz was

put up, initially, in a home packed with Jewish refugees. Living on charity, he did the best he could, continuing his analytic training with Karl Landauer, another refugee analyst who formerly, along with Frieda Fromm-Reichmann, headed the Frankfurt Psychoanalytic Institute. Fritz palled around with a ham actor who had the unusual ability to fart melodies and had an affair with a somewhat hysterical married woman. Six months later he sent for Laura and Ren, and together they managed to find an unheated attic apartment to live in.

Conditions became progressively worse. Neither he nor Laura (who, by now, had received her own degree) were permitted to work. They had no money. Whatever pieces of furniture and books Laura managed to get out of Germany were sold so that they might eat. Living in an unheated flat, Fritz would get up at five or six each morning to light a small stove. Laura would scrub floors, something she had never done before, in freezing temperatures. On rare occasions they would buy Ren a banana, which was, for her, "an absolute luxury." More turmoil ensued when the woman Fritz had had his affair with started to make trouble, for Fritz was quite discreet and secretive about any extramarital involvements in those days. Laura's suffering a miscarriage and having a subsequent depression added to the family's woes.

Fritz knew they had to leave, to get as far away from the impending holocaust as possible. He had some correspondence with A. A. Brill, the dean of American psychoanalysts, who was willing to help him come to the United States. But then, Ernest Jones, who worked hard to help the refugee analysts, told him of a position in South Africa. Recalling his previous aversion to New York and filled with some romantic visions of Africa, Fritz chose the latter.

4

South Africa

Determined to hurdle the language barrier that contributed to his earlier isolation in New York, Fritz taught himself English during the three-week voyage to South Africa
aboard the *Balmoral Castle.* Upon arriving, his instant language program brought about instant success. The contrast
between the poverty of Holland and the wealth Fritz and
Laura acquired in Johannesburg was mind-boggling to
them both.

Almost immediately, both of them established full-time
practices. The founder of The South African Institute of
Psychoanalysis in 1935, Fritz sought to establish a training
center for potential analysts. His title was more impressive
than the fact that Fritz was, at the time, the only psychoanalyst in the country. On August 23, 1935, their second
child, Steve, was born. Within one year they managed to
build the first Bauhaus style home in a wealthy suburb,
replete with swimming pool, tennis courts, ice-skating
rink, a housekeeper, two servants, and an imported nurse
for the children.

In addition to his work, his new found wealth afforded
Fritz a great opportunity for playing. There was swimming, skating, tennis, Ping-Pong, vacations to Durban and
other areas on the coast to enjoy the Indian Ocean, drives

to Zululand, and flying lessons. Fritz became so proficient a pilot that he intended to fly his own craft to the Psychoanalytic Congress in Czechoslovakia in 1936, failing to do so only because someone outbid him on the purchase of the craft, offering more than Fritz felt it was worth. So he returned to Europe as he had left, by boat.

Fritz had prepared a paper to deliver at the Congress entitled "Oral Resistances." Although he did not realize it at the time, that paper would eventually come to lie at the heart of his first book, *Ego, Hunger and Aggression,* for "Oral Resistances" stressed the unique importance of the infant's relating to the world through the intake of food and the relationship between the adult's eating habits and his or her current interactions with other people.

At the time, analytic doctrine was that "resistances"—the patient's holding back in treatment—were related directly to early toilet-training habits, where children would spite a disciplining mother by withholding their feces. Fritz, hoping to make a contribution to analytic theory, wrote of how these same resistances could be seen even earlier in an angry child's refusal to take in nourishment.

He had traveled four thousand miles to attend the Congress. Not only did he hope to have his paper welcomed, but he wanted, as well, to meet with Freud himself. For hadn't he, Fritz, established a new branch of The Master's mission in South Africa?

Neither of these expectations were met. He was given a curt, cool, four-minute audience with The Leader while standing in Freud's doorway, a foretaste of the icy reception his paper later received from most of the other analysts in attendance. An "I'll show you—you can't do this to me" hurt reaction followed.

In addition to his disappointing meeting with Freud and the lack of respect his paper received from his peers, Fritz was greatly disheartened to find Wilhelm Reich, the analyst who had given him so much, withdrawn, morose, and barely capable of recognizing Fritz.

From the Congress on, the negative influence of Freud

began to exert itself. Fritz's work was to be forever more marked by his taking frequent swipes at orthodox psychoanalysis. His love/hate relationship to Freud was most accurately described by Fritz himself:

> Many friends criticize me for my polemical relationship to Freud. "You have so much to say; your position is securely grounded in reality. What is this continuous aggressiveness against Freud? Leave him alone and just do your thing."
> I can't do this. Freud, his theories, his influence are much too important for me. My admiration, bewilderment, and vindictiveness are very strong. I am deeply moved by his suffering and courage. I am deeply awed by how much, practically all alone, he achieved with the inadequate mental tools of association psychology and mechanistically oriented philosophy. I am deeply grateful for how much I developed through standing up against him.

Fritz was away from his family for about three months. In addition to the time passed at the Psychoanalytic Congress, there were visits to family and friends in other parts of Europe. In Holland he saw Liesel, Laura's younger sister, and alludes, in his writing, to the possibility of having a brief interlude with her (". . . we had some lovely encounters. Compared to Laura's heaviness, intellectual and artistic involvement, she was simple, beautiful and flirtatious"). After the Congress he went off to the Hungarian mountains with Ernest Jones and some sympathetic colleagues.

His return to Europe led Fritz to realize that his newfound security was little more than a house of cards. His antidogmatic thinking, influenced by dissidents like Horney and Reich, was evident in his paper. The response of his fellow professionals led him to a point where he would no longer be comfortable in or welcome as a member of the psychoanalytic establishment. His personal mentor, Reich, was not in the proper place or proper frame of mind to provide any support or guidance. And the time spent away from his family caused him to recognize that he didn't miss or need them—that they were a habit more than a passion, an obligation rather than a solution. Laura was the closest friend Fritz had allowed himself since Ferdinand Knopf had been killed in the war. Now, however, this relationship seemed to be dying as he apparently developed a typical case of seven-year restlessness and hungered for new adventures and new stimulation.

In both Germany and Holland the family had been close-knit. This was partly a result of the newness of the relationships and partly a result of banding together against the adversities brought on by the Nazi terror. Laura, after her spontaneous abortion in Holland, soon became pregnant again. Fritz, then almost forty-two years old, was opposed to being a father for a second time. He could sense his own growing short temper around children and also wanted more time for himself, not less. He suggested the possibility of a legal abortion to Laura, but she was against it. She promised Fritz that a second child would not restrict him and that she would assume full responsibility. Fritz was unwilling to push hard to interrupt the pregnancy because of Laura's previous depression over her loss in Holland. And Laura was firmly committed to having another offspring.

"From my mother," said Renate, in recalling those years, "and from what I see of photographs, Fritz adored me. He carried me around on his shoulders and showed me off to everybody. I know that up until age four we were close. He cared. Up until then I had everybody: my mother, my father, my nurse, and the black man who worked for us. Then my brother was born. My mother had to divide her time between work, Steve, and myself. Next my father took off for Europe and the Congress. He came back a very different man. I've been furious with Fritz ever since.

"There were a few pleasant moments afterwards. I remember that we went for a walk in the field near where our house was—a lovely place with a roof garden, tennis courts, and swimming pool. And I was walking ahead of him in the tall grass, a bitty six-year-old having a lot of fun.

Other times he'd take me to restaurants and hangouts. We'd have lunch or he'd get me an ice cream soda, meet friends, and play chess. But these were the only contacts we had. I often felt lost at these places, particularly when there were all adults around."

Although Fritz came to have nothing but scorn for Renate in later life and described her, in *Garbage Pail*, in both a fleeting and contemptuous way, he also acknowledged a great fondness for both her and Laura at the time of Renate's birth. "I even began to reconcile myself, somewhat, to being a married man. But later, when I was blamed for anything that went wrong, I withdrew more and more from my role as *paterfamilia*."

Laura herself had a busy schedule and was unavailable for full-time mothering. When Steve or Ren cried or complained or seemed at loose ends she, possibly out of her own sense of guilt, faulted Fritz for his even lesser involvement. This, in turn, only seemed to establish a vicious cycle with Fritz removing himself even more from contact with his children. Fritz came to resent what he felt to be a clutching, symbiotic relationship between Ren and Laura in which Laura would act as The Supreme Giver and Comforter and Ren would be The Perpetual Taker and Sufferer. Although this may have satisfied Laura's desire to see herself as a good mother and Ren's childish desire to be pampered, the bond between the two of them left Fritz out in the cold. He also, no doubt, resented the extra burden of his second child and begrudged whatever attentiveness Laura gave the two of them.

In any event, he became increasingly detached, both emotionally and hourly, from his family. The next four years were spent pursuing projects that did not involve the others. Fritz had his patients and Laura had hers. Meals were often taken separately, as patient schedules had priority over family interaction. When they did dine together, Fritz and Laura discussed their clinical work or read books or newspapers.

The type of professional life Fritz led in South Africa is

best described by the following passage from *Garbage Pail:*

> I was caught in the rigidity of the psychoanalytic taboos: the exact 50 minute hour, no physical eye and social contact, no personal involvement (counter-transference!). I was caught by all the trimmings of a square, respectable citizen: family, house servants, making more money than I needed. I was caught in the dichotomy of work and play: Monday to Friday versus the weekend. I just extricated myself through my spite and rebelliousness from becoming a computing corpse like most of the orthodox analysts I knew.

Fritz kept going through the motions, but his heart was obviously not into being a suburban husband. Each Sunday night, Laura had an open house, creating, as best she could, a cultural salon in the generally dreary South African ambience. Fritz participated when he felt like it and was brusque and unavailable when he didn't. For amusement he continued at his sports, had a number of sexual encounters with the children's nurse, and tried his hand at directing some amateur films and plays.

In a more serious vein he decided to develop his therapeutic ideas. Freed by geographical distance and cultural isolation from other analysts, his therapeutic style softened, became more flexible, more experimental, and more open. Enlarging upon the paper he presented at the Congress, incorporating the helpful elements of his work with Reich, and including some of his familiarity with existential thought, he completed his first book, *Ego, Hunger and Aggression,* in 1940. Subtitling it *A Revision of Freud's Theory and Method,* he was, while on the attack, not yet willing to make a clean break. Initially published in Durban, South Africa, in 1942, it established a position that set him still further apart from other psychoanalysts when, in that work, he challenged some fundamental Freudian scripture. For one, he declared that Freud oversexualized life. He began by pointing out the obvious: how self-preservation (hunger) takes precedence over species preservation (sex), and that our developing attitudes toward food—the behavior patterns surrounding eating—set a precedent for the way we relate to the world that is more basic than later developing sexual motivations.

After opening the motivational system beyond Eros (sex) and Thanatos (aggression/death) by including *hunger,* he went on to postulate an endless series of motivations that flow, one into another, from moment to moment. He stressed the importance of *present time* and criticized Freud for being preoccupied with the past and Alfred Adler for overstressing the future. His awareness of polarities (opposites) made him point to the areas that the *psychoanalysts* (*mind-dissectors*) left out, namely, the *body* and *synthesis* (the importance of new experiences).

He denied the usefulness of the analytic theory of Transference. That concept states that the neurotic tends to see present-day people in terms of the early figures of his life. If a woman's father was cruel, she sees the analyst and others as cruel. If her mother was overpossessive, other older women are seen that way. Analytic treatment dictated that the therapist be a neutral blank screen, the better to have the patient "transfer" these attitudes, which could then be analyzed, appreciated, and dispelled. Fritz took a different tack, pointing out that the "cruelty" or "overpossessiveness" was more readily related to the patient's unacceptable impulses:

> The whole complicated process, both aspects—the cruel father and the cruel analyst—boil down to the patient's own personality. In other words: dealing with the transference means an unnecessary complication—means a waste of time. If I can draw water from a tap in my room, it is unnecessary to go down to the well.

He also made a case for ending the artificial anonymity of the analyst with this argument:

> The orthodox psycho-analyst will agree with me when I introduce another formula for termination of the analytical cure by maintaining that not only has the psycho-analyst to understand the patient but the patient has to understand the psycho-analyst. He has to see the human being and not a

screen upon which he projects his "transferences" and the hidden parts of his self. Only when he has succeeded in penetrating the veil woven out of hallucinations, evaluations, transferences and fixations, has he learned to see things as they are: he comes to his senses by applying his sense. He achieves genuine contact with reality in lieu of a pseudo contact with his projections.

The final section of *Ego, Hunger and Aggression* he entitled "Concentration Therapy." Within these pages Fritz elaborated upon those concepts that, when attended to, brought him some peace of mind. These had to do with focusing awareness in the present moment, stopping unproductive historical ruminations and blame, and realizing the nature of projections. This part can be read either as a unique self-help book or as a primer which underlines and explains the "magic" that Fritz performed in his subsequent work with patients. Chapter by chapter he suggests procedures to help the reader realize the importance of the moment, of internal silence, of simple task observations, of body concentration, and of how one externalizes inner conflicts.

On January 19, 1942, the year his book appeared, he volunteered for service in the army. The wheel had come full circle as he now joined the English side in a war against the Germans. For the next four years, until February 20, 1946, he served, alternately, near Pretoria, Potchefstroom, and, from May 1945 on, back in Johannesburg as a medical officer. The work was routine and uninspiring. Rarely home, prior to his return to Johannesburg, he and Laura pursued largely independent lives. As his hated father had done before him, Fritz drew still further away from his own family.

"Basically he wasn't around very much," recalls Steve. "My major recollections are of him coming and going and not being there.

"He'd come maybe once a month, or every few months, on a weekend pass. My mother would have men friends visit and they would stay for a few days when my Dad was in the Army. They'd play Ping-Pong with me and were nicer than my Dad was most of the time. I was nine years old, so I enjoyed them.

"As far as I can recall, I was never spanked by him. He'd yell, occasionally, if I would do something that would annoy him. The only thing that I can remember that annoyed him was making noise with my friends kicking a soccer ball around the backyard when I was six. He'd tell me to be quiet, because they both had their offices in the house. That's my recollection of my parents during my elementary school years. Even in older years they had the office in our home. I could never walk in the front door to the bedroom or dining room without going through the waiting room. Many times there were patients waiting to see the doctor. Life centered around them seeing patients."

If Steve remembers his father with empty detachment, Renate recalls him with fear and dislike.

"I was often sent on vacations to dreadful farms, places I hated and where I felt like an outcast. I don't remember Fritz paying very much attention to us. He was an absent father, very involved with his own work. But during the war he was hell when he was home. *'Thou shalt not exist. Thou shalt not have any friends unless I say so.'* Things like that. With him, practically everything was 'No.' With Laura it was invariably 'Yes.' No middle ground.

"I know that I was always afraid of Fritz—terrified of him. He'd hit the living bejeesus out of me. He never touched my brother. Fritz had a temper you wouldn't believe.

"I remember the first time he lost his temper. I was five years old and he locked me up in a garage for the whole afternoon. I don't remember what I did. John, the gardener, wanted to let me out but he said, 'I can't. I'll lose my job. He'll fire me if I let you out.'

"The first time he actually hit me, my brother was bugging the hell out of me. He was turning the radio up loud and I wanted it turned down. There was a pen lying about and so I jabbed Steve with it. Fritz hit the shit out of me to the point where my bones rattled. Another time, my mother was away somewhere. My nurse was at the table, my father was at the head of it, and I heard him grunting and snorting while he was eating his food. I leaned over and I said to the nurse, 'Hey, Mira. Poppy eats like a pig.' She told him this. Back to the box room again. This was a smaller room when we were living in another house.

"And another thing that confused me. We moved to this shitty house at the outbreak of the war. Fritz had a package of flags from all over the world. Every day my friend Peggy and I would decide to wear different flags to school. Each day I'd pick out two flags and we'd wear them. One day I happened to pick out the swastika. I didn't know what the hell it was. I'd never seen it before. Fritz shook me until I rattled like a skeleton. I pissed in my pants. I was so embarrassed. He never told me the reasons why. Now I understand that. But you don't do that to an eight-year-old. You explain why it's not right."

Fritz's reaction to the Nazi banner may not have been a thoughtful one, but it is certainly understandable emotionally. Had not both his mother and sister Else perished in the Ravenstadt concentration camp? As for his quickness to hit, one might also point out that Ren doesn't recall being struck by him before the age of seven, and even then the episodes that come to mind are fewer than can be counted on the fingers of one hand. What is undeniable in both Steve's and Ren's reflections is the lack of warmth, lack of communication, and lack of love that existed between their father and themselves, together with Fritz's unwillingness to work to bridge that gap.

Although Renate's terror cannot be dismissed, it would be hard to make a case for Fritz's being an ogre. Ren herself contributed to their negative interaction, her "Poppy eats like a pig" remark being a forerunner to later, periodic goadings. Just as Fritz felt that his mother helped foster his dislike for his own father, he also speculated that Laura subtly aided her children's dislike of theirs. Steve, for example, claims that Laura told him Fritz never wanted a second child and tried to have her abort him.

By the time he was discharged from the service, Fritz had decided that it was time to leave South Africa. The Perls had already abandoned the palace they had built at the time of World War II, since gasoline prices prevented patients from driving out from Johannesburg, so that was no longer an attachment. Jan Smuts,* the prime minister, for whom Fritz had great respect, had died. Both Fritz and Laura experienced the country as a cultural wasteland. And Fritz sensed the growing, indigenous brand of South African fascism—all the more repellent since he had fled to Africa to avoid Hitler's tyranny.

Fritz's plan was to go to America alone, establish a practice, and then send for the rest of the family. His leaving was marred by another tussle with Ren, one that underscored both the bitterness and desire she had for him: "The last time he hit me I was fourteen. It was a week before he left South Africa. I had some friends coming over and he didn't want me to have anybody. I said, 'Look. A boy's coming over to join us. I do not know his telephone number. We are going to be on the other side of the house. We will not disturb you.' He said, 'You are the most selfish child that I have ever met in my life.' 'And you,' I answered, 'are the grouchiest old man that I have ever met in my life.' With that he went Zap—right in front of my girlfriends.

"I did not talk to him for a week, until the day he left. Then I offered him a piece of chewing gum because I didn't want him to go off to America while we were on bad terms. But as the years went on, our periods of not talking got longer, somehow."

Fritz's friend and benefactress, Karen Horney, was already in America. So was Paul Goodman, whose articles

---

* Smuts, in his book, *Holism and Evolution*, stressed that all phenomena must be studied and understood in terms of their organic unity, not merely in terms of their parts. Gestalt concepts have much in common with Smuts's *Holism*.

had captured his imagination and whom he was eager to meet. Karen agreed to be his sponsor. Because he was not able to come to the United States directly due to an anti-Semitic American consular official, he took a troop ship to England and then voyaged to Canada, staying in Montreal for as few days as it took to secure proper papers to enter the United States.

The twelve years he spent in South Africa led him to formulate all the basic ideas that underlined what he would later call *Gestalt Therapy*. It had also led him to realize that the roles of father and husband gave him little satisfaction.

Yet, these same years cost him much. Like Sisyphus with his stone, Fritz had first seen his world come tumbling down during World War I. He pushed his rock up the mountain and rebuilt, only to see the Nazis destroy what external supports he had created for himself. The same pattern repeated itself with even greater losses in South Africa, where he lost his psychoanalytic reputation, his home, his practice, and the affection of his children and was beginning to lose his wife.

So here he was—an unhappily married fifty-three-year-old man, with a daughter nearly fifteen, an eleven-year-old son, and an evolving therapeutic approach that was still in the process of being born—once more upon unfamiliar shores, preparing, once again, to roll the stone back up the mountain.

5

New York

For a while it was touch and go as to whether Fritz would stay in the United States or return to South Africa. He arrived in New York in the summer of 1946. The city of noise, concrete, big buildings, oppressive heat, and unfriendly faces reaffirmed the previous distaste he had felt during his 1923 visit. He fled, almost immediately, to the home of his brother-in-law in New Haven, where Robert Posner lived with his own family. New Haven was to prove equally inhospitable.

For one thing, Laura's brother never liked Fritz, resenting, perhaps, Fritz's seduction of his sister twenty years earlier. Add to this his wife's passion for tidiness and Fritz's extraordinary sloppiness—from unmade beds to clothes left about to cigarette ashes strewn everywhere—and it is easy to understand why they eventually asked him to leave. Professionally there were also disappointments. An opening for a professor of psychiatry at Yale, a post Fritz coveted and was considered for, went, unfortunately for him, to someone else. Lacking professional or personal support, Fritz was about to return to Johannesburg when he met Erich Fromm. Fromm had read *Ego, Hunger and Aggression* and was impressed.

"Don't go back," he told Fritz. "I promise you that within three months you'll have a practice of your own."

So Fritz returned to New York and, with the help of Fromm, Clara Thompson, and other members of The Washington School of Psychiatry (later called The William Alanson White Psychoanalytic Institute), had a flourishing practice going within three weeks. After firmly establishing himself, he once more sent for his family. Laura and the children arrived in the fall of 1947, fifteen months after he did.

The ten years that Fritz spent in New York were a time of ferment, great upheaval, and marked change in direction. Throughout this period Fritz struggled to end the discrepancies between his private and professional life—to allow himself to be more of a person as a therapist and more of a therapist as a person. The decade also witnessed the formal birth of Gestalt Therapy. It ended in 1956 when Fritz decided to leave Laura.

The William Alanson White Institute, a neo-Freudian group, adhered to Harry Stack Sullivan's theories, which stressed the importance of interpersonal relations. Fritz still had a couch but began to make ever-increasing use of face-to-face encounters (his own face now sported a moustache) as well as delving into group therapy. His exploration of and openness to interpersonal relations, both in and out of practice, was a bit too open as far as the White Institute crowd was concerned, causing that association to be short-lived.

He started, at first, to lead a professional existence similar to that in Africa: a slave to his rigid schedule of seeing patients weekdays during the winter months and of spending the summer months in Provincetown, where he and Laura rented a cottage next to Clara Thompson, the major figure at the White Institute.

If his physical proximity to Clara was designed to further his goal of affiliating himself with more openminded psychoanalysts, his plans backfired. Fritz was now daring to be less devious, and he began to publicly reach out for other women in direct proportion to his loneliness, isolation, and dissatisfactions in living with Laura. Although the Freudians and neo-Freudians both proclaimed a reverence for honesty and integrity, and although each claimed sexual impulses to be a natural and acceptable part of life, neither group relished the idea of being associated with an openly sexual being. Yet here was Fritz, acting on these feelings, virtually in Clara Thompson's backyard.

Dwight McDonald, the critic, recalled summers spent in Provincetown in the mid to late forties: "Fritz had a terrible reputation . . . some 'mad power over women' in spite of the fact that he wasn't terribly attractive even then. Any woman would remember him. He had 'hand trouble.' "

Or, as another friend, the educational innovator, Elliot Shapiro, put it: "He was quick to fondle. Right away, almost without introductions."

The White Institute's unwillingness to grant him full membership proved to be one of the factors that liberated him from slavery to orthodox hours and a conventional practice. The other, and more telling, influence was his association with Paul Goodman and the new bohemians around him.

Goodman—writer, critic, teacher of literature, gadfly of the establishment, and darling of the New York intellectual set—met Fritz and Laura in late 1947, shortly after Laura's arrival. Just as Fritz had read and admired Paul's works while he lived in Africa, so had Paul read and admired *Ego, Hunger and Aggression.* The Perls' provided Paul with sympathetic ears and a therapeutic setting in which he might organize his chaotic, albeit creative, life. He, in turn, drew them into his counterculture circle of writers, actors, musicians, and thinkers, giving them their first intellectually challenging and exciting company since leaving Germany.

The group that centered around Paul consisted of several dozen people and included such future luminaries as Merce Cunningham, John Cage, George Dennison, James Agee, Dwight McDonald, and Julian Beck and his wife, Judith Malina. Most of these people were a generation removed from Fritz and Laura. Each of them was, in his or her own way, dissatisfied with the forms in which they were cast, objected to the limits placed upon their lives and their art, and struggling to achieve some breakthroughs. In this they mirrored Fritz's sentiments. They shared a belief that new forms might develop through *honesty* and *experimentation*. Candor was required to demonstrate the banality, bankruptcy, and hypocrisy of existing social and artistic structures. Experimentation, both in life and in art, might point the way toward richer expression and greater and more natural satisfactions.

Paul Goodman was the "leader" (if such a group might ever be considered to have one—the "center" might be a better term) of this group of American Bauhausers because of his range and his outspokenness. He was everywhere at once, writing essays, plays, critiques, and books, being a student of music and dance, politics and education. An avowed bisexual, he thought nothing of discussing his homo/heterosexual nature either privately or publicly on a college campus or in a television interview. He felt that his outspoken candor might pave the way for others to accept their true selves without shame instead of play acting at being plastic people from some radio soap opera. Moreover, Goodman articulated the desire of this group to end the discrepancies between their professional lives and their private lives. Thus, the Becks attempted to make their Living Theater *real:* to involve actor and audience in actual dialogue, all the while struggling to bring artistry and dramatic truth to the casual rap, the business meeting, or the luncheon engagement.

The stress on honesty and on exploring the limits of behavior and feeling led, as well, to a fair amount of sexual "game playing," in which, according to Julian Beck, "whether you will or will not fuck somebody is both ambiguous and terribly interesting, and becomes a terribly important matter between any number of other people." Along with these sexual games, there were sporadic at-

tempts to lead open, nonpossessive sexual lives and to
explore the limits of sexual pleasure—from heterosexuality
through bisexuality to homosexuality—both in individual
couplings and in larger groups.

The relationship between Fritz and these young bohemians was a very positive one insofar as each gained rein-
forcement in their attempts to explore their limits. Whatever doubts arose in Paul's circle concerning the rightness
of their endeavors were allayed by the presence of this
prototypical, older European psychoanalyst. And Fritz's attempt to explore living/therapeutic styles beyond the
scope of his psychoanalytic background were legitimatized
by the community.

"I'm not just a crazy analyst going off half-cocked," he
might well have told himself, "for here are a group of very
creative people exploring the same ground."

For Fritz, this association reinforced his belief that psychoanalytic anonymity was unnecessary and encouraged
his attempts to make therapy more a part of life. He was to
permit himself ever greater freedom in reacting spontaneously and experimentally with patients—challenging and
overcoming all his preexisting limits, including the taboo
against sexual intimacy. He was to become *Fritz*, not some
die-cast, type-cast, unnatural, anonymous therapist figure,
but permitting his cynicism, tenderness, humor, gruffness,
paranoia, and lustiness to come through with the patients
he was treating just as he did outside the office.

In social settings he allowed himself, in ever-increasing degree, to make diagnoses, offer the same prescriptions, and proffer the same candid analysis that he previously permitted himself in his office.

"He put me down pretty badly a couple of times," remembers Judith Malina. "I wasn't really afraid of him because he was a little bit on the make for me, so that I could
always excuse his remarks as based on unfulfilled desire.
He said that I had a horrible mouth and that I should spit
at people—that I should express my venomous hostility.

"And he always said these things in the presence of

other people. He didn't say this just to me, like in a psychological session. But he said this in a moment when I was feeling gloriously beautiful or grooving, or surrounded by my lovers, or something."

Similarly, he once walked up to Nina Gitano, another member of The Living Theater, during an intermission of Claude Frederick's *The Idiot King*, put his face right in front of hers, and told her, as she was about to go out and do her big scene, "Your performance stinks."

By giving people gratuitous, professional analysis of their behavior in social situations he, like the younger members of the circle, struggled to bring his "acts" together and to lead one life instead of two.

Without doubt, these new revolutionaries overdid things at times. As Judith Malina analyzed it: "Fritz was into a kind of style that most of us were into, sort of a forties' nastiness—the kind of clever conversational chatter that consists mostly of insulting somebody. You used to hear it on the late night talk shows where they had bantering insults, said crushing things, or tried to outwit people. And Fritz was a great star at this sort of public bitchiness."

But such overreaction is the way of revolutions. And Fritz's mind was such that he eventually caught the nature of the new game known as *Outspoken Honesty*, the new trap that the group found itself in.

"Eventually it lost its popularity," continued Judith. "Thank God. Also thank people like Fritz who got away from that and pushed all the rest of us away from it and gave us a little insight into our bullshit. Certainly the insights that he showed us were also insights into a former self that were only too apparent, a socially witty, domineering person with all the falseness of manner, all the game playing, who was what we used to call absolutely 'Divine' at parties."

Fascinated from early adolescence by innovative theater, Fritz spent a fair amount of time with The Living Theater. Julian Beck recalls him hanging out at rehearsals and stagings, commenting on theater in general and their acting in particular. And, of course, he spent time with them socially.

"It became clear to us that Fritz was looking at that time and talking—with a kind of deep and moving excitement but also a great vagueness—about wanting to do some kind of directing or something with the actors. He had something in mind that was half-way between the kind of performances we were doing and therapeutic sessions."

In his personal life, the same dramatic sense was evident. "He was always," added Julian, "trying to bring the meeting, the encounter, to its frontier. And the device was always honesty, frankness, and a certain shock technique. These forms of address were very important to our own work, for instance, in *Paradise Now*, where many of the scenes are concerned with bringing that kind of candor and that kind of honesty into a direct I-and-Thou relationship between the actor and the audience. I think that Judith and I learned much about this as concept and reality through Fritz."

Paul Goodman's influence upon Fritz was not limited to introducing him to his friends, the Becks, his other social contacts, or his life style. Laura took Paul on as a patient. Within two years Paul began training as a lay therapist, joining a growing number of lay and professional people who met, as a group, with Fritz and Laura on a weekly basis. Included in this group were Elliot Shapiro (the man who later championed community-run schools in New York City as the initial principal of Intermediate School 201), Paul Weisz (a physician turned therapist turned Zen student), Isadore From (an avowed homosexual, one of Fritz's first American patients, and one of Fritz's close friends), and, later on, Ralph Hefferline (a university professor and, along with Paul Goodman, a collaborator on Fritz's second book) and Jim Simkin (the first Gestalt Therapist with a Ph.D. to work on the West Coast).

The group was started by Laura in 1950 as a professional therapy training group at a time when Fritz took off for Los Angeles with Isadore From, for, in spite of the social and professional stimulation he was getting, Fritz was restless. He had never liked the city of New York itself. He also felt hemmed in by his relationship with Laura, as he delved deeper and deeper into sexual exploration.

Isadore's twin brother, Sam, lived in Los Angeles. The brother was the lover of Christopher Isherwood. Fritz was quickly accepted by the intellectual "gay" set, which, aside from providing him with a number of patients, also provided him with a number of bed partners. Fritz, as both a sensualist and constant explorer, was not one to let any opportunity for sexual adventure pass.

His interests, of course, went beyond finding new sexual playmates, for he could do this to a certain extent in New York. What he wanted, by this time, was to spread the word of his nascent therapy and find fellow professionals who would accept his *Here and Now* approach. In that regard, Los Angeles was a fiasco, for he turned most of the therapeutic community off. They objected strongly to what they considered his lack of professionalism: his solicitation of patients at social occasions, his fraternization with other patients, and his open sexual enjoyment of both men and women. His style was so offensive to them—that "honest rudeness" which he brought from the East—that his message was never attended to. Yet what other way was he to be if he dared combine his social and professional selves in one package?

Laura came out and spent two months in Los Angeles that summer, but had no desire to play the Queen Bee to a nest of homosexuals. She returned to New York in the fall, followed in short order by Fritz.

On reentering the New York scene, Fritz got together with Ralph Hefferline and Paul Goodman and outlined a book which he invited them to coauthor. The work would serve as the basic tenet of their new therapeutic approach. Hefferline, who taught psychology at Columbia University, tried Fritz's Concentration Therapy exercises with his students with good success and elaborated upon them. He was, along with Fritz, to write these up as the first part of the book. Fritz, with disheveled notes and lots of ideas, planned to complete the second and theoretical section. Paul, an experienced writer, was to do the editing.

As it turned out, Paul wrote nearly all the second half and Ralph all the first, for Fritz, upon returning from the West Coast, continued to commute there several times a month in order to terminate his unfinished social and professional business. What Fritz did contribute were the ideas and the title for the new approach—*Gestalt Therapy*—over strong objections from Laura and his coauthors. To Laura, the approach had little relation to the academic Gestalt psychology she had studied in Europe. Paul thought the title too esoteric. Ralph was for calling it *Integrative Therapy*. Arthur Ceppos, of Hermitage House, published *Gestalt Therapy* in late 1951. In the beginning of 1952, Fritz and Laura established the *Gestalt Institute of New York* in a new home and office complex at 315 Central Park West.

He was proud of his new therapy and hung a shingle outside the building, *Dr. Frederick S. Perls/Gestalt Therapy Institute of New York*, that was three times larger than the professional signs hung by any of the other practitioners in the building. Yet pleased as he was, the inside of the Institute failed to match The Grand Plaque upon the building wall.

"He would always look for a bargain," according to his son, Steve. "We ate out frequently, but we always ordered the cheapest thing on the menu. He was never interested in spending a reasonable amount of money to get something—whatever that something was. When he and Laura outfitted their office, Fritz found some unfinished furniture. He sanded it and painted it and made it look reasonably okay. But my conception, if you're trying to start a New York Institute of Gestalt Therapy, is that you do so by trying to make it look fairly well put together rather than a fly by night outfit. But that didn't matter to him. Even with speakers of hi-fi components, which he really liked. Until the end of his life he would hunt around for used bargains. Very seldom would he buy anything new. He just wouldn't spend money."

Nor did he spend any more time with his children in New York than he did in South Africa. Steve, again: "I remember a few times asking him to show me how to drive. He said that I was too young to get a driver's license. When I was finally old enough, he gave me a few dollars and said 'Here. Take driving lessons.' Which wasn't a big thing, but significant to me because I felt that this was one thing he could have taught me, for he was a good driver and liked to drive. Even after I got my license he didn't want to lend me the car. The message I got was 'I don't trust you.'"

If Fritz was uninvolved with Steve, he was doubly so with Renate. He even failed to attend her wedding to a young art student named Arthur Gold. The reason? He didn't like him. His excuse? He had a patient. It was as if Fritz's only progeny was his new therapy, not his flesh and blood offspring.

Although the impact of *Gestalt Therapy* was, initially, almost nil, a few people in regions remote from New York did become aware of the new school—some through the book, some by happening to hear of the approach while at Columbia or otherwise passing through the city, and some through Paul Goodman's larger public platform. It was not too long before Fritz began traveling from city to city on a "milk run"—to Cleveland, Detroit, Toronto, Miami—running small groups for those professionals and laymen interested in Gestalt Therapy. In addition, he took advantage of observing, attending, and being affected by such pioneers as Charlotte Selver (Body Awareness) and J. L. Moreno (Psychodrama), studying Dianetics with Arthur Ceppos, and being turned on to Zen by Paul Weisz, his friend, confidant, and fellow Gestaltist in New York.

In the psychological realm, Fritz's thinking was

strongly influenced by these various approaches. Fritz might be likened to a vacuum cleaner which searches out and sucks in new material, new thoughts, and new ideas. He continually absorbed useful concepts and techniques and added them to his own central core. This attitude toward new approaches is best summed up by an introduction he wrote to Dr. J. A. Winter's *A Doctor's Report on Dianetics:*

> At the time when psychoanalysis itself was commonly dismissed as a "crackpot" theory, I learned not to be intimidated by name calling. As one who has attempted to make contributions to psychoanalytic theory, I realize now, as I realized then, that the science of psychotherapy is not a closed or finished one. The division of psychotherapists into mutually hostile "schools" has been more destructive to the young science of psychotherapy than the earlier hostility of the layman; each school in its battle against the other has acted as if it had all the answers and, for the most part, has ignored insights of a rival school. Name calling has become a substitute for independent thinking, the life blood of any science. The interests of science (as well as those who come to its practitioners for help) demand that I remain sensitive to the ideas of others. Insights, even though badly or inadequately formulated, are worth investigating. The history of science is full of examples of valuable discoveries made by those who were not aware of their full, and most important, significance.

Fritz was particularly intrigued with L. Ron Hubbard's *Dianetics*—later referred to as Scientology—and was one of the first people audited by this procedure. The Dianeticist's technique of emotional recall of past disturbing elements *in the present time,* as though they were happening *now,* in order to erase and eliminate these influences through emotional catharsis, was clearly evident in Fritz's later work, as was their insistence on communicating, on taking responsibility for one's own feelings. Thus, a Scientology student would say, "I feel uncomfortable when I am around you," rather than "You make me feel uncomfortable."

Paul Weisz introduced Fritz to Zen. "Fascinated with Zen," Fritz wrote, "its wisdom, its potential, its nonmoral attitude," he attempted to create techniques "of opening up this kind of self-transcendence to the Western man." More than any other practicing therapist, he managed to bring about a "marriage," to use Alan Watts's term, between psychotherapies East and West, between psychoanalysis and living totally in the *Here and Now* (in a Zen state of enlightenment).

"In his sessions in the early fifties he was never interpretive," said Elaine Kempner, a Gestaltist who trained with Fritz in the early days, "nor had he yet developed his *hot seat* technique. Instead it was 'What are you doing now? . . . What are you experiencing? . . . What are you feeling?'—all awareness techniques. He philosophized as well, talking about Gestalt Therapy as the *Here and Now* and that everything exists in the present moment. If the aim of therapy is to enable people to get through their impasses at the places they are blocked and stuck, they are blocked and stuck at this moment in time. He also stressed, much more than he did subsequently, the encounter between patient and therapist. If you were his patient he would quite explicitly work with your projections of what you thought was going on in him—all the things you were making out of him—and then he would tell you what he was actually experiencing.

"I remember working with him one time in Cleveland. I was depressed. He was a very impressive and a very frightening figure to most of us in those days because he was a very confronting, sharp, sometimes quite hostile person, sometimes quite paranoid. Anyway, I was claiming that he was never feeling anything but good. After I finished, he said, 'That's your fantasy.' Then he shared his own state, which was depressed, feeling pretty down, and anxious."

Fritz's willingness to share his own feelings was a further departure from Freudian technique, which insisted upon the analyst's anonymity. Another advancement occurred in the mid-fifties, when Fritz introduced the idea of having patients *be* (act out) the people, moods, and things in their dreams. Prior to that, the New York Gestalt group had *interpreted* dreams as indications of the ways by which a person might fulfill himself in the real world, already a step beyond the Freudians' attempts to analyze dreams for "deeper" meanings.

One of the things that Fritz became increasingly aware of as he traveled about the country was that he was received far better on the road than he was at home in New York. In later years Fritz established a reputation as a person who couldn't take criticism. That came, undoubtedly, from having had his fill of it from his wife, his colleagues, and his students at the New York Gestalt Institute from 1952 through 1956.

Although the Institute began under Fritz's and Laura's aegis and the training group was led, officially, by Laura, it soon developed into a peer session. As in all groups, a distinct pecking order developed.

Elliot Shapiro is a giant of a man who looks today a bit like Lyndon Johnson did in his heyday, but radiates warmth, informality, and gentleness. Quick to laughter, truly modest, and with no bones to pick, he described the situation that existed: "Laura was the leader of the group and the two big brains were the two Pauls—Goodman first and then Weisz. The group was very quick to hit and hit hard, to cut through the 'bullshit,' as Fritz would say.

"My remembrance of Fritz was that even when he was angry he seemed to be in good humor; that when you talked directly to him, even very, very critically, his response bordered on a joke, as it were. While Fritz, at first, had an aura of deep respect due to his *Ego, Hunger and Aggression*, he lost it rather quickly. Eventually, Paul Goodman's comments in the group, even about treatment, were listened to a little more carefully than were Fritz's.

"In Fritz's work with people he exhibited a mischievousness the way a little boy might in order to catch your attention and point out certain elements in your behavior or attitude. He was most often right. But at the same time, the need came more from him and not so much from the therapeutic situation. He was being a little tiny bit malicious, but it was a maliciousness that had some humor about it. He wanted you to see something, especially if you were egregiously bullshitting. But it was also, partially, to enter into a somewhat longer relationship—on a teasing basis—wherever that would go. Maybe, finally, to an affectionate relationship.

"I remember and always marvel that Fritz was constantly coming up with a new idea. Whether the idea seemed worthwhile or not, I really cherished his ability to look at things freshly. There were times he would come in eager to be with us because he really felt that he had something to share; that this was a real jump in therapy. Perhaps his ebullience turned people off. One doesn't think of an intellectual as being ebullient. And when it came out with great good humor and with a few Anglo-Saxon adjectives being thrown in at the same time, we didn't pick it up as part of an intellectual style. Maybe that was because there was something talmudic about us; that we considered an intellectual to be someone who pulls at his beard.

"Fritz was in the position of being a prophet without honor in his own home, really. He would come back from his tours around the country and come into the sessions again with new ideas—like the idea in dream analysis of making believe that you are every part of your dream—being every character and even pieces of furniture in the dream. He was criticized even for that in this group. The criticisms seemed to me, at that time, 'professional.' At one point I recall Fritz saying to Laura, 'You always knock me down.' I caught that with a certain surprise because I hadn't felt that, hadn't been aware of such an attitude on Laura's part toward Fritz.

"He'd come back with a great deal of satisfaction of being successful here or successful there. Then he would get hit very hard, especially by Paul Goodman. And what Paul would say very directly to him is 'You're saying this or using this device because you don't really have a verbal

gift. . . . You're not really an intellectual and you therefore depend on a technique.' This was picked up by a
number of the members of the group from time to time so
that after a little while, it seemed to me, Fritz had a feeling
of 'Who needs this? After all, I'm going around the country, having a certain amount of adulation. I come back here
and get insulted all the time.'

"If you ever get to be the parent of adolescents, you'll
see the same thing. That's really what was happening at
the time."

In 1956, after four years of this treatment, Fritz decided
to leave New York, migrating to the warmth and ocean
waters of Miami.

I met with Laura Perls on two occasions in the winter
of 1972–73 to talk to her about Fritz. She was a smartly
dressed tiny woman with short-clipped white hair, sparkling brown eyes, and a warm and cordial manner. Elegant
where Fritz was coarse, smiling while he often scowled,
intellectual whereas he was intuitive, proper while Fritz
was ribald—it is easy to see how the two of them comple-
mented one another. Photographs and posters of Fritz
adorn the walls of her office-apartment on West Ninety-
sixth Street. Her interpretation of Fritz's move to Florida
was far from flattering: "I think he left New York because
he wasn't the only one . . . was not the only big fish—not
the leading psychotherapist, nor even the leading Gestaltist. What he showed, afterwards, was that he would rather
be a big fish in a comparatively small pond in Florida or
the West Coast. But when the operation became bigger
and there were other people involved, either in New York
or at Esalen, he couldn't stand it anymore."

Although that analysis may contain some kernel of
truth, it seems to me to miss the point and contains, perhaps, a mixture of Laura's feeling of superiority and the
hurt reaction of an abandoned wife. Clearly, New York
was a no-win situation for Fritz. The pleasure of his friendships with "Isad" From and Paul Weisz and his involvement with The Living Theater was more than offset by the

consistently negative feedback he was getting from his peers. Much of this resulted from a rivalry that developed between Fritz and Paul Goodman in which Paul was readily besting Fritz. Paul was more Laura's kind of person: cultured, refined, academic, a prolific writer, and a "real" intellectual. The two of them formed a mutual admiration society with Paul respecting his ex-therapist's "genius," and she his. Paul dedicated his best-known work, *Growing Up Absurd,* to Laura. In groups, Paul expressed with waspish and direct tongue many of Laura's quietly felt attitudes regarding Fritz. Instead of awarding kudos for Fritz's enthusiasms and accomplishments, the Gestalt group, led by Paul, threw tomatoes.

Laura has the quality of gentility and of intransigence that made it difficult to ask her highly personal questions about her life with Fritz. She was reluctant to talk about him and seemed unwilling to elaborate upon any details of their personal life that might reflect, adversely, upon herself in any conventional sense. For example, Fritz made a total of four brief and passing references to her in *Garbage Pail.* In one, he wrote about having "voyeuristic compulsions centered around Lore." I asked, on our second meeting, what this phrase referred to.

"I don't know what he meant," Laura gently smiled.

Two of Fritz's outstanding qualities were the strength of his sexual drive and the range of his sexual interests. During the years he and Laura lived in New York, tales of their amatory escapades ran rife. How did this affect their marriage?

"You know how stories spread," Laura answered, implying that rumor far outdistanced fact.

Arthur Ceppos, who had some familiarity with the New York Gestaltists, doubts the many stories that he, too, heard. "With the exception of Paul Goodman, most of those people just talked a good sexual game."

Ralph Hefferline's impression of Laura was that of a "deeply conventional person."

Still, Marty Fromm (the woman he subsequently fell in

love with) says Fritz told her that his and Laura's sex life was always very rich, varied, full, and included other people.

For me, the *details* of Fritz and Laura's sexual relationship are unimportant. I can appreciate the fact that it is nobody's business but her own. Nonetheless, attitudes toward something as fundamental and as "animalistic" as sex are indicative of more general attitudes toward life. Certainly, when a husband is such an avowedly open sexual being, his wife's perspective in this area might provide important insight into even more basic aspects of their marriage. One element that seemed illuminated, for me, by Laura's parrying my questions was her concern with respectability and her image.

And why not? The fact of her being a psychotherapist aside, she is also a woman, a wife, and a mother. How many women, one wonders, would relish being married to a man who had such a reputation for sexual adventures with countless other people? Who among us could readily endure the knowing smiles, the perpetual gossiping, the smug condescension that others might register? How is one to justify a marriage to a man who loses no opportunity, in his autobiographical ruminations, to declare his lack of passion for his spouse? How is one to contend with all these elements and at the same time behave and speak as a highly cultured woman, an understanding wife, and a person who has her own house, psychologically speaking, in order?

The causes of marital discontent were many. Where Fritz wanted real adulation, Laura seems to have offered studied support. She gave this "support" because she felt, empathically, his deficiency in this regard and because, at least initially, she loved him.

Yet this "giving" to compensate for and heal his weakness offered a steady unspoken reminder that "You are, indeed, an inadequate person. But my compassion, perceptions and interventions will eventually make you well."

I could sympathize with Laura's well-intentioned motivations and told her that it sounded like she was a good mother to Fritz.

"I was that way from the very first," she answered. "I protected Fritz from any kind of attacks from the outside. He didn't realize how many people attacked him. First my family. And then people who relied on him in some way and from whom he then withdrew or resented in some way. I was continuously protecting him. Even when he was rather hostile. And I'm still doing it now that he's dead."

Fritz may have worn blinders when it came to self-respect, but he had an uncanny sensitivity to the transactions people tried to engage him in ("agendas," or "manipulations," as he contemptuously called them). Instead of a "thank you" for her well-meaning efforts, Laura received the sort of scorn that an adolescent boy reserves for his protective mother.

When Fritz, Ralph Hefferline, and Paul Goodman were working on *Gestalt Therapy,* Fritz told Ralph that Laura "wanted to keep me tied to her apron strings."

"That made it sound," said Ralph, "like he wanted her to be Mommy—or she wanted to be Mommy—and he wanted to be a big boy. I don't know about that, but it certainly seemed that a great deal of what he did was flamboyant acting like he was a big boy."

Sensing the dynamics behind Fritz's cavalier responses, Laura persisted nonetheless.

"Fritz had a carry-over of his father's attitude toward him, which was always denigrating. His father called him a 'piece of shit,' which was terrible. If I did anything it was to counteract that—to give him a feeling, or get him to the point where he could get a feeling of his own worth. But when I said anything that was at all critical, he felt completely devastated. As if I was calling him 'No good.' And I certainly never did. Not even at the time when he was most hostile and rejecting."

But again, her solicitousness reflected adversely upon

Fritz's strength. It was this motivation and his response that led to their never-ending "Can you top this?" game.

Fritz told many people that he felt at a competitive disadvantage with Laura, who could out "one-upsmanship" him. Indeed, many of Laura's comments contain sweetly voiced put downs. Take this remark, when I commented that Fritz seemed like a very lonely person to me: "He was very narcissistic and I think most genuises are in a way. They are self-involved. And whoever could go with that, he thought he loved. He loved being loved. But he couldn't take any kind of criticism."

It is not so much that Laura is correct or incorrect in her assessments. For me, it is what particular truths about Fritz stand out in her mind that is of importance, what it is that is "foreground" for her.

In commenting, for instance, about Fritz as a clinician, she had these critical remarks to make: "Actually, long before Fritz was in medicine, let alone in psychoanalysis, he was in the theater. He was in the Reinhardt school. He wanted to become a director. And he did. That is what he fell back on, in the end, in the last three years or so. And that is when all the films of him were made. Unfortunately, people think that this is all there is to be done . . . the hot seat and the empty chair. Yet this is just a way in which he could keep himself from getting involved."

One impression that I have of Laura is that she resents, somewhat, the fuss that is made over Fritz, resents the fact that he achieved the credit of being the founder of Gestalt Therapy, and feels that she and Paul Goodman, her friend and protégé, were not really given their due. To her, it must seem like a cruel accident that Fritz, this impulsive, vain, restless, and somewhat slipshod man—a man who couldn't even make it as the kingpin of the New York Gestalt Institute—should achieve all the accolades as the founder of a "New School," when she, Paul, and the others knew as much, if not more, about these same concepts. It must have hurt additionally to see their academia outpaced by Fritz's show business style. Still, she might, to herself, take credit.

"You take Laura," said Arthur Ceppos, "and she'll give you Laura. She made him, which was unquestionably Fritz's biggest hangup. He knew that she didn't make him. But not only did she insist that she did, but she represented that which, to a very large degree, emasculated him. And this was the phony academic achievement and approval. So it was quite a struggle for Fritz, who was so talented, with Laura always projecting that she was the scholar and he was an uninformed, relatively illiterate person who was dabbling in psychology, and that his particular recognition was only due to the aura which came from her and kind of touched him. But he was aware of it. He tried to fight it. He fought it very beautifully once he left New York."

Fritz claimed that he left New York to get away from Laura. But, according to Laura, "He never really left me. He just stayed away from home longer and longer. He was like Peer Gynt, the character he always wanted to play as an actor, the eternal wayfarer who always comes home to his mother, and later, his wife. Even in his final illness he sent for me."

If Fritz was playing Peer Gynt, as Laura claims, she was certainly being Solveig, the good wife/mother who always accepted him back whenever the wayfarer returned. Whenever he came to New York to visit or work, he stayed at her place—even after his unflattering descriptions of their life together in *Garbage Pail*.

Gestalt Therapy presumes that when we invest emotion upon someone else, it is often *our hidden unresolved self* that we see in the other person. Using this principle as a guide, it is interesting to review not only what Fritz and Laura accused each other of, but of how very similar, in many ways, they were to one another.

Laura, for instance, critizes Fritz for his narcissism, and yet she can be affectionately recalled, by Elliot Shapiro, to have a similar quality.

"Laura's vanity was not to be right all the time, but to let you know that she could do something very, very well. She always indicated that she did things very, very well and had great talent. It didn't come out as heavily as Fritz experienced it, and in fairness to Laura, she wasn't *that* boastful. It wouldn't be deadly or anything. But she did a tiny bit of name dropping. And it was always her name."

Or take this description from Rae Perls, Laura's daughter-in-law: "Laura is very much upper middle class. She is a Queen who sits on a throne, equal in size and height to Fritz's. When she comes to visit us, she is the Queen coming for rest. We serve her, take care of her, and she bestows her favors upon us."

"Like Fritz." I rejoin.

"That's right," Rae laughed, "and then she'd criticize him for it. She always did. That was one of the funny things. He'd come down and make nasty comments about her. And she'd come down and do the same thing. He'd accuse her of not listening and she'd accuse him of not listening. You could just run down the list of mutual complaints."

Marriage, for Fritz, failed to provide those elements he was searching for: a sense of an accepting and adoring family that would treasure him. The same, of course, might be said of Laura.

Why, then, did she endure so many insults, so many meanderings, so little appreciation herself?

"I asked Laura once," said Elaine Kempner, "why in hell don't you divorce this son-of-a-bitch?"

"Because," she answered, "he's the most fascinating man I've ever known."

Fritz's fascination with Laura, however, had run its course. The changes that he put himself through during the previous ten years—experiences that made him both more authentic and less acceptable to his wife—had convinced him that it was time to part. At sixty-three years of age, the gypsy was on his own once more.

6

Miami

Fritz's coming to Miami meant not only withdrawing from Laura but also withdrawing, in large part, from his professional scene and accepting, to an extent, the fact of his old age and the likelihood that Gestalt Therapy would never achieve the major impact he intended it to have.

Physically he was feeling poorly. In New York, periodic anginal pains had led to a diagnosis of heart scarring. He was unable to take the cold winters and tired of being the outsider, fighting for his new therapy to not only survive, but also grow. And its growth seemed imperceptible.

Gestalt Therapy had been in print, now, for five years, but outside of New York there was little movement in the direction of Gestalt Therapy to show for it. A Cleveland Gestalt Institute had started in 1954, but it was, as far as Fritz was concerned, more under the influence of Laura, Paul Goodman, and Paul Weisz who, along with Fritz, visited and taught there regularly.

The cities Fritz visited alone, he met only with lay groups. Although he was willing to pick up any support he could get for his ideas, he was nonetheless disappointed that he could not be more involved in the training of therapists. Every therapist he worked with might carry his message to hundreds of potential patients and colleagues alike. Doing demonstration groups for laymen seemed far less important.

He fully expected to end his days in Miami, not in any melodramatic way, but, given his poor health and his advanced age, he planned to live in semiretirement until his heart gave out.

Miami had been one of Fritz's circuit towns. He looked forward to its warmth and to ocean swimming, about the only sporting pleasure left that he could enjoy. But instead of air and lightness, he frugally opted for a cheap apartment which he rented from a former patient. It consisted of a very small living room (where he conducted his therapy sessions and listened to music), an even smaller area that doubled as a kitchen, and a dark bedroom that admitted no light either day or night.

It was a most depressing environment for him to live in. He went out for meals and spent great periods of time alone. His bitterness over being unappreciated—of going nowhere slowly—resulted in his alienating the professional community almost immediately. He expected brickbats and he got them, being seen as a sharp but critical, contemptuous, and arrogant person with an enormous chip on his shoulder. He ran one group a week and had very few private patients, living, for the most part, as a hermit.

Every six or seven weeks, when his isolation and boredom got the best of him, he would leave for a short circuit to those cities where Gestalt groups had formed: New York, Toronto, Cleveland, Detroit, and back to Miami. He might, on the road, share an imtimacy with an old lover, but for the most part he was even turned off to sex, fearing that the excitement might precipitate a heart attack.

For nearly two years he lived this way, withdrawing, more and more, from work, from play, from sex . . . from life. And then, in December 1957, he met a thirty-two-year-old woman named Marty Fromm, "the most significant woman in my life," and he was once again *involved*. She was to be the spark that reignited his passions, unsettled him with jealousy, and placed him back in motion.

The following excerpts are part of an open letter that he wrote to Marty in *Garbage Pail:*

Big Sur, California

Dear Marty,

When I met you, you were beautiful beyond description. A straight strong Greek nose, which you later destroyed to get a "pretty" face. When you did this, when you had your nose baptized, you became a stranger. You had everything in excess—intelligence and vanity, frigidity and passion, cruelty and efficiency, recklessness and depression, promiscuity and loyalty, contempt and enthusiasm. . . .

When I look back on our years, what comes up first is not our fierce lovemaking and our even more fierce fights, but your gratefulness: "You gave me back my children."

I found you despondent, nearly suicidal, disappointed in your marriage, chained down by two children, with whom you had lost touch.

I was proud to take you up and to mold you to my and your needs. You loved and admired me as therapist and, at the same time, became my therapist, cutting with your cruel honesty through my phoniness, bullshit and manipulations. Never was so much equal give and take between us as then.

Then came the time when I took you to Europe. Paris, some insane jealousy bouts on my part, some wild orgies, exciting, but not really happy. That happiness came in Italy. I was so proud to show you real beauty, as if I owned it and to help you overcome your mediocre taste in art. Of course we got drunk with Venice and . . .

That Aida performance in Verona! And ancient Roman amphitheater holding twenty—thirty thousand people. . . . Voices floating with gripping intensity over us and through us. The finale: torches flaming into infinite space and dying voices touching eternity.

It was not easy to wake up to the hustle and bustle of the leaving crowd. . . .

Our nights. No pressure to go home, no fear of getting too little sleep. Getting the last drop from our experiencing each other. "Tonight was the best" became a stock phrase, but it was true, an ever-increasing intensity of being there for each other. There is no poetry to describe those weeks, only amateurish stutter.

In this life you don't get something for nothing. I had to pay dearly for my happiness. Back in Miami I became more and

more possessive. My jealousy reached truly psychotic propor-
tions. Whenever we were separated—and we were most of
the day—I got restless, checked up on you, drove several
times a day by your house. I could not concentrate on anything except: "Marty, where are you now, with whom are you
now?"

Until Peter came into our life and you fell in love with him.
He did not care much about you. For you, he was a respite
from me and my torturing. He was easy-going, an entertaining
raconteur. It was impossible to be bored in his presence. He
was young and beautiful and I was old and vicious. To com-
plicate matters still further: I, too, was, and still am, fond of
him.

The heavens caved in for me. I was left with debasing myself on the outside and nursing wild revenge fantasies on the
inside.

All attempts to break off with you failed. Then I did something which, looking backwards, appears an attempt to com-
mit suicide without the stigma of such a cowardice.

I survived those operations. I survived our separation. I survived our final fights and reconciliation. I am here and you are
there. It feels good and solid whenever we meet again.

Thank you for being the most important person in my life.

Fritz

I telephoned Marty in October 1972 and asked if I
might meet with her. She is willing to do so. A month later
I board a plane and fly to Miami.

How am I to describe her in a way that would do her
justice? Mother, egoist, handsome woman, speaker of
truths, it is easy to understand Fritz's fascination with her.

She lives alone in a meticulously kept home. Her apartment is simply furnished in contemporary fashion. A
lovely Japanese style drawing adorns the guest room that I
occupy. It is a birthday greeting from her daughter and her
boyfriend. The following inscription is nestled between
delicate tree branches:

Hi Ma!
Have a delicious joyful day
We miss and love you incredibly mucho
Your biggest fan club (California branch)

Artfully and painstakingly made up, Marty, at forty-eight, is still a beautiful woman. Her short black hair has not a streak of grey, and her eyes sparkle. When we meet, she is wearing a green African print mu-mu style dress with a long slit up the side that accents a well-turned leg. Later, she put on a diaphanous orange shift that reveals her shapely breasts. And when we go out for dinner, she wears a smartly tailored slacks and shirt outfit.

There is still a lot of Bayonne in this transplanted New Jerseyan. An associate professor of psychology at Miami-Dade Community College, she is street smart, wise, and tough in the Northern big-city manner. And she is phenomenally outspoken about her desires.

"What's in it for me?" is her attitude in speaking about Fritz. Almost everyone I've interviewed has undoubtedly considered that question, yet she is the only person to raise it up front.

Money?

Well there is none.

Recognition?

That will have to do. After all, the book will be written anyway.

"Fritz liked what he saw of himself in me," she says.

Indeed, when Fritz described her as having "everything in excess—intelligence and vanity, frigidity and passion, cruelty and efficiency, recklessness and depression, promiscuity and loyalty, contempt and enthusiasm"—if you substitute "coldness" for "frigidity," Fritz might just as well have been describing himself. I am reminded of a line in a poem that a friend once wrote: "I see myself reflected in your gaze and call it love. . . ."

I see them both as egocentric, sensual, honest about their most self-seeking motivations, and very tough, shrewd businessmen. There is also, in Marty, a warm motherly quality. I am seated in her most comfortable chair, mixed a respectful drink, and am amply fed throughout my weekend visit.

There are distortions in Fritz's "open letter" to her, she

tells me, and errors in the actual sequence of events. Yet, if that's the way he experienced the situation, she is willing to accept his attitudes.

Marty had first met Fritz casually and socially. When he mentioned his group, she decided to see what it was like. Attending one session, she felt moved, emotionally, and decided to continue coming. Her participation was marginal, however, until her daughter began acting "crazy"—showing signs of hyperactivity, nastiness and untouchability.

At school, her child screamed, cried and vomited to the point where Marty felt obliged to keep her home. She brought her daughter to a pschologist and entered individual psychotherapy with Fritz, seeing him anywhere from three to five mornings a week, "and all I did was cry for my $150."

Severely agitated and depressed, Fritz initially helped her by giving her a perspective on the psychologist's treatment of her offspring. Marty felt this man was acting cruelly to her child. Fritz gave her a paper to read, entitled "Support Through Non-Reassurance." She allowed her daughter to continue with this therapist, and, within a month, she was back in school.

> As for me, I was my mother's child. I was really a terrible person in all ways. I was frigid and vicious, ugly, sharp, sarcastic, hateful, turned everyone off and knew I was turning everyone off yet had no way of doing anything other than what I was doing. I was filled with a great deal of personal despair that was never shared with anyone and hugged the fantasy of suicide very close to me—always knowing that I did have an out when I got so hateful that I couldn't stand myself. For I obviously wasn't doing anything right but was turning the world off.
>
> My daughter's breakdown brought it all to a head for me. My first reaction was to really hate her, because "How could she do this to me? Now the whole world knows that even the surface of this beautiful family and lovely home and my well-organized life and functioning is absolutely based upon quicksand." And with all these people about me that I felt superior to, obviously their kids weren't having breakdowns at

the age of six. Mine was, and everyone was shaking their heads. Her breakdown exposed my act. She showed me up.

Fritz did a lot for me. I asked him to come to my house, see my daughter, and tell me what he saw. He was never interested in children, but he said, "Yes," he would. He came for dinner. We weren't lovers. He came because I asked him to see her. So there was always contact with my family from the moment I started in therapy. He didn't like my family scene, but he would come and be part of it from time to time during all the years we were together. Those were the practical things he did with me. Much more long range was dealing with my mother and my relationship with women—all of which were connected to my relationship with my child.

Within a month we were in bed together. That was strange.

Fritz kissed everybody. When I left his office, feeling depressed much of the time, and he kissed me goodbye, it gave me a feeling of great warmth, teddy bear cuddling and comfort. But suddenly it became very much of a man/male kiss. I got out of there one day and drove home absolutely dazed. I was very nasty when he did that. I looked at him and I said, "I need a therapist, not a lover," and stomped out of the room. I had a dream that night. A very obvious sexy dream about Fritz and my husband. I came back the next day in therapy and Fritz said, "What's happening? You're looking everyplace but at me today." I would not tell him. Finally, grudgingly, I came out with the dream. He listened to it and we talked a bit about it. I had been very protective of my husband—never talked about him out of a sense of loyalty. You must also understand that I never had a friend. I had a terrible life and never shared it with anyone—partly because none of us talked about our husbands or our sex life but of safe things like children, politics, and the state of the world.

Fritz said he knew, afterwards—when we finally got to talking about my husband's and my sex life—that when he first saw us together, he saw a Queen and a Frog. And how can a Frog fuck a Queen? And the other thing was the seductiveness of my husband . . . how good he was to me. My mother was very cruel to me. It was nice to have somebody who was so kind to me. And the less he functioned sexually the kinder and kinder and nicer and nicer and softer and gentler and understanding he was toward me. I would do things that I didn't understand at all, like really beat on him sometimes—really hit him. Just to get any kind of response from him. Now I understand why I did it, but then I was appalled. He's such a nice man, what am I pummeling him for? But I never acted out any of my aggressiveness and frustration of not getting laid and not having any kind of sex life. Because I didn't know anything about what I was supposed to have. All I knew was that the image we were making for the world was something like, "He's so nice and Marty's so terrible, what does he possibly see in her?" That was what I imagined people saw in the two of us.

After I told Fritz the dream, I went home and decided I would take him as a lover. I was much sterner then and came in to the next session with my diaphragm. After the session, when Fritz kissed me, he was suddenly over me but we were fully clothed and never fucked. I think he was testing me. A session or two later, we were intimate.

Even after we became lovers I was still very much the patient, seeing him three or four times a week. My husband was paying for it until much later, when I complained about it. "I don't like it. How come I'm paying for sessions if I'm doing such nice things for you?" Because at that time I was doing things such as cooking for him, taking care of his laundry— things that were easy for me to do and hard for Fritz to do.

What we did for each other sexually was absolute, sheer magic. Fritz came to Miami to die. His heart was bad. So when he touched me, he was also wary of getting into me. He was worried about his heart pounding. Was he really going to have a heart attack and die? Yet there was enough sex, attraction, magnestism, excitement, and magic that made it another world type of sexual existence together. For I was dead and absolutely frigid and not going to let myself get all excited if all I could have were my husband's twenty-nine-second touches. Fritz was similarly fearful of getting excited. He didn't know if he wanted to live again. He made his peace and was in Miami to die. He was going to eke out his last few years and live minimally and take care of himself and not get involved in pushing Gestalt or pushing sex or living with zest as he had done all of his life. He was sixty-five when we met. Yet our sexuality was just amazing.

We were together for hours. That was part of Fritz's Pygmalion act of turning me on to sex. It gave him much pride and joy in melting me. And it melted him too. However that wasn't the way we verbalized it or how he thought of it. It was, "He's doing something for me." And with his developing me sexually, we also introduced other people into our relationship sexually. It was Fritz's insistence on turning me on to all the variations on a theme. Everything that existed he wanted me to taste. And he wanted to be the manipulator and puppeteer who was pulling my strings.

So he found other women and he found other men and he found combinations and he found drugs. And he was doing this "for me." He had been through everything before except drugs. The kind of sex life that he had with Laura was always very rich and very varied. I realize now that Fritz didn't do anything for me. What he was doing was for himself. I was young and beautiful and I provided lots of access to lots of scenes Fritz wanted. So I did as much for him in producing what he wanted as he did for me in turning me on to the world.

There were no rational explanations for the magic that happened between us physically. Fritz was older than my father and not as beautiful. So it could not be explained externally.

Another thing we did a lot together was go to the movies. I enjoyed that, too. The advantage of having a lover who was older than my father was that we could go everyplace together . . . and we did. As crazy as I was about what people would say and think, in my own head my rationale was "the worst they can say about me is that I'm too dependent on my psychiatrist." That's the worst they could say. Because look at this deteriorated old man and look at beautiful young Marty. We just didn't match. That gave us freedom to do many things together. As my therapist he'd come to the beach with me, the cabana, he'd come to the house for dinner, he'd come to parties occasionally, that I made, and be on the fringes of my ongoing social life—as much as he wanted to be.

I never functioned better in my life than in those years, in the sense of doing lots of things I had to do. I ran the house and the maid and our Jewish upper-middle-class social life and children and chauffeured everybody about and went back to school immediately after seeing Fritz. One of the early things he said to me was, "Marty, the basis of your neurosis is boredom." The message I got was, "I may be crazy but I'm not stupid. I can do something about that." So I went back to the University and made up sixteen undergraduate credits in psychology and twenty-four graduate credits. And still spent anywhere from three to eight hours a day with Fritz.

One of the nice things we had going was that he asked me to criticize him. He also fought back, hated and resented it, but he asked for it and came back for more. For all our personal relationships were subjected to therapeutic scrutiny.

Whatever we did outside of therapy became foreground in the next therapy session, and that's how I came to act as his therapist. Fritz was closed in many ways and put limits on what we talked about together in our personal lives. There were no limits when he was my therapist. But there were limits to gossip, chitchat, asking him questions, draining him, talking about my kids, or chatter outside my formal therapy.

About six months after we were together, he decided to leave Miami to push Gestalt Therapy again. He got an offer from Vin O'Connell in Columbus, Ohio, to be a training psychiatrist at one of the large mental hospitals there. That was an offer Fritz could not resist. For once he wouldn't be playing with dumb-bunny patients but would really be affecting psychiatry with Gestalt. And that was his baby. That was always his major interest—to put Gestalt on the map. There was never any thought of his taking me with him. Just, "I'm going to Columbus to be a training therapist."

I screamed and cried and ranted and raved. "How could you do this to me? How could you leave all your patients? You're letting me down." I got from that a very important message in terms of learning what responsibility means—a hard lesson, but one I have not since forgotten. And the lesson was, "Marty, I did for you what I could while I was here. I'm not responsible for you. I don't owe you anything. Goodbye." I sure learned a lot, for I've come to adopt that too.

Vincent O'Connell, a therapist friend, offered Fritz a chance to train psychiatric residents at the Columbus Psychiatric Clinic, Columbus State Hospital. Fritz's willingness to take to the road once more was undoubtedly related to his increased feeling of vitality engendered, for the most part, by his close involvement with Marty Fromm.

Upon arriving in Columbus, he stayed with Vincent and his wife, April. For three or four months he was quite happy, training residents, running groups, and rekindling his passion for Gestalt Therapy. Indeed, his involvement in his work was so intense, April O'Connell finally threw him out, not being able to take Gestalt Therapy for breakfast, lunch, and dinner.

Marty came to visit Fritz and helped him relocate,

equip and organize a new domicile. The new address was to be a most temporary one, though, since Fritz remained in Columbus for only nine months in all. During the last three months he was on the road more often than in Ohio, visiting Marty in Miami and starting up his milk run once more.

In the winter of 1958–59, he returned to Florida. He came to discover during his separation from her that Marty had become far more important to him than he had realized. This was not just another casual affair. There was, instead, both love and a gnawing neediness that resulted from her fulfilling desires that he had previously ignored.

What was there about Marty that melted Fritz's isolation? Over and above her physical beauty, he found a kindred spirit, another human being whose soul had never been shared. She was someone who felt a great deal of appreciation for the wisdom and perspective he gave to her and who showed her gratitude and love by fussing, feeding, aiding, and tidying up after him—small comforts, perhaps, but things that Fritz hadn't experienced in years. Moreover, she was, perhaps, the first woman he had known who was intellecutally stimulating and yet uncompetitive; he could argue with her and accept her divergent opinions without feeling put down.

He appreciated Marty's nerve, honesty, and toughness. She was always ready to speak her mind and give him a fair fight. There was none of the "I'll protect your poor self-esteem" attitude that Laura fed back. Nor the envy.

Fritz, always the teacher, also wanted Marty to be a Gestalt disciple. He continuously bounced ideas off her and clarified much of his own thinking through their discussions and her questioning—for half the time she had little idea of what he was talking about.

Marty's appeal rested, as well, in her being a fellow adventurer, someone who derived pleasure and excitement in challenging conventions and taboos. She was excited by the concept of sleeping with her therapist, delighted by the fact of loving and turning on to a physically unattractive man more than twice her age, intrigued by the idea of their illicit romance, and bold enough to join in Fritz's experimentations with lysergic acid.

Upon Fritz's return, he and Marty found an apartment on the beach, a scant five minutes, by car, from where she lived. It was light and airy, sunny and bright—a most pleasing place for them to spend more time together. For more than half a year, things went exceptionally well. But by the fall of 1959, their relationship began to unravel.

The catalyst that served to tear Fritz and Marty apart was LSD—the mind-expanding psychedelic agent that Fritz, always the bold experimenter, hoped to use to gain fuller awareness of himself. It is likely, however, that even without the drug their intense relationship would have ended, as it posed great problems for Fritz, problems that caused him as much anguish and pain as he had suffered with Lucy, the adventuress he had known in Germany.

Fritz was a man who suffered greatly, in his life, from unrequited love. He had missed the love of his father, had played second or third fiddle for his mother's love, had had few friends as an adolescent, had lost his closest pal in the war, and had always experienced himself as an ugly toad. As he grew older, he learned to live without feeling close to his peers, his wife, or his children. He endured this deprivation by preaching, *"I do my thing, you do yours. . . . If we meet it's beautiful. If not it can't be helped."* Yet here he was—wanting, desiring, and needing another person—and unable to adopt his own "Truth" when his wishes weren't met.

Fritz was caught in a difficult ethical and social dilemma. As a therapist and a philosopher he knew that his Gestalt idea of "do your own thing" made sense for those he worked with. As a needy man, his heart demanded that Marty be obedient to him. These oppositional forces were responsible for one of his few lapses as a therapist. Ordinarily, Fritz saw others clearly because he had no need for them. Now he vacillated between being helpful and demanding, which caused both of them much anguish and

confusion. Months went by before he eventually chose the
proper path and withdrew from this insoluable bind.

Our roles started switching and changing when I called him
on his role of being a perfect therapist. We always had formal
sessions, face to face; he was the therapist and I was the patient. As a therapist he was perfect. He said all the right
things in terms of philosophies, values, and attitudes which
were very different from the way I was raised and could really
help me disengage myself from my major worries and responsibilities and the burdens of the weight of the world that I
carried with me. For I was assuming responsibilities for everybody, and everything he said began to make sense and
began to make life easier for me. Words are important, you
know. *Responsibility* and *obligation* and all the things I was
doing.

Then we would switch from our hour or two of formal therapy. We were then personal and lovers and into each other in
all ways. The discrepency showed up immediately in things
like money and in things like sex. I had the perfect *therapist.*
He told me I should fuck around. It was really a crazy thing to
tell me. He created problems I didn't really want. I'm "supposed" to fuck around because my therapist tells me that. And
I was suddenly the most lucious flower that thousands of bees
started buzzing around. For the first time in my life I was into
sex. I must have smelled it and looked it and showed it. My
husband would come home from work some days and say,
"You're so beautiful." And I would look at myself and see that
I really was glowing and melting and people were responding
to it.

So I'd come to his home and talk about this man or that, one
invitation or another. One voice said, "Yah. Fuck him." And
the other voice said, "How dare you leave me alone? How
dare you do this to me?" Depending on which chair he was
sitting in. In the therapy sessions he'd then say, "Okay.
Express resentments." I would, and each time he'd say,
"You're absolutely right." I'd think, "Swell. We really have
our lines of communication open and he really does understand the double messages he's feeding me which really are
driving me crazy." And then we'd go through the same thing
again.

Yet my problem was that I did not trust what I saw because
Fritz was the official psychiatrist who I did trust. Brilliant, a
genius, absolutely valid as a therapist. I couldn't doubt that.

What I doubted was my perception of reality. When it came to a showdown on whose perception was really accurate, I gave him lip service, and I backed down. So I really reinforced my own neurosis, in terms of not trusting me. I never gave up my perceptions. Fritz's admiration of me was for my clear thinking—cutting through shit and seeing what was happening. Yet then I didn't trust my perceptions, because they differed from what he was telling me was going on. And he's my psychiatrist. He knows what he's doing.

He really became psychotic when we started taking LSD together. But that was only part of it. Even before he started taking drugs he was psychotic, and it primarily manifested itself towards me and throughout his life in terms of paranoia.

I had an enormous number of things to do and we still spent a lot of time together. But if I was due at 10:30 and came at 10:45, I was late. Of course, the more demands he made on me, the later I would keep coming. I had lots of good excuses. I was running a home and kids and chauffeuring and going to school and writing papers and meeting people. And it was a burden for me, his happiness revolving around my presence. He lived for my getting there, physically. He was fine when we weren't together, knowing I was doing my busy things. But he would invent "Who is she seeing? What is she really doing?" That kind of paranoia. And it was ridiculous, because I was leading a busy compartmentalized life occupied with *things*.

Fritz took acid first alone and then he introduced me to it. When we took our first trip, when the day was over, he looked at me and said, "Well, Marty. You're certainly a lot less crazy than I imagined and I'm certainly a lot more crazy than I imagined."

We took acid together but Fritz frequently took it alone. Because I was busy and wasn't around and Fritz was alone, didn't have much of a practice, and did have a lot of time. Fritz got into drugs even more heavily when he first moved to California. He tripped every other day. In Miami he was tripping on Sandoz acid once a week. This was in fifty-nine, before the psychedelic revolution. Only a few people were into it.

He saw acid as a tool to get into his psychosis. He loved to use it, loved to become raving mad and get into his animal qualities. He loved to rant and rave and play act. He always had very violent tragedy-Queen experiences with huge sobbings and great traumas and memories and feelings—much of it about his father. But instead of being a tool to work through his psychosis, acid exacerbated his paranoia. Now I had a full-blown psychosis to deal with. For his focus in life was me, and our situation became worse. He became more and more demanding and I more and more surreptitiously spiteful. The crazier he got the less attractive he was to me and the more I resented our role reversal with me being therapist and he patient. I felt, ME ME ME. I PATIENT.

That fall of fifty-nine was difficult, with Fritz getting into psychedelic drugs so heavily and my becoming more and more uncomfortable and feeling very very crazy. I was aware that something terrible was happening to me, that symptomatically my neurosis was a lot worse than it had ever been. The symptoms had changed, but what I had now were a lot more physically involving and terrible. And they had to be taken account of. When I was dead and frigid and miserable, that was okay. I didn't know there was anything else. Now I wasn't vicious or dead or mean or miserable, but anxious. Terrifying anxiety attacks. I still wasn't getting along with people. I had no contacts, was phobic of everyone. Nobody knew about me and Fritz, and I was more devious and more sneaky than I had ever been in my life.

I was pretty devious about exposing myself before, anyway. Now there was a lot more I didn't want exposed. Nobody knew we were lovers. My whole life with my husband had been kept secret and I was totally dependent, therefore, on one person in my life for any kind of contact, communication, sexuality, aliveness. My keeping our life a secret served Fritz's needs as well. He never said, "Why don't you leave your husband? Why don't you tell him?"

Fritz no longer had the aura of "My psychiatrist is going to save me," because something pretty terrible was happening to me and my psychiatrist was pretty crazy. And I knew it, finally. For he wasn't doing any of the things he was telling me to do.

Suddenly, Peter appeared out of the blue. He came five thousand miles from Europe to put himself in therapy with Fritz Perls. This gorgeous man walked into group one night and I thought, "very interesting." It never occurred to me to make it on my own. I need someone to go to. I obviously wasn't going to go to my husband or anyone I knew. And here was a lovely man, who was young and beautiful and vibrant and exciting and alive. We met in group a few times and then Fritz disappeared. He went to New York over Christmas and did his little tour. So Peter and I were alone, without Fritz around, for about two weeks. We did see each other and play with each other, but Peter had some difficulties at the time so we never made it.

When Fritz came back he imagined what was going to happen. Out of the whole group we were the only people that he cared for. He loved Peter and he loved me. The rest of the group were background for him. He came back in very bad condition. Very paranoid. "What have you done?"

I told him about Peter and me: that we liked each other and played with each other and that Peter was all the things that I wanted—that Peter was good to me. And Fritz was very cruel to me. It was so nice being patted on the head again. Peter was like a good Daddy to me and Fritz like my mother—a very cruel mother.

Fritz also came in hemorrhaging very badly from his ass and insisted that we go to bed together. In another part of his book he mentions how hard that was on me. He knew it. I am the cleanliness and Godliness lady. And he was disgusting and dirty. He always was disgusting and dirty and he smelled. So he came back from his sojourn just absolutely filthy and unkempt. And on top of everything he's laying in a pool of blood.

That was a very hard thing I did but I knew it was very important for him. Young, beautiful Peter was around and Fritz needed me in his bed then. So we slept together. Fritz's rationale for his piles was totally unmedical and insane: it was fine bleeding from his ass because it had never been hemorrhaging, and bleeding from his ass was okay because it would keep him from having a stroke and a hemorrhage in his head. And this is a doctor? I heard this for two years knowing it was crazy. But with the pool of blood I could finally say, "This is crazy. It's about time you went to a doctor and investigated the source of this bleeding."

All this happened simultaneously. There were a lot of horrors of a physical nature going on. Fritz was in the hospital. Peter and I were out in the world—were not locked up. We'd visit him in the hospital and he'd call me day after day—really scared and lonely and phobic about me and Peter. At that point I told him that Peter and I don't go to bed and we don't even play. It was really just nice being with him and talking to him. I felt very virtuous and very self-righteous because we weren't fucking but really dug each other and especially grateful for meeting someone else in my life who was not

crazy and could give me some perspective about Fritz. Because Peter was the only person who was now into our secret.
It was a relief. He was the only person who could give me
feedback. Like which one of us is crazy, me or Fritz?

Fritz came home from the hospital (his hemorrhoid operation was successful although he almost died on the table from
an anesthesia reaction) and started recuperating. I started taking care of him—not full time. For I was looking after everybody and doing everything. Shortly after, I got a phone call,
and he said, "I'm not at home today. I'm again in the hospital." There was a great deal of anxiety in his voice and in his
tears. Because there were real physical problems as well as
the anxiety of Peter and I being on the loose in the world and
he not being around. His bladder, kidneys, and urethra had
clogged up so he had been in excruciating agony all night. In
the morning he called a doctor who got him to the hospital
and immediately performed a second surgery on him. So
within two or three weeks Fritz had two major surgical procedures in and around his genitals. One was a prostatectomy
and one a hemorrhoidectomy. That really gets any man—and
certainly a sixty-six-year-old man whose involvment in sex
was so consuming it was staggering.

Again surgery and recuperation were going nicely and
again Fritz would demand to know what I was doing. And I
was seeing Peter and talking to Peter. We visited Fritz sometimes separately, sometimes together. One day I got a call. It
really sounded like he was dying. Essentially the call was,
"Make a choice. You can have me or Peter but you can't have
both of us."

Of course I knew that there was no choice. We were a very
strange triangle. There was never any doubt in my mind as to
who was doing what to whom and what the priorities were.
Peter wanted Fritz, Fritz wanted me, and I wanted Peter.
Those were foreground for each of us. I wanted Peter as a life
raft. It was either him or I'd have nothing again except my
husband and that whole shit family scene and I'd be totally
isolated and alone again. Peter had come over five thousand
miles to work with a therapist and it was too bad that the therapist chose to spend two weeks in a hospital. But he was just
biding his time until Fritz was well enough to work again.
Sure, I was bright and interesting and nice to have around.
But that wasn't why he was in Miami. So I said to Fritz,
"Okay. I choose you. I'm not going to be left without anyone.
Because Peter wants you." I wasn't going to be left without an
outlet because I still didn't have a friend.

We really had to start from scratch—like the beginning of something—because something else had ended. And we still wanted each other. So Fritz's "suicide attempts" that he refers to in his letter to me in *Garbage Pail* were his viewing the hemorrhoidectomy and prostatectomy as things he did to himself. But when you're nearly seventy years old, those things happen.

Shortly after, Fritz left for California. Wilson Van Dusen had invited him out. California was again a place where he might be able to get back into the professional community. Another of his fantasies in going was starting a Los Angeles Gestalt Institute with Jim Simkin. Going to California meant ending his professional isolation in Miami.

But we never really left each other. We always managed to see each other after he left Miami. At least once a year he'd come to Miami or I'd go to the West Coast or we'd meet in New York. He always called occasionally. So we were always in contact, even when the intensity lessened. I always felt that if the chips were down and I really needed a person, Fritz would be there for me. We left each other by plan.

We ended up on very good terms. Because Fritz's final gift to me was that last summer in Europe. We had five marvelous weeks together, as marvelous as the previous winter had been horrid. We ended up so close and loving and attuned and sexually alive with each other that parting from him in New York was at a very high point in our relationship. He stayed in New York at Laura's to prepare to return to California and I caught a flight to Miami.

Fritz was a very good therapist for me in the beginning. He was helpful to me with my daughter, with my relationship with women generally, with turning me on to sex, with providing me with clues that there was another way to live that was totally different from what I was used to. And that was easy and nice. I knew that his message was real though I didn't know if I'd ever get there. Because he certainly wasn't a model. So what I created of myself is me. And God damn it, I did that alone.

7

California

Wilson Van Dusen, author of *The Natural Depth in Man*, is a large, affable, unpretentious man in his early fifties. There is a softness, earnestness, and appreciation of simplicity both in his tone of voice and in the things he speaks of. One is more likely to see him as the proverbial Dutch Uncle, to mistake him for a friendly neighborhood pharmacist, than to recognize him as the influential phenomenologist that he is.

In the late 1950s, Wilson and his family were living in Ukiah, California. He was the chief psychologist at Mendocino State Hospital, a psychiatric facility located in redwood forest country, some hundred miles north of San Francisco. Fritz and he were to meet, by accident, at The American Psychological Association's annual meeting in San Francisco in 1958, where Fritz was a minor participant on a Psychodrama panel. Minor or not, Wilson says Fritz's comments at that meeting "struck me like a thunderbolt."

Fritz was preceded at the conference by a young psychiatrist active in the peace movement who talked both publicly and privately about saving the world for peace. Being a Californian, he was known to many of those in attendance. Fritz, who was living, at the time, in Florida, had no knowledge of this man's personal affairs. Yet he began to talk about what he noticed in this young doctor's voice, about the desperate wailing that he heard.

"I was terribly impressed," said Wilson, "because Fritz was seeing well beyond what everyone else had seen. Suddenly, the whole course of the conference turned. For this man happened to be in the midst of a divorce, his family was breaking up, he was in difficult straits economically, and there *was* a wail there. The whole peace argument of the man was undercut by Fritz's pointing to the emotional basis underneath it. Fritz did several things like this and in a way took over the conference."

Wilson approached Fritz after the panel ended and talked of his desire to learn what Fritz had to teach, for what Fritz was practicing related to the existential *life-is-lived-NOW* philosophy Wilson was interested in.

"I talked to him about what he was doing. He said that he knew he could do it well but that he considered it a kind of trivia. I had to argue with him. 'Fritz. Your trivia is very enlightening to people. Could you show us more of this trivia?' He didn't think much of it at all."

Fritz always had doubts about his personal worth, doubts that would clearly manifest themselves by his believing that he was not entitled to the love of a beautiful woman, that his memory was faulty, or that his penis was inadequate. Indeed, using one of the principles of Gestalt Therapy, his paranoia might also be seen as a reflection of his own low self-esteem projected onto the world at large. "You're not worth much," he could hear his fellow professionals whisper. "You're nothing but an undisciplined, cantankerous, and lecherous old man." The fact that part of the world might actually have mirrored his inner view of himself in no way detracts from the idiosyncracy of his low self-image, for Fritz, had he respected himself more, might have chosen to look in a different mirror.

Before going to Florida, Fritz had never doubted the validity of Gestalt Therapy. This was, in fact, the one thing he could believe in. It was only after beginning to experiment with lysergic acid that the usefulness of his work began to come into question. The flood of thoughts and images that LSD released made Fritz cognizant of the lower functioning of his ordinary mentality. It brought him close to the awareness of cosmic consciousness—that oceanic feeling of being part of every bit of universal energy—although he never seemed to have fully entered that state of being. Approaching such revelation, his earthly task of being a "psychotherapist" must have seemed petty and relatively insignificant. How could he, afterward, take his work so seriously? What justification was there for his two voluminous books, *Ego, Hunger and Aggression* and *Gestalt Therapy,* when his drug experiences made him realize that all his thinking could be more simply stated in a seventeen-syllable Haiku.

Still, Wilson Van Dusen was impressed and, upon returning to Mendocino State, talked the hospital administration into having Fritz up as a consultant on a fairly long-term basis. The offer, coming after Fritz's surgery and in the midst of his despondency regarding his hopeless and helpless involvement with Marty, was gratefully accepted. In early 1959, Fritz left for California. He lived with Wilson and his wife, Marjorie, for nearly six weeks.

Fritz was now tripping on Sandoz acid several times a week, an unsettling experience for anyone, let alone a sixty-seven-year-old man. The result was deeper despair and deeper suspiciousness. Having separated from Marty, he was also looking for a sense of connectedness and of family. These twin elements often opposed one another, keeping him in his private limbo. His loneliness drew him to others, but his paranoia—his fear of getting hurt should he love too dearly—made him keep these others at a safe distance.

Fritz, for example, had a justly deserved reputation for being indifferent, at best, to children and was a failure as a father. But during the nearly two months that he lived in Ukiah with the Van Dusens, he established very affectionate relationships with their daughters, Cathy and Joanne. Marjorie recalls them clambering up on his lap, where he would patiently play with them and indulge them with gifts.

"He was like Santa Claus in person," recalls Cathy, a spirited nineteen year old who was five at the time. "I remember his taking me to buy a dollhouse and furniture. Parents can't get their kids everything and he was saying, 'Pick out anything you want. Any furniture.' And I thought that was really neat."

During Fritz's stay, Wilson witnessed first hand Fritz's contradictory nature. There was, for example, Fritz's unwillingness to accept his fading sexual energies in spite of teaching people to accept themselves as they are.

"I was alone with him one evening," remembers Wilson. "I was sitting in the living room. We were both very conscious of the fact that we were alone because usually my family was around. And he came in with his pulse beating very fast. He was very excited. I had this strong feeling that he wanted me to do something sexual with him. I knew it. He knew it. It was not said and I just couldn't. It was not my cup of tea.

"I think he had been trying to masturbate and couldn't make it. He couldn't get a climax or a hard on, I don't remember which, or both. This really bothered him. It meant he was kind of finished. He told me that one of the things that bothered him was that he couldn't masturbate anymore. I said, 'My God, man. You're nearly seventy.'

"He once described himself as a cross between a prophet and a bum. It came from Laura Perls. He felt that it was correct and I feel it is correct.

"That prophet side was his mastery in observation of the *here and now*. That's where he was a prophet and the greatest I have ever known, and that was his major contribution. The bum was a very sensuous man who was somewhat lost and alienated in his own inner life and desperate in his own way. Grabbing and wanting reputation.

Wanting me to do a book for him. Wanting me to start a Gestalt Institute. And I sat back and thought to myself, 'Why? For Fritz? I'm not interested in spending my life decorating Fritz's name.'

"I saw him as a brilliant person, very intelligent, somewhat detached, and unable to bridge the gap with others. He was very clever about the gap. He could use it, work with it, illustrate it, make you feel it, but was not well able to bridge it at all.

"If I could have given Fritz one thing it would have been to be content with the *here and now* himself. He was terribly well off. He never needed to work again, which has been a problem in my life. He had so much money stashed away in stamps and other kinds of things. He eventually came to have plenty of reputation with his books and his Institute and yet he was so unhappy."

During his stay, Fritz grew fond of Wilson and valued his kindness and independent thinking. He would ride off to work on the pillion seat of the younger man's motorcycle, learning to trust Wilson's handling of the machine. Wilson, in his turn, valued Fritz's unique ability to describe the obvious in both professional and social situations, his ability to capture the significance and implications of surface behavior.

"I recall very well the first session at Mendocino State. I had gathered together the principal administrators of the hospital. There were between twelve to twenty-four of us in the big room. We were all sitting in a circle, all professionals, mostly psychiatrists. Fritz came in. Someone started talking. Fritz raised his hand as if to say, 'No one is to say anything.' And then he went around the room describing what he could see in each person. It was shocking, really shocking. While I knew everyone there, I had not told him anything about these people. Yet his descriptions of what he saw accurately reflected each person's life and character. Each member of the group in turn. Bang. It just shook each one of them.

"On another occasion, Fritz and I were at a restaurant with my wife and kids. I don't know if Fritz was paying for the meal or not. Likely not, if I know Fritz, for he was a taker. He would take as much as he could from you, absorb your support, your time, your energy, and anything else, and the reward was that you were in the presence of a great man. Anyway, we were sitting and eating and I was very much involved in trying to be as good as Fritz—to catch up to Fritz, learn from Fritz, even show him that I was cleverer in a few things. So while he was deep in the midst of a bowl of soup, which I knew would capture his whole attention, I carefully observed the waitress.

"Later, when the waitress came to the table, I described what I could see in her. I was very clever and perceptive. Fritz never even stopped slopping up his soup, but he said 'Ah, yes. But what you missed was this, that, and the other thing.' And I think he was right. So I permanently considered him to be a great observer. This I saw as his greatest skill and it partly came from his utter detachment."

Marjorie Van Dusen did not have the same ability to detach herself from her observations of Fritz. She had certain expectations of guests in her home among which was cleanliness, "thank you's," and the other social amenities. These Fritz was either unable or unwilling to fulfill. By failing to display sensitivity to her needs, Fritz eventually lost the nurturance that the Van Dusens provided him.

There was, for instance, Fritz's eating ritual. He wrote, in both *Ego, Hunger and Aggression* and *Gestalt Therapy*, of the symbolic importance of thoroughly chewing and digesting one's food and of how this served as a model for the way one chews, assimilates, and integrates other knowledge and information from the world. He himself practiced this with a religious vengeance. Wilson Van Dusen witnessed Fritz's mealtime rites regularly during the weeks that Fritz lived with him.

"We had to learn that his eating style was somewhat

unusual. Eating was a very sacred ritual for him, and we didn't bother him with any chit-chat or anything else. He was going to chew away. He could be quite cruel at the table until he finally conditioned you to behave the way he expected you to behave. And that was that you don't bother him with anything, for he was engaged in a very gustatory, concentrated thing.

"Over and above all that, he lived sort of like a pig. In his room he just dropped everything. It got dirtier and dirtier and dirtier. The bed was never made, just messed up. You either took care of him or you let it go to rack and ruin. That was his style. He didn't believe in social graces. He felt that they were phony."

"He was completely lacking in social graces," added Marjorie, a thin, animated woman who believes in the old-fashioned virtues. "This came somewhat as a shock to me. I had preconceived notions about people and I expected him to react as a guest and he did not. I expected kindness and consideration and certainly didn't get anything like it. So I heartily disliked him.

"My feeling now was that the way he acted was just as phony as the way I expected him to act. You can break your neck to be a slob—which he did, I believe—to make a point."

Fritz antagonized Marjorie still further with unsolicited Gestalt Therapy feedback whenever she reacted in ways he disapproved of. Like April O'Connell, Fritz's hostess in Ohio, Marjorie tired of Gestalt Therapy "morning, noon, and night." Nonetheless, Fritz persisted in trying to enlighten her. During one of his gratuitous feedbacks, Marjorie got so mad at him that she picked up the sugar bowl and threw it at him.

"He threw up his hand," said Wilson, "and she managed to hit his watch with it, which knocked the workings out of the watch. Exit Fritz. Later, he mailed the watch back—all those pieces in a box—as though I'm supposed to pay for it and repair it. And I'd been supporting him for over a month. I sent the watch back to him with no note, because I expected him to repair his own damn watch."

In *In and Out the Garbage Pail*, Fritz tells us:

> I took an apartment in San Francisco. Two of my hangers-on followed me; otherwise I had not much of a practice. I did my thing in the hospital and did not mind driving a hundred miles through the beautiful redwood country. There I became fond of Paul, a psychiatrist who loved farming and rearing children. I believe he has eleven of them by now. We played quite a number of exciting chess games.

"Paul" is Paul Frey, who, along with Fritz and Wilson, worked at Mendocino State. I doubt whether three more brilliant minds ever worked alongside one another in the field of human understanding.

If relationships are to be measured in terms of mutual respect, harmonious interactions, intellectual stimulation, and empathic vibrations, then Paul Frey had to be considered one of Fritz's closest friends in spite of the limited amount of time they spent with one another. The fact that Paul, at thirty-four, was half Fritz's age imposed no barrier to the synchronicity that existed between them, for they both seemed to vibrate to the same iron string.

An unassuming, red-headed, bearded, plain-spoken man, Paul today is a psychiatric dropout. In 1959, the year Wilson brought Fritz to California, Paul had just completed residencies in pathology, internal medicine, and psychiatry at Dartmouth before heading out west to work at Mendocino State Hospital. In addition to his rich educational background, his familiarity with the fields of philosophy and psychiatry (he is an authority on Freud, having an encyclopedic recall of all Freud's works and many of those written about him), Paul possesses uncommonly common sense. Refusing to speak the language of the "intellectuals," he nonetheless remains one, as he succinctly describes Fritz's approach in his own pop idiom: "His bag, essentially, was to introduce people to existential experience. Gestalt means the sudden awareness of the here and now as a real thing, which you can experience with LSD in a more far-out sense.

"I was in one of his sessions in the summer of fifty-nine. His thing was to become provocative and for you to get mad at him or in some other way invest affect, and then for you to reverse roles—where he'd say, 'Okay. So I'm mean. Be me and be mean.' And you'd do something he did to someone else and all of a sudden you'd see that he had you way out on stage in total silence. And you'd say, 'Wow. What got me mad about him was me.' Or things like that. And he could do that. He was really good.

"If somebody would just sit there, folded up, like you and I are sitting now, he'd do the same sort of thing. He would just mirror you right down to the glance, just like that. You'd smile, he'd smile. Back and forth. Most people, when they get into that, it makes them very nervous. It's called *hearing one to death*. He could do it silently, verbally, anyway. It was just him. It was his natural thing.

"The first time we met was when Van Dusen and Mrs. Van Dusen brought him to our house. We sat at the table by ourselves. The kids were all in the kitchen. My wife came along. She did the cooking. There was a funny rap there. I said something to him when I introduced him to her and my wife took it amiss. It was something she didn't like. He immediately picked up on that and said something to me that would have left it wide open for her to blast me back. But she didn't. And then he went no further. We were instantly into the here and now. In other words, he detected a slight thing between me and my wife. He was instantly on to it to exploit it. But since she recognized that would lead to trouble, she didn't say anything. He instantly recognized that she recognized that. And we went right into whatever else there was.

"He was cool at that. If he felt that you didn't feel like hassling, he didn't hassle. But if he felt that you wanted to, he would grease the skids all the way. He was a clever fellow.

"Fritz liked emotionality because he was such a

header.' He was a total, calculating Freudian and he didn't like that. That's why he enjoyed intense emotional relationships with as many people as possible. When he was alone, he was a lonely intellectual, like Goethe. We talked about that. He said the same thing that every German used to say. 'Ah. Every German used to talk about Goethe at the breakfast table.' And he was like that, too. He could continue into that for three straight hours, quoting Nietzsche and Goethe in German.

"Every great man is a tragic figure in some sense, because to get as many turned on as he did, you're going to have to be sure that he was sensitive to all sorts of really bad things. Freud was a tragic figure. Fritz, too. Anybody who has ever experienced life. Because you're participating in something of which you know nothing. You think, one day, you've made a rational decision and then you discover five years later that it wasn't rational. There is no such thing as rationality in my opinion."

Like Fritz, Paul was, and still remains, a compassionate skeptic. Wary of most psychological medicine men peddling their quick cures, he had, at first, the same wariness regarding Fritz. "You see a lot of these therapeutic hustlers come through with their particular bags," he said.

"But when he talked to you it was real. You could tell he wasn't bullshitting you. On the other hand, if you started playing games with him, in the least little bit, boy would he come back hard. That's why we got along. We both operated the same way. And we never had a hassle. He was my friend from the first minute I ever met him.

"To me, Fritz was a friend; an old man with grey hair and a German accent who was like my father. My father died when I was very young. And then there was my grandfather. I've always been very respectful of old men and always liked them. And I just plain liked him. He could be *hurtlicht*. You know what *hurtlicht* means? Courtly. Polite. He could put it on, yet it was real."

How is one to reconcile Paul's report of Fritz's social graces when the Van Dusens witnessed the exact opposite? The answer lies in Fritz's multifaceted personality, one that dared to contradict itself and allowed the situation to dictate the response. As Emerson has stated:

> A foolish consistency is the hobgloblin of little minds, adored by little statesmen and philosophers and divines. With consistency a great soul has simply nothing to do. He may as well concern himself with his shadow on the wall.

One of the bonds between the two men was their willingness to mix it up when it came to affectionate teasing, as they both enjoyed bantering repartee greatly.

"One time we were in one of these Sensitivity sessions. There was a big circle of people. He was putting a guy on and it was just so nasty that I was getting mad at him. I stared at him. I don't think I said anything. And he said, looking at me: 'I see murder in those eyes.'

"I said, 'Maybe you do. But maybe you see a mirror, too, hah?'

"And he goes, 'Touché. Touché.'

"There was also the story of The Intractable Schizophrenic Woman. It was a dirty trick, but we just wanted to see what he would do. Here was the scene: He came up here, doing his thing, turning people on, doing sensitivity groups periodically. On this particular occasion there were a tremendous number of hospital employees—technicians, social workers, doctors, residents, anybody interested in the subject. And he was going to show off his technique with the patient. Now we knew enough about his bag to know that there are some people that it just doesn't do anything to or for. And they are the true schizophrenics. They have that glacial quality about them, like the ocean, almost. So we picked out one of these for him—Van Dusen, me, and a group of us. And she sat there, like a rock.

"He did everything. She crossed her legs, he crossed his legs. She picked her nose, he picked his nose. She'd scratch her ear, he'd scratch his ear. He just did everything he could to make a fool out of her. And nothing happened. This went on for maybe forty-five minutes. Finally, he said, 'Okay. . . . Be crazy if you want to.' And he walked away. To applause."

Aside from their contacts at Mendocino State Hospital, Fritz, over the next year and a half, paid seven or eight weekend visits to Paul's home—visits he looked forward to in spite of the three-hour bus ride. To be in the presence of Paul, his wife, and twelve children, to satisfy his intellect with good conversation, to enjoy Paul's playing Chopin for him on a dilapidated piano, to engage in chess games where the old fox was perpetually outfoxed, and to settle down for dinner gave him profound, if fleeting, moments of satisfaction.

Paul laughed, recalling their chess matches, about the artful ways in which he would defeat Fritz.

"He was chagrined. He was a sore loser. He didn't kick the board off or anything, but he would make these put-down remarks. And I would outfox him in the cleverest way.

"I was always a good chess player. And I know how old men play. They get tired. So anyway, I would make a very sophisticated move in the midgame, somewhere. I would always enjoy complex midgames. I would avoid trading and get a whole series of infinitely complex possibilities set up while he was trying to simplify it. Then I would cause him to trade the wrong way. He caught on very fast. Maybe the very next move he knew that it was downhill no matter what he did.

"Then he'd say, 'Ach. Sometimes I don't like to play chess.'

" 'Well, you know what Freud said,' I'd answer. 'When you win it's the most interesting and best game in the world. And when you lose it's a waste of time.'

"And he said, 'Exactly right.' "

In their conversations the two men shared a mutual interest in the meaningfulness of their lives and their work.

Paul was involved in lysergic acid research at Mendocino State and became a conduit for the drug for Fritz, who also shared some of his LSD experiences.

Fritz was envious of Paul's wife when she took lysergic acid during one of his visits and had a blissful transcendental experience. And he respectfully questioned Paul about his mystical experiences.

"I've always regarded myself as a Christian," said Paul, "but I went further. I said things like 'Christ is magic and transcends us.' Being an intellectual doubter, Fritz would ask me *why* I believe, *what it is* I believe in fact, and *what it does for me.* Things like that.

"I'd tell him of certain experiences, describing LSD trips, but it's indescribable. Something really happened and I experienced it and it was real. But I can't really tell you what it was like. And that was the way I spoke to him about my views on Christianity."

Fritz, for all his own experimentation with the psychedelic drugs, had little or no experience with the Beyond. He could never transcend his own ego, and arrogantly believing himself to be Everyman, claimed that the Beyond was a fantasy. When Fritz tripped, he never saw God or felt himself one with Creation. Instead, he played out emotional scenes regarding the facts of his birth, experienced the paranoia that others were threatening his ego, felt himself to be a fraud, and, on one occasion, played chess with himself with Fritz on both sides of the board. It was Fritz, Fritz, Fritz—always in the way—always preventing that fusing, melting, ego-death that is part of the religious/mystical experience. He reached for it repeatedly but always came away empty-handed. It was exactly as Wilson Van Dusen described it: "Enlightenment can be gummed up by reaching for this overwhelming state. The more effort you put into it, the less of anything is there. It comes, if you're lucky, when you're not doing a damned thing. It's the idea of *Grace*. It finds you. The more you try to find it, the more you create the obstacle."

"Fritz had a lot of bummers on acid," according to

Paul, "the negative Jew trip where he'd conclude 'I'm just another Jewish Charlatan.' "

This feeling of being a charlatan was undoubtedly reinforced by the philosophical conclusions they would arrive at when discussing the relationship and nature of mental illness and psychotherapy. In an existential sense, Paul recognized that a man was neurotic only because he thought of himself thusly, and that therapy consisted of one person in the role of helpless patient consulting someone else who played the more arrogant role of therapist. He saw this interaction as an essentially destructive process, since it reinforced "illness" (the patient, by turning to a higher authority, keeps himself in an inferior, dependent, one-down position).

Paul came to feel that if there was anything he had to teach it was by example, not verbiage, and that to charge people for conversing with them was a "rip-off." He was to make, instead, a commitment to real work—to farming, carpentry, and raising children—so that when he talked with you it was as a fellow traveler upon life's road and not as a guru.

Paul was to involve himself so fully in the elements of basic living that he remains, to this day, an obscure figure to the larger world. Willing to talk freely to anyone who seeks him out, he nonetheless is not looking for converts and has started no new psychotherapeutic school. He seems capable of practicing what Fritz Perls preached: the ability to live in and be content with the present moment of existence. He currently lives in a barn that he converted, with children, chickens, and sheep running through his home. He butchers his own hogs, raises his own vegetables, and teaches his kids all the basic fundamentals.

"You could drop his children high up in the Amazon basin," claims Wilson, "and they would all survive."

Fritz left the Bay Area for Los Angeles in late 1960, partly because consultation funds at Mendocino State ran out and partly because the paucity of his practice made

him restless. Jim Simkin, his friend and former student
had already established a solid, reputable practice in the
City of the Angels. Jim, as straight and conventional in his
own life style as Fritz was unorthodox in his, was able to
help Fritz get started.

"He rarely came without a gift," said Jim, a pleasant-
looking man of average height, average weight, and
average features. "Which is so unlike Fritz. People don't
know this side of him, for he could hound you for a nickel.
When he came to Los Angeles in 1960, I had been in practice about a year and a half. He asked, 'How are you
doing?' . . . 'Could be better.' . . . 'You need some
money?' . . . 'Yeah. I could use some money.' . . . 'Here.'
And he gave me a thousand bucks, which was a big chunk
of dough in those days. 'You pay me when you get it.' "

Jim helped Fritz, initially, by convincing him to cut
down on his use of LSD, for it was clear to Jim that Fritz's
experimentations with that agent had not only adversely
affected his relationship with Marty Fromm and the Van
Dusens, but had prejudiced severely his subsequent per-
spectives and dealings with others.

"He got paranoid while he was on drugs," Jim reported, "and vicious. People were 'always trying to take
advantage' of him, 'trying to steal' his ideas, his theories.

"*He* always had to have the advantage. He would do
the taking advantage of and then project that and experience it the other way. The dynamics of the Injustice Col-
lector."

The second way Jim helped Fritz was to provide him,
again, with some brief but meaningful sense of belong-
ingness. As with the Van Dusens' children, Fritz, who ordinarily had little tolerance for youngsters, allowed a fa-
milial rapport to develop.

"The kids loved him," Jim continued. "All three of our
daughters. He had a delicious sense of humor. We had a
parakeet that our little daughter taught to say, 'Dr. Perls.
Quack, Quack.' And Fritz could hardly wait to sit in front

of that bird and hear him say that. He enjoyed those human touches, sitting around the table and being part of a family where he felt welcome. That aspect of him is also not well known. He didn't show that often and was, instead, the gruff guy. When he left Los Angeles, he gave one of my daughters his television set."

Lastly, Jim helped Fritz relaunch his professional efforts: "We started a study group. In less than a month there were ten top-notch people in training: Bob Gerrard, Walt Kempler, Ev Shostrum, and others. And within eight months a second group started. Fritz was still difficult in the way he conducted himself in public, but not quite as impossible as when he was in L.A. in the early fifties. More sure of himself and less angry and belligerent."

Although it may have seemed that Fritz was reestablishing himself, in actuality he was doing little more than relocating—as he did when he gave up on New York and moved into semiretirement in Miami.

"But he was always impatient," Jim continued. "He started Freeway routes. He would go out on the San Bernardino Freeway—go out to some hospitals and private groups, pick up some consultations along the route, and maybe stay overnight. He did the same thing on the Santa Ana Freeway. Things didn't build up fast enough and he was also getting fed up with what he called the psychiatric racket. So he decided to go on a world trip. He left in sixty-two, turned over part of the practice to Walt Kempler, who took the San Bernardino Freeway, and I took the Santa Ana Freeway. When he came back, fifteen months later, I still had the Santa Ana Freeway going."

Fritz's dropping out was similar, in many respects, to that of Paul Frey, reflecting the lack of belief each came to feel about the validity of their profession. But, whereas Paul found an alternative life style, Fritz did not. His subsequent experiences, however, gave him renewed respect for quiet *Here and Now* living and enabled him, upon his return, to work, again, with some measure of good faith.

His round-the-world sojourn was by boat—from the Orient, to the Middle East, Europe, and New York, before returning to California. The high points of his journey were Kyoto, Japan, and Elath, Israel, an uncanny coincidence for a man who later jokingly described himself as a Zen Judaist.

Fritz spent two months at the Daitokuji Temple in Kyoto, immersing himself, with a gentle cynicism, in Zen training. He was particularly delighted when the Roshi, on giving him a simple *koan*—"What color is the wind?"— seemed satisfied with his response of blowing smoke in the Roshi's face. But it was the tranquility of Kyoto, the city of Temples and the seat of Zen, its unhurried nature, and the friendliness in its citizens' faces that appealed to him the most.

The same tranquility was rediscovered in Elath. Fritz, who had periodically dabbled in painting, took it up more seriously there, inspired by the colors of the Red Sea. Painting, however, failed to offer the same satisfactions that he had as a practicing therapist. Elath is a drab, dusty, hot city, where he remained for a month after discovering a colony of American beachcombers *doing absolutely nothing at all and apparently quite content in their lack of "productivity."* It was Friz's first contact with beatnik culture.

"To find the beachcombers was an event," he wrote. "To find people who were happy just to be, without goals and achievements."

Fritz returned to Los Angeles somewhat less ambitious and less despairing than when he had left. He was now seventy years old and had demonstrated, to himself, that he could survive apart from his role of therapist/teacher. He seemed more resigned than ever before to the idea of being unremembered for his work on earth. It is one of those perpetual paradoxes that, when least desirous, desire is fulfilled. So it was for Fritz.

Substituting, one night, for a vacationing Jim Simkin, Fritz met Bernard Gunther, a member of Jim's Wednesday-night group. In the group that night, Bernie, who later became The Esalen Institute's resident masseur, experienced living in a perpetually flowing *present*, a feeling he had known before only under the influence of psychedelic drugs. He was so excited by this experience that he arranged to transfer to a group that Fritz led. The more Bernie admired Fritz, the more cavalierly Fritz seemed to treat him, so much so that it often bordered on contempt. How ironical, in view of the fact that Bernie played such a catalytic role in Friz's eventual fame.

Fritz wrote, with biting undertones:

> In one of my groups there was a guy who was involved in a number of "far out" things—yoga, massage, therapy, Charlotte Selver's sensory awareness. His name is Bernie Gunther. He is a good *entrepreneur*—not very creative, but capable of synthesizing and putting to use what he takes from different sources. He, like Bill Schutz, certainly turns people on. I have little doubt that he will climb up the ladder to the top.

Bernie tried to spend as much time with Fritz as he could, to absorb, as completely as he was able, Fritz's Gestalt message. He seemed willing to ignore, avoid, or overlook the ungracious personal feedback he received. Shortly after beginning in group, for instance, Fritz was attempting to put Bernie in touch with his capacity for aggression.

"He conned me into that 'Louder' business," said Bernie, an unusually soft-spoken, soft-stepping, muscular man. "I was into weight lifting and was a husky guy then, and one time he asked me to pound the coffee table that he had. I pounded it and he said, 'Do it again.' He kept egging me on until I broke his coffee table into a thousand pieces. Everybody was quite impressed except Fritz and myself. He was pissed because I broke his coffee table, and I was afraid he was going to make me pay for it, which he eventually did."

At other times, Bernie attempted to get closer to Fritz by remaining after group meetings and watching wrestling matches on television with him—a pastime Fritz enjoyed greatly. Except that Fritz "didn't like to talk very much, at least not to me.

"I used to go to dinner with him. Gestalt therapists in those days were hard guys. They were really into that *here and now* thing. If you didn't have something to say that they thought was totally relevant, they wouldn't answer you or they wouldn't talk to you. So I remember those awful meals when that used to happen.

"Eventually I decided I wanted to help him spread Gestalt Therapy and so I put on a seminar for him at a place called Books in Review. It was a classical bookstore run by Harry Hill, the sort of place where if a new book came in, Harry, who knew all his customers, would let those people know who might be interested in it. Alan Watts would come into town every three months and give lectures upstairs, in the balcony. I knew people from having taught Yoga in town and having worked with Charlotte Selver. Harry had lists of people from the Watts lectures—people in the pre-Humanistic swing. So we had a fantastically successful lecture—a standing room crowd. Somewhere between fifty and a hundred people in a small room.

"He was really pleased, because he didn't think, at that time, that he was a particularly good lecturer. And he was quite nervous, something that in the later years he had gotten over. But he was really nervous that first night. Afterwards, I was talking to him—he always used to call talking, 'shitting'—and he would say: 'Jesus. I was really shitting well tonight.' And he really did flow very well. The series went very nicely."

Chait's Hot Springs Hotel, in Big Sur, California, was inherited by Michael Murphy, a recent Stanford graduate and former student of Alan Watts. He and his exclassmate, Dick Price, were running the place as an inn, which they would rent to people interested in holding seminars in areas that later came to be subsumed under the term *The Human Potential Movement.* Chait's, before long, changed its name to The Esalen Institute, after a local Indian tribe, and set its own course instead of being available for charter.

In Christmas of 1963, Gene Sagan, a Bay Area psychologist, rented Chait's to organize a program called "The Education of the Imagination," sponsored by the Berkeley Education Extension. It was an interdisciplinary conference designed to introduce to one another people who were in the cutting edge of their professions: people from the theater, dance, music, sociology, psychology, and body awareness. The program was not open to the public, but was strictly for people in what was to become "The Movement." Each would share with the others—for room and board—what they were into.

Fritz and Bernie were both invited. Bernie fell in love with the place and persuaded Mike Murphy to let him stay on and free-lance with the Inn's guests and do some "massage, sensory awareness, Yoga, and a little Gestalt.

"Fritz didn't like Esalen at all," Bernie continued. "He thought it was a screwed up place, pretty primitive, with a lot of dropouts running around."

Bernie was still imbued with the idea of putting Gestalt Therapy on the map and was interested, personally, in more Gestalt training for himself. During one of his visits back to Los Angeles, he pressed Fritz to establish a training group for therapists at Big Sur.

Fritz was initially against the idea, but Bernie persisted, pointing out that The Esalen Institute was ideally located, being half way between San Francisco and Los Angeles.

"You organize; I function," said Fritz, finally relenting.

Bernie was to organize quite well. He cleared the project with Mike Murphy and Dick Price, sent out a mailing, made some phone calls and collected registration fees. When Fritz returned to Esalen in the summer of 1964, he was not simply one among many, but was there to teach Gestalt Therapy to people who had come up solely to see and work with him. On second inspection, given a chance to "do his own thing," the ambience had apparently changed, for he wrote:

The target Esalen scored a bull's eye with the arrow Fritz Perls. A landscape comparable to Elath; beautiful people on the staff as in Kyoto. An opportunity to teach. The gypsy found a home and soon a house.

He found something else as well. A respite for a sick heart.

8

The Esalen Institute, Big Sur

Esalen is a cliffside community situated along Route 1, a third of the distance from San Francisco to Los Angeles. Behind it loom the Big Sur Mountains. In front lies the vast Pacific.

There is a heaven/hell atmosphere to the place, from its Edenesque grounds to the Beelzebub smell of its hot sulphur baths. I arrived there on December 23, 1972. The next evening, Alan Watts, dressed in clerical garb, conducted a mock Christmas Eve ceremony—half pagan and half Christian, rich in ritual and mysticism but poor in following orthodox religious custom. Those who live, work at, or visit Esalen profess a love of nature and man. Yet, the quality of this love is offensive to Bible-thumping fundamentalists, for Esalen is a temple of sensuality as well as of the spirit.

"People expect life to be different here," says Suzanne Williamson, a displaced Yankee who works in the office. "It isn't. It's just more intense.

"We have the same rip-offs, deceits, backbiting, gossiping, and criticizing that goes on in the outside world. Only it happens under maximum view and is subject to closer scrutiny."

"Your style doesn't change so much," added Carole

Rosenblatt, another young staffer, "it's just that you come to see it more quickly."

Esalen was the better mousetrap that finally brought the world to Fritz's doorstep. The Institute itself is small— comfortably accommodating up to sixty people. By utilizing Southcoast, a motel down the road, somewhat over one hundred people can be housed, if necessary. Although these numbers are not large, Esalen's popularity and year-round operation, from day-long to month-long programs in the areas of psychology, mysticism, the humanities, and the arts, results in several thousand people passing through each year.

Esalen burst into the public's consciousness in 1966 because of its utilization of novel and exciting ways of waking us ordinary mortals out of our deadened, somnambulistic state. Willing to allow any approach that might turn people on to life, nature, harmony, freedom, grace, or awareness, the Institute offered workshops in Yoga, meditation, sensory awareness, Encounter groups, massage, religion, nude therapy, etcetera, etcetera, etcetera. Fritz's Gestalt Therapy groups were just one of these etceteras.

Esalen psychologist William Schutz wrote a best-selling book in 1967, *Joy*, which explained some of the encounter techniques he was utilizing at the Institute. The interest in that book contributed, of course, to Esalen's ever-growing fame, as did the movie *Bob and Carol and Ted and Alice*, a gentle comedy of what happens to two couples who turn on, at a fictionalized version of Esalen, to the concepts of *honesty*, *sensuality*, and *following your feelings*.

To be sensitive to the needs of your body, follow your impulses, and start to relate straightforwardly was a most appealing notion to many people in the 1960s. Doing this in groups *with other people* made the concepts even more enticing. For the malady of the times was alienation accompanied by a quiet, ritualized despair.

Large sections of the population had been through the psychoanalytic mill and found it left them unfulfilled.

They might have come to recognize the causes of their complexes, but had failed to achieve a more zestful existence. Even more souls considered themselves normal and felt no need to see a therapist. Yet these "normals" also sensed a lack of excitement in their lives—so hooked in were they to their time/performance slots in our mechanized society.

Esalen was open to Everyman and Everywoman. To attend their programs required only curiosity. If anyone were willing to say, "I could get even *more* out of my life," that person was welcome. One no longer had to wear the label "neurotic" in order to try to feel better. Many were attracted by this possibility. For the decent home, decent job, decent car—the end result of a materialism that was supposed to make life richer—had left us poorer instead. Not only had meaning disappeared from life's labors, but, given the mad scramble for goods and resources, we had forgotten how to share ourselves with family, friends, and neighbors.

Esalen's twin promises of a freer lifestyle and freedom from alienation were as appealing to those over twenty-five as was the flower child movement for those who were younger. No matter that most of Esalen's leading gurus were, like Fritz, similarly alienated. It was the very depth of their own alienation that impelled them to search for new ways of overcoming it, to replace interpersonal isolation with decent contact.

It was Esalen's institutional success that, in large measure, enabled Fritz, at the end of his life, to gain the respect and appreciation that he sought and deserved; that, plus his way of being and his influence upon the other members of the staff. Fritz worked with many of Esalen's future group leaders, influenced their styles, and, through them, spread his legend and his "truth."

"A big part of Fritz's story was that, especially for a psychiatrist, his life was so different, so damned colorful," said Abe Levitsky, San Francisco Gestaltist and former student of Fritz's. "The fact that he lived at Esalen in almost a public way. The fact that thousands of people encountered him at the lunch table and dinner table and at the festivities in the evening and that sort of thing."

"And that sort of thing" included flapping like a seal in the baths, performing therapeutic "miracles," leching after scores of young (and not so young) beauties, and dealing with both staff and seminarians with such regal aplomb and disdain that people were perpetually aware of and expecting the unexpected from this theatrically exciting septuagenarian.

It was, then, not so much that a "new" or a "different" Fritz arrived at Esalen, but that he was performing his usual act under a microscope through which ten thousand eyes eventually peered.

Fritz spent five years at Esalen, offending some and intriguing others. It was hard, however, to ignore him or to remain neutral. As Mark Mann, one of the staff, remarked to a newly arrived seminarian: "That's Fritz Perls. Some people think he's a genius. I just think he's a dirty old man."

Fritz eventually went through three phases at Esalen. The first was a period of short-tempered, introspective nastiness which lasted through most of 1965. Part of this mood can be directly attributed to his health, part to the small demand for his work, and part to his usual defensive come-on in a new social/therapeutic location.

Fritz's heart condition had deteriorated steadily since his departure from Miami and Marty. Anginal pains were so bad, in 1963, that Fritz seriously contemplated suicide. When he first arrived at Big Sur, his condition was so poor that he could not walk down the slope from the lodge to the baths. Special arrangements were made to allow him to drive his Volkswagen to the bathhouse.

He had been living alone, prior to Esalen, for years. His diet was poor. Never preparing his own meals, he ate at the local diner or some other greasy spoon. His hours were similarly irregular, for there was not much of a schedule to build his time around.

Because of his lack of stamina, Fritz asked for Jim Sim-

kin's assistance at the training workshop that Bernie
Gunther had organized. This circumstance heralded the
offensive qualities Fritz displayed during the early part of
his residence.

"The reason I organized that workshop was that I
wanted to become a Gestalt therapist," said Bernie. "My
deal with Fritz was that I would get this whole thing
organized and he would let me take the course. And he
said, 'Fine.'

"But he was going to co-lead with Jim Simkin. And Jim
Simkin was very uptight about anybody doing Gestalt
Therapy who didn't have an M.D. or a Ph.D. He told Fritz
that if I were in the class, he wouldn't teach with Fritz. So
Fritz told me I couldn't be in it after organizing this fucking thing. I was really very salty toward Fritz. That was
our first big run-in. As far as I was concerned it was just a
dishonest thing on his part. The rationalization he had
was, 'Look. I'm not willing to give up Simkin just for you.'
And my thing was, 'Fuck it. There wouldn't have been
anything if it wasn't for me.' "

Simkin's insistence that all Gestalt therapists hold le-
gitimate post graduate degrees was particularly ironic,
since his mentor, Fritz, could not have met this qualifica-
tion. Fritz's M.D. degree was never recognized in this
country. His Ph.D. was an honorary award in 1950 from
The Western College of Psychoanalysis, a small Los
Angeles school unrecognized by any bona fide national
accrediting body and currently unlisted in the Los Angeles
telephone directory. Although proudly listing his Ph.D. on
all his later publications, it was apparently as bogus as a
three-dollar bill.

Fritz's harshness was invariably in direct proportion to
his own neediness, and he was particularly needy at this
time. His attitude and bearing discouraged those who
would place him in the role of a nurturing parent or a reas-
surer. He treated such requests to suck his symbolic teat
scornfully or with a logical argument: "What do you need
me for?" he might ask. "What do you need your parents

for? You've got eyes and ears and energy. What do *you* want to do? Why not say goodbye to us authorities, throw us in the garbage pail, and do things and solve problems on your own?"

"He had," reports Abe Levitsky, "an overemphasis on the issues of autonomy and self-support which, I feel, he was almost obsessive about and reflected his own unresolved problems of dependency. This probably had a great deal to do with his rejection of my depression when he worked with me. Or anybody's depression. It made him impatient."

Impatient or not, Fritz also knew that self-pity was a dead end in depressive states, and he bent over backward to avoid encouraging it.

Fritz was in a bind when it came to neediness. Wanting something from others offended his sense of dignity, his idea of taking care of one's own business. His association between desiring support from others and being undignified came, most likely, from his expectations of unrequited love. It is easy to conjure up undignified images of reaching out to people for a loving embrace and finding that the parties you reach for turn their backs on you and move quickly aside. Fritz lived through many such experiences. Little wonder, then, that he had a great reluctance to express his own neediness.

He was once quite harsh with Diane Reifler, a woman who participated in one of his weekend groups. Subsequently they were intimate. Fritz later invited her to take part in a month-long training workshop he was giving at Esalen. She went up to work on the hot seat and started out by saying, "I want."

"And he really zapped me. Because I said 'I want. . . .' The first two words out of my mouth. Like 'How dare you say *I want?*'

"He was angry, I think, because I wasn't fucking him during that month-long program. I didn't want to, then, but he might have expected that I would. And I didn't make any overtures toward him. I think he would have liked me to make some overtures but I didn't. He was really caught in his own stew, because he wouldn't ask me for greater closeness."

This instance clearly illustrates his *Neediness Paradox*. Fritz wanted, but wouldn't ask. And so he condemned the wantingness of others.

One legendary tale of Fritz the Terrible is told by a former assistant who wished to remain anonymous:

When I came to Esalen for the first residence program, he was beginning to record his work. He spent five thousand dollars on videotape equipment. He was very tight, and when he spent that much, he really was involved. Yet he couldn't get it to work properly. I told him I had been an electronic engineer for fifteen years. That's how I became his cameraman. For two or three months I recorded everything he did. It was right, for me. The residence program had just fallen apart and it was a good experience for me to learn Gestalt.

I liked him a lot. He once called me "twentieth-century man, scientific and aesthetic."

Then one fine day a woman named Marsha Price appeared, zipping down the hill in a red Ferrari with a "Whoopee, I'm here." She soon saw that the energy at Esalen was where Fritz was, and she registered for all his workshops.

In her second month there, she wanted more of a work relationship with him, and he hired her as my assistant, for he was turned on to her. Marsha and I became really close friends and Fritz seemed jealous. She wasn't into fucking Fritz but was playing with him.

One day the camera broke. The videotape also needed overhauling. I told Fritz that Marsha had a station wagon and that we'd take it down the coast and stay for a few days. We stayed an extra day and a half in my home town. When we returned, he was furious. He was incoherent, jealous, and fired me.

It was out of nowhere. Fritz had previously talked to me about starting a production company and was I interested. I even began to get some of my own stuff to improve his equipment. I had no idea he was so concerned with Marsha. So I said, "Okay. I'll go up and get my stuff—my microphone and my mixer."

"You're not going into that house or I'll call the sheriff."

I was hurt so I pulled some little boy stuff. I said to Fritz, "You can't have it. . . . You can't do that."

"Sue me."

So I did. Afterwards I went off to lead some groups for the Peace Corps. I came by a month later and was sitting in the lodge with Selig, the gardener, and some exceptionally wealthy society ladies. Selig had brought them in and they were all in a twitter.

Selig was selling them on the tranquility of our harmonious relationships at Esalen. Out of the back of my eye I saw Fritz opening his mail. Selig was saying, "We have ex-bankers, space engineers, ex-convicts . . ." and as Fritz opened his mail he turned red and went into a big puffing up of his chest. He had gotten the court summons. I feared an attack. He stalked across the room, walked right up to me, and whonked me with the flat of his hand.

This seventy-three-year-old man just started hitting me and screaming, and I finally pushed him back. Selig came between us.

"I'll see you in court," I said.

"Over my dead body."

We reseated ourselves and Selig continued his talk without a broken word as though nothing had happened.

The next day, while I was walking toward the lodge, Fritz, in his Fiat, came at me. I jumped away at the last moment and threw a rock at his rear window. We were never close again.

Several weeks later Fritz did show up in court. I had sued for $100 although he owed me a bit more. He walked into court wearing a grey sharkskin striped suit. His hair was neatly trimmed. This was a very different man—*Dr. Perls*. No one had ever seen him except in a jump suit. And he acted maligned.

He went on and on about how he had been ripped off. The judge interrupted: "But do you owe him money?"

"Maybe. But not $100."

He was gently admonished to be specific. He felt he was training me and the equipment was the price I paid. Not having all my sales slips, I showed receipts totaling $37, and I got part of my money.

There are other accounts of Fritz the Opportunist, although much of Fritz's opportunism came from simply utilizing people that he had little respect for. You, I, or others might not care to accept favors from people who curry favor with us in spite of our open dislike. Fritz would. His attitude might best be described as, "If you choose to be my doormat, I will willingly wipe my feet upon you whenever they are soiled." He treated Bernie Gunther that way. In some respects, his relationship with Laura might be viewed from a similar perspective, for in spite of his insulting references to her in *Garbage Pail*, she continued to make her home available to him and he continued to use it. Yet, for all his brusqueness, there was always the opposite side.

"Fritz was interesting in that sometimes he could be very sweet and very vulnerable," added Bernie Gunther. "One day a lady came to Esalen who read palms. Fritz was usually very down on anything metaphysical or mystical, but he consented to have his palm read. And this woman said something which touched him a bit and has always stayed with me. She said: 'You have all this veneer, all this armor, all of this external defense. And underneath you're just absolutely soft. Like a crab with a soft body and a hard shell.' "

Fritz's half-moon house was built, in 1966, upon the highest point of the Esalen property. He was very proud of it. Directly below are the baths, the sulphurous vapors rising straight up to the deck. Off to the right are the living units for the seminarians, and further down the same road is the lodge, which houses the office and the dining room.

Dick Price lives in Fritz's house now, enjoying its sunken double-sized bath tub, its stone walls and cedar siding. Blue morning-glories climb about cast-iron railings by the door and about the deck, which juts out toward the sea. Scrub trees and brush cover what varies from a straight drop to the ocean to inclines of forty-five degrees.

Standing outside, the eye is inundated with greens and blues. Cats walk about—one of which is pure white, like Mitzie, Fritz's cat, who he claimed was his guru. Bees are sampling the nectar of some brilliant red flowers. Daisies are in bloom by the stone steps that lead to the door.

Dick Price, red-faced, slim, with grey hair, blue intense eyes, and a hurried and energetic voice, ushers me inside to speak about Fritz.

The interior of the house consists of one large room, rounded and wood-paneled in back, with an expanse of glass in front that faces upon deck, sky, and sea. This is where Fritz lived, conducted his workshops, and listened to recordings of Mahler, Mozart, and Brahms at dusk. Two small bedrooms are tucked into each side of the moon's crescents. Dick speaks: "The way we operated back in 1964, we didn't have any resident staff. I think Bernie had just come in residence, but the place was open to outside leaders and open to programs whether or not I liked them. Esalen was operated to allow a number of independent scenes to go on. Mike and I would go along with them as long as they were within reasonable grounds. So at first, when Fritz said, 'I want to live here, ' I said 'Okay.' He has a draw. I didn't know him that well. His name might be good for business. I didn't have that strong an opinion of him at first. I grew to dislike him during that first year and a half that he was here. And then at the end we grew very close and loving.

"When he first came here he was drawing four or five people to his workshops. Almost two years later he was still only drawing thirteen or fourteen. And then his curve went up so quickly that at the end, if you let it go in sixty-nine, Fritz would have drawn two hundred or three hundred people.

"But as I said, at first I didn't trust him. I saw him putting people down and having very little patience. If someone was obviously disturbed and came to see him and Fritz wasn't interested, I'd see him just turn away. It was almost brutal. But in the context of the group I saw him as loving and patient and sensitive. It was just like a coin turned around. All the things I thought he was utterly without, in the course of a group he had with a richer degree than anyone I had ever witnessed.

"My background was one of Buddhist studies, so what I also saw, almost immediately, was the parallel between Fritz's awareness training and *The Heart of Buddhist Meditation*—a text that claims to be based upon the discourse of Buddha twenty-five centuries ago. Here was a book, apart from the lack of interpersonal possibilities, but in terms of awareness exercises, that could be used as a textbook in Gestalt. So naturally I went on to train with Fritz.

"I had learned that Fritz was not easy to deal with in a business way and yet this was my responsibility. We paid leaders on the basis of how many people came to a workshop. Fritz would come back and say 'I don't trust your count.' Finally I would tell him that 'I will not pay out until you come back with your secretary and we go over it person by person by person. And you will not get paid until we have a mutual agreement.' I can't think of any other leader we had to do this with.

"With Fritz you learned that you had to establish this immediately. Because he'd say, 'You paid me for sixteen people and I had seventeen people.' I used to feel, 'Well, he doesn't have a group this week. I'll handle my business with him now,' for our business would not be more than an hour a month. But I quickly learned that No! The time to get him was when he was doing a group and feeling good and involved. Without a group Fritz became very very bitchy. Not so when time went on, but certainly in the years, say 1964 and '65."

To fully appreciate Fritz, one needs to appreciate paradox, for paradox abounded during Fritz's initial phase at Esalen. In regard to his work, Fritz wrote the following:

> My function as a therapist is to help you to the awareness of the here and now, and to frustrate you in any attempt to break out of this. This is my existence as a therapist, in the therapy role. I haven't managed it yet for many segments of my life. You see, like every other psychologist or psychiatrist, I solve my problems to quite an extent *outside*. The fact that I'm so happy in integration means that my own integration is incomplete.

Fritz not only taught out of his own familiarity with conflicts, but also as a way of alleviating them. Leading groups, for Fritz, was more than an occupation. It was also a form of self-therapy, one of the ways he solved his problems "outside."

When working, Fritz was excited, happy, integrated, and in contact with the world. When idle, his thoughts left the *here and now* and wandered to what could have been, real or imagined injustices he suffered at the hands of others, what might yet be, and his shortcomings as a father, husband, guru, and friend. As Dick Price noted, the time to discuss business with Fritz was while he was working, for when he was unoccupied he was usually unapproachable, nasty, or highly suspicious.

"Fritz," said Dick, "used his groups for personal awareness exercises. He was very, very sharp and present and I could just see him become vitalized in doing his work. He wasn't bitching that the house wasn't complete or that 'Esalen isn't all that I would want it to be.' He would become utterly present. And in becoming utterly present he energized himself, using excitement and interest and all the things he talked about."

Fritz's tendency toward paranoia is a perfect example of *not living in the moment*. When one becomes paranoid, one is trying to *figure out* what the moment *means*. The same holds true of his hunger for new experiences. As Jim Simkin has said, "He would want more than what was there. And he would imagine that there was more"—the Divine Discontent that Julian Beck referred to.

By making his therapeutic focus the awareness of the here and now, Fritz disciplined himself to be cognizant of the present moment so as to reflect it back to those he worked with. When he focused his own awareness this way, his fantasies, preoccupations, suspicions, and painful memories all fell by the wayside. Little wonder, then, that Fritz needed to teach for his own peace of mind as much as others needed him for their greater contentment.

To imply, however, that Fritz's therapy served little more than his own needs denies the benefits that countless people derived from it. It seems to me that Fritz's brand of Gestalt served the needs of therapist and patient alike. To argue over whose needs had primacy is as pointless as pondering the question, "Did the chicken precede the egg?"

Much of Fritz's inner struggle was between what he called his Topdog and Underdog (what Freud referred to as Superego versus Id, or Eric Berne labeled Parent and Child). The Topdog was the moralist, the perfectionist, the internalized parent. The Underdog represented the impulsive, self-seeking, instinctual attitudes that are often frowned upon by parents or society.

One patient who worked with Fritz complained of feeling nervous and tight in her arm. He asked her to tighten *his* arm. As she squeezed, she relaxed markedly.

"Aha," said Fritz. "Because you did to me what you usually do to yourself. This is the golden rule in Gestalt Therapy: 'Do unto others what you do unto yourself.'"

This is exactly what Fritz did with his Topdog/Underdog conflict. He externalized it and played both roles toward others. Among the professional community and the world at large, he was Underdog: wild, woolly, impetuous, creative, rebellious. And with many of his patients, he became Topdog: authoritarian, unsympathetic to certain feelings, and critical. With patients his natural tendency was to frustrate (Topdog). In his personal life he wanted the Underdog's support.

Instead of berating himself for still having dependent feelings, he would rather turn his scorn upon dependent men who occupied his hot seat. Rather than torture himself for his manipulative tendencies, he would rather twit this quality in others.

Why not forgive and forget all these shortcomings both in himself and others? Because he was a perfectionist. That's why he cautioned against being one. And he was still, as a therapist, more aware of liabilities than assets.

Such is the nature of paradox. The more you try to explain it, the more absurd it becomes.

It was during this first year and a half that his health steadily improved. Being out of the Los Angeles smog, eating decent meals, sleeping and rising on a regular basis, and spending much time in the medicinal baths all contributed to his increasing sense of well-being, as did the slow but steady build-up of both his work schedule and acclaim. Credit is also due to the work that Ida Rolf did with him.

Ida, a contemporary of Fritz's, practiced "Structural Integration." He knew of her from his own interest in body/movement/posture. What she did might be compared to deep-muscle massage coupled with chiropracty, in that she would "tear away" the fascia that unnaturally bound down certain muscles, enabling a new and more natural alignment and posture to emerge. She came to Esalen in 1965, primarily to work with Fritz on his stooped posture and sunken chest. Her work (along with the supportive Esalen ambience) was so effective that his heart no longer pained him.

"You know, Dick," he said to Price, "I was able to walk up and down to the baths today with hardly a beat dropped."

"He was like a kid when he was pleased by something," Dick reminisced, "and he claimed that Ida gave him the last six years of his life."

Fritz, by his remarkable response, gave Ida and her therapy—better known as "Rolfing"—their claim to fame.

In addition to the mellowing that came with regained physical health, his growing acceptance by the Esalen community, and the opportunity to work more regularly, Fritz was also vitalized by his reinvolvement with artists— most notably Ann Halprin, the founder and director of The San Francisco Dancers Workshop. His developing closeness to her gave him an opportunity to do group work with her dancers in terms of using movement to have them integrate emotionally unfinished business—work that satisfied him greatly because of his special delight in creative theater and because of the unique wedding of aesthetics and Gestalt Therapy that he might preside over.

Fritz's being in residence did not, in any way, hamper

his outside travels, and he frequently journeyed and worked in both Los Angeles and San Francisco. It was during one of his visits to the Bay Area that he met Ann. A slim, graceful woman with short sandy-colored hair, open, curious eyes, and an expressive mouth which radiates, at rest, a warm, soft smile, she was in her mid-forties at the time. She speaks of Fritz lovingly, clearly missing the presence of a cherished friend: "In my own way I had deviated totally from traditional theater, from traditional dance, and was searching for all sorts of new resources to work with what I called a humanistic approach to theater. Someone told me, 'You would be interested in Fritz.' So that's how I happened to go to him while he was coming up from Esalen to give workshops here.

"The first meeting I had with Fritz came when I was very heavily involved with the theater. I was giving a performance at the time. Many of the things that we were doing were so far ahead of ourselves that we were only being appreciated by a very small group of people. We never got the support that we needed to maintain the continuity of our work. It was as if we were too far out all the time.

"I remember the day I came. I was really hurt. Because I felt I knew what we were doing, and I couldn't understand why the critics didn't understand and why we weren't getting more support. I was feeling pretty upset and brazen and sort of furious with the world. And this man, who I have since learned to love and appreciate, John Enright, was in one of these first groups. He arrived at this group in a black suit and a white shirt and a tie and black shiny shoes and black silk stockings. And he was sitting sort of upright in his chair.

"We were all waiting for Fritz to come, and I was sitting next to him. Something about the look of that man sitting there like that, wearing those kind of clothes, just freaked me. All my resentments about not being understood, about 'Who's crazy? Is he crazy or am I crazy?' just triggered me off. So I stood up in front of this man and I started to rip my clothes off. I was just glaring at him in the eye as I pulled this off and that off, until I stood in front of him stark naked. I stood there very brazenly, and then I sat down.

"And he started to cry. Tears started streaming from his eyes. I didn't know what to do when he started to cry. I didn't expect that. It's like whipping a dog that goes limp on you. I was so irritated that he didn't yell at me 'Stop that'—or something. Instead I got this terrible reaction from him that just took the wind out of my sails.

"Fritz was standing in the door. He had been on the way in and saw the whole thing. I sat down and crossed my legs as if to say, 'Humph.' And Fritz came in, having seen everything, and said, 'So why are your legs crossed?'

"I thought I was so flipped out. He implied, 'You think you're so far out? Man, you're just as uptight as he is.' So that was my first dance with Fritz at a workshop he gave in San Francisco.

"Our next interaction occurred in another group session. I was sitting next to a fire and I was terribly turned off by some person who was working on their craziness. I just made a circle around myself on this thick carpet and I kept looking at the fire. I was very unconscious about what I was doing.

"Fritz came over to me. I didn't even notice that he had left his chair. But he came around the room, sat behind me, opened up his legs to kind of embrace me with them, put his hand on my hair, and said, 'and I am your Guardian Angel.'

"What was so unique and phenomenal about that was that I was fantasizing that I was the burning bush. It was in relation to a whole Biblical allegory about the burning bush, Moses, and the Guardian Angel. And he, somehow or other, was able to pick up these messages. He knew my fantasy. When he said, 'and I am your Guardian Angel,' something in me just snapped, and my whole relationship was established at one moment—my feeling of being able to believe in him, to trust him, to marvel at his creativity

For it was not that I was a mystic and felt that he had mystical ways. I just knew that he was such a master that he knew me. He plugged into my Jewishness, he knew my background.

"He could see subtle, subtle messages in your body. He could read expressions in your eyes, in your mouth, and all around your cheeks that were uncanny, they were so perceptive. He had a way of going right to the center of your soul and just splitting you open in a fraction of a second. Because he could see you so clearly.

"We developed a tremendous love for each other. He was never cruel to me. I didn't understand that, because he could be so cruel to people. I've never seen a man who could be so sarcastic, so belligerent, so nasty, and get people so frustrated that they would be ready to assault this poor old man. I saw somebody, in one group, pick up a heavy ash tray and throw it at him. And he'd say, 'Hit me. Come on, hit me.' I know that was one of his techniques. I could see he was doing this and it was very courageous. He had some woman choking him at one time. 'Go ahead and choke me,' he taunted. And I'd sit there petrified."

These new opportunities for creative work reinstilled, in Fritz, both energy and passion. Esalen, he wrote, had "become a symbol very similar to the German Bauhaus, in which a number of dissident artists came together, and out of this Bauhaus came a re-catalyzation of art all over the world." The Institute, he felt, would, through its diversity of programs, similarly recatalyze psychotherapy. It was "a symbol of the humanistic revolution that's going on."

By 1966, the old revolutionary was feeling his oats once more. It was Berlin after the First World War, New York in the early fifties, and then some. For he himself could now enjoy the role of one of the leading formulators of this new way of thinking. He was no longer simply one of the crowd.

9

Missed Connections

What prevented Fritz from finding a sense of family with his own children? Why would a man who resented his own father's aloofness be remote from his own son? Was Fritz not guilty of the same *stück scheisse* feedback toward his daughter that he suffered at Nathan's hands?

It does not suffice to attribute these paternal shortcomings to his marital discord with Laura, to his greater interest in his work, or to his advanced age on becoming a father. My quest for greater understanding of the disconnectedness that existed between Fritz and his offspring led me, of necessity, to Ren's and Steve's doorsteps. I discovered, in the process, people of sensitivity and warmth, came to empathize with Fritz's longing for greater closeness with Steve, and felt saddened by tales of their missed connections during Fritz's Esalen years.

I was unprepared for my meeting with Ren (Perls) Gold at her suburban New Jersey home. Laura, ever protective, had told me that she preferred I didn't contact Ren, that her daughter was "precarious," and intimated that talking to her about her father might be an unsettling experience for her. Ren's brother and sister-in-law, while good enough to direct me to Renate ("she would be even more upset if a book came out about Fritz and she wasn't asked to comment"), also hinted at serious personal problems. It was both a great surprise and a great delight to meet Ren, for she failed to live up to any of these catastrophic billings.

Ren Gold reminds me of Ethel Merman. A big, brassy, attractive forty-one-year-old, with a rich laugh that erupts from her belly, she exudes warmth and theatricality. On both our first and subsequent meetings she was artfully, dramatically, and colorfully dressed in long flowing robes, wearing large summer earrings, noticeable pendants, and chunky jewelry.

There is a cozy and intimate quality in her home. She is a child/Queen who obviously gets from her immediate family what she stopped getting from Fritz and Laura when she turned four. Art, her husband, is a soft and gentle man who seems to defer to her. Her younger daughter, Leslie, a beautiful twenty-two-year-old, fetches cigarettes for Ren and serves hors d'oeuvres that her mother had previously prepared. The three of them speak frankly about the most intimate details of their personal lives— like three adolescents, sharing stories and giggles. But Ren is clearly the leader of the gang.

I cannot believe she has had any emotional problems and tell her so.

Oh no, she insists. She has. For over a decade she never left her house.

Never?

Well hardly ever. She had unnamable fears of something awful happening to her if she ventured beyond her doors. Only recently, after therapy, has this begun to dissipate.

But aside from that, was she as rational, as available to her two daughters, and as capable a homemaker and raconteur as she is now?

Yes, came the affirmation of all three. She entertained, ran the home, laughed, cried, loved as she does now.

So what was so dreadful? How was she so "ill"?

Well, she couldn't go outside and felt limited and panicked by this symptom. Laura came over frequently to comfort her and, for years, supplied money to meet the expenses of the Gold's household, which were, in the past, invariably beyond their means. Fritz had shelled out money, at first, too, but eventually got fed up and stopped because he felt it was going into an empty well.

"With my father I always had to grovel. If I was a good girl he gave me money. The money came in handy, but I think a little affection and a little interest would have been much more helpful."

Fritz was also contemptuous of Arthur Gold, Renate's husband.

"Why didn't he like you?" I asked.

"I married his daughter. That was the first thing. And then there wasn't any hero worship coming from me. When we first got married he would ask me for advice—for criticisms of his paintings. It was the one common ground we had. He took my criticisms very carefully. But beyond that he was very disdainful of me, looked down on me, and would shit on me every chance that he had. He tried to throw both Ren and me out, he called us leeches, parasites. He called us parasites while I was going to art school and had no income. He knew I had no means of support. We were living with him in a brownstone in Manhattan, and he picked on us at our most vulnerable point. Well, maybe we were parasites. But he invited us to live with them when he knew I had no income and Ren was pregnant."

One wonders, of course, who did the actual inviting. Knowing of Laura's solicitousness toward Ren, I can only assume that she extended the invitation, with Fritz begrudgingly going along.

Ren complains that Fritz never took note of her desires: "We were up in Greenwood Lake once and Fritz came up to spend the night with me there. He was disaster. The only good thing about it was that I made a good dinner. After I put the kids to bed I turned the television set on, and trouble began. Everytime you'd begin to understand something, he'd switch channels.

"At 7:30 he went to bed. But I wanted to watch television. The cottage had no curtains and no doors. So I'm sitting there with my ear to the television set; I can't see the picture, and he's yelling at me, 'Turn the damn thing off!' So I turned the damn thing off. Now who the hell goes to bed at eight o'clock? I had a little radio and took it under the blanket. I, the mother of two children, had to go hide under a blanket to listen to a fucking radio because he didn't want any noise. Or running out in the rain to shut the windows of his car. I did it because I was scared."

She complains that he never took note of her children: "The last time Allison, my eldest daughter, saw Fritz, she was there with a girl friend. He went over to the friend and said 'Hello Allison.' He couldn't even recognize his grandchild."

She complains that he never took note of her home: "Our final meeting was an absolute utter and complete disaster. We had just moved into our house and he had just been to Esalen. We decided to have people in—my mother, my aunt Grete, and Fritz. When Fritz came in, I said, 'Would you like to sit down first or see the house?' He said, 'I don't care.' I said, 'In that case, see the house.' But he never did make the effort to walk through the house."

And she complains that he never took note of her: "My mother always said that he thought that I was beautiful. Why didn't he ever tell me? To me, I was always shit. He gave me two compliments in my life. One when I was thirteen going on fourteen and we had a big Russian to-do at the City Hall in Johannesburg—before Russia was the enemy. I was taking ballet. And there were all these Russian and South African dignitaries. I was the best jumper of the group and got a lot of compliments for two jumps. And he was bragging about me.

"The other time was when he came back from Israel

and brought back all these paintings, which I thought was the biggest shit I had ever seen. I had been painting at the time myself. I didn't like my paintings. I'm not a good painter, but a 'cute' one. But he said, 'There's one thing that you can do that I don't have the guts to do. You *dare* to use color.'

"During most of my life there was simply almost no communication between us at all. I certainly tried. I wanted closeness with him. I heard that a patient of his brought along his girl friend to either Cowichan or Esalen, and that he threw her out—she reminded him of me. What can I say about him? I loved him very much and tried to get his attention. I never could and it turned into hatred.

"In the last six years that Fritz was alive we didn't even talk. I hadn't read *In and Out the Garbage Pail* before he died. And after I read it, I thought that if he weren't dead, I'd kill him. His few remarks about me were a total wipeout."

And what were Fritz's complaints about Ren? Basically they boil down to her failure to take note of him except to ask him for things. Two proud and stubborn people—each unable to give the other the adulation that they wished.

Having had warmth and closeness until she was four, Renate, I imagine, found it hard to give it up. She reacted, instead, as any child might, with hurt, anger, and displays of sassiness. Her later adaptation to life, including her "illness," enabled her, apparently, to get the concern, attention, and financial support ordinarily reserved for loved children or handicapped adults.

Fritz was never sympathetic to her underlying desire to be pampered and cared for. He responded, instead, to her surface behavior with irritability and, later, contempt. This, of course, only perpetuated a vicious cycle of more demandingness and more contempt until an unbridgeable gap was erected between the two of them. Once, upon seeing his daughter twelve years after her "illness" began, he said, quite scornfully: "What's the matter Ren? You still can't go to the movies?"

"That was the only sentence he ever issued about it," Ren indignantly said.

Fritz never recognized the positive elements in his daughter. He saw only one aspect—her desire to suckle—and failed to realize that she could also suckle others, that she provided (and shared) a cozy nest for her family, that she had charm, humor, warmth, generosity, and a stage presence every bit as impressive as his.

Part of Fritz's failure to understand Ren and Steve related to his high expectations of them. Fritz treated his progeny not as children but as adults. He expected them to exercise the restraint, maturity, and self-sufficiency of twenty-year-olds while they were still in their pre-teen years. And he was intolerant of their inability to do so.

He failed to satisfy a child's normal greediness for favors, affirmation, and affection and, instead, dealt with this with the same "Why expect anything of me?" attitude that any reasonable adult might adopt toward another grownup. When one adult doesn't get decent stroking from another, he or she can always move on and find more affirmative companions. Children, unfortunately, can't find new parents.

Even more damaging than his unrealistic expectations were the convoluted and painful attitudes he had toward himself. On the one hand, Fritz had no sympathy for his own need to be cherished and couldn't, therefore, be sympathetic to that need in others. And on the other hand, Fritz's wanting center stage was so powerful—he was such a big kid, in this regard, himself—that these rival needs of his children for center stage were simply pushed aside.

Thus did Fritz, who felt so resentful toward Nathan's neglect of him, become so self-absorbed that he acted as an unwitting conduit in visiting the sins of his father upon his children.

He saw in Ren the "bottomless well" that he himself shared and he hated her for it. He saw her as a parasite who took from Laura. Yet he himself would perpetually free load off Laura: use her apartment, get her to drive him

places and pick him up, to cook, clean, and wait upon him,
and to provide hospitality in return for the pleasure of his
company. As he later wrote:

> If you have hate for something there,
> This is yourself, though hard to bear.
> For you are I and I am thou.
> You hate in you what you despise.
> You hate yourself and think it's me.
> Projections are the damndest thing.

Fritz would not be direct in asking for affirmation, love,
or adulation because it offended his sense of dignity. Yet,
as he received this recognition in later life, he softened,
considerably, in terms of responding to this need in others.
He became increasingly comfortable with his own nedi-
ness as the degree of his "want" lessened with his fame.
At the end of his life he was more capable of acting fatherly than he had been in his younger days.

Fritz knew that he was a terrible father and tried, at
least with Steve, to lessen the gap between father and son
and to show that he cared. With age he found he was missing "what might have been."

He made small, unasked for monetary gifts whenever
he visited Steve and his family, a clear symbol of love
when one is so patently frugal. Steve Perls, for instance,
rarely asked his father for anything and fully recognized
Fritz's difficulty in giving. Once, twelve years into his
marriage, Steve turned to Fritz for a loan. He had just
finished school and needed a car to get to work, but he was
hurting financially.

"Fine. What do you want?" asked Fritz.

"Just over a thousand dollars," Steve answered, "and
I'll pay you back over a few years.

"And he said 'Fine.' He took his checkbook out and
wrote a check. I was shocked but accepted it. Later, I
started to make a payment back to him and sent him a first
check. But he said, 'Forget it. You don't have to pay it back
to me.' Which surprised me."

His daughter-in-law remembers his second and last visit to Albuquerque.

"We were sitting in the dining room. Some mutual friends were with us that night. I made the comment that it would be fun to just earn $50 that I could go and blow— do whatever I wanted with it. And that took his fancy. He asked questions like, 'What would you do with it if you had $50 absolutely unattached to anything?' I told him what I'd do with it, and he thought that was neat, I guess, for he took out his checkbook and he wrote a check to me, Rae Perls, for $150—a hundred more than I had even dreamed of. And he said, 'This is yours. This is for you. It's not for anybody else. You just do what you want to do with it.'

"One friend, Larry Bloomberg, said, 'I'm going to check up on you in a couple of months to be sure that you didn't buy groceries.' And he did. But Fritz never asked. And I had fun with it. I bought books. I bought lingerie. I nickled and dimed it away and had an absolutely marvelous time."

Unfortunately for Fritz, these financial gifts were usually interpreted by Steve as conscience-clearing money. Neither Fritz nor Steve could openly ask for the other's appreciation. Nor could they express their own. Fritz would keep a photograph of Steve and his family on display at his home, but he would never display open affection.

Steve is a thirty-seven-year-old man of average size and shape. Stoop-shouldered, shy, polite, gentle, and friendly, he looks, behind his glasses, a lot like Fritz did in his early years. The heads are shaped the same, with ample noses, sparse hair, and deeply set large eyes. The difference between the two men is that whereas Fritz would stare at you intently, Steve frequently—almost uncomfortably—looks away. There is a note of apology in both his tone and manner. One would never suspect that he is the president of The New Mexico Psychological Association, nor that he heads a manpower training program at the University of New Mexico's Medical School, teaching seventy "dropouts" skills as mental health workers.

I spent two days with Steve and his family in Albuquerque in December 1972 and was most impressed with his thoughtful and disciplined decency. Driving his blue and white Pinto with red trim, relating stories of managing his son's Little League baseball team, picking up his kids after school and dutifully inquiring about their day's activities, he seemed to be the stereotype of the All-American Father and Husband—so different, in that respect, from Fritz.

Steve appears detached and reluctant to need others. He is a man, I suspect, who would have to know you for a long time before he would allow himself to count upon you as a trusted friend. This impression was reinforced as he talked about his life, for "once burnt, twice careful."

Steve, never having had Ren's early "good years" was, perhaps, somewhat less disappointed in his father's unavailability. Instead of Ren's demandingness, he denied his desire for parental closeness, went his own way, became his own "parent," and adopted a cool, aloof, live and let live attitude toward Fritz and Laura. His quality of "I do my thing and you do yours" was more acceptable to Fritz and accounts for why he never treated his son with the scorn he reserved for his daughter.

Steve left home for college when he was eighteen, two years before Fritz left for Miami, and aside from vacations has seen little of either parent since. He met his wife, Rae, at Antioch, when both were attending that small progressive school in Ohio, and married her in his third year. Moving on to the University of Chicago he received a master's degree in educational psychology and a doctorate in counseling psychology. From there he went to Oregon and, some years later, to New Mexico.

"I got angrier as the years went on because Fritz finally began paying more attention to me after I got my doctorate. The attitude was 'you weren't any good until you a least got your degree.' I got the feeling, partly confirmed by him, that if I became a Gestalt Therapist, everything would be groovy. But unless I became a practicing therapist, I didn't have much worth. I was always torn between wanting to go in that direction and gain his approval and feeling that's not really me. So I resisted it.

"I never knew what kind of behavior was acceptable in the sense of what will please him; how can I get his attention. What would be good enough, both to him and my mother, to really merit their attention? I was on that quest for a while but in the last few years realized it was stupid. Because even when he was alive there was really no way I could please him. Eventually I discovered that when I acted in my own interest instead of trying to please him, that that would please him more. So I started not to pay attention to him in terms of getting him to pay attention to me.

"I used to brood on the question, 'Why can't he just pay a little attention to me? Why couldn't he come to my high school graduation?' He did come to my Antioch graduation, which surprised the hell out of me. And he came to my marriage, which was also in Ohio. But those were the only big time occasions he got involved in. Otherwise he was either too busy or off somewhere else. But in Albuquerque I gave up the thoughts of how to get him involved when I began to enjoy what I was doing.

"The contact with my family has always been limited, especially with my sister. My mother would visit me about once a year wherever I was—in Oregon or here. Now I'm part of her route. She won't come and visit me any other time except when she goes to Los Angeles or San Francisco, which is usually about the end of February.

"My Dad would come and visit the last few years of his life. He started to get more involved with me partly because I was getting into things that involved therapeutic activities, but even more because my wife was interested in being a therapist and had the potential of being an excellent therapist, which she now is. Fritz spotted that and worked with her, coming in as you came in. He would fly in one evening and leave the next day. But those few hours would be very important hours, both for me personally, but more for my wife because of the kinds of things she picked up and the training he gave her.

"He'd come in and the conversation would usually turn to me at some point. How am I doing and how am I feeling? During the last six or eight years he would ask me about myself and focus in on me. There was more of an interest in the last few years.

"I was never out to Esalen while he was alive. It was the same old business of my resisting going even though he had invited me because he hadn't *actively* invited me. He said, 'If you're around, drop by.' He didn't say 'I'd really like you to come by and see what we're doing,' or anything like that. It was our usual interaction. I didn't have much money at the time, though money wasn't everything. I think it was much more of a contest than actual money. A few dollars can get you there if you want to come. I'm sure that if he said, 'I'll pay your way if you want to come,' I'd have come. But that little contest was going on.

"I phoned him in Chicago during his final illness. He was pretty sick, but at that time he didn't know what it was. He said that he felt pretty weak and tired and he really couldn't talk very much. I remember thinking something to the effect of, 'Would you like me to come and visit you?' I remember being in a bind, then, because I was thinking that I didn't want to say that I was interested in coming to see him, for that would imply it was pretty serious—maybe near death. Yet if I didn't say anything, that means I'm not interested. In the end I decided not to go. If I didn't take the trouble to see him at Esalen a couple of years earlier, when we could have interacted with each other, why run to a deathbed sort of thing?

"When I think of myself as a parent I can either reject or model myself after my parents, as can all of us. I know I don't want to be·like him. And I know I haven't been like him. Maybe I've gone to the other extreme, but I do things

with my kids; I enjoy being with them. I think it's important that they feel that someone cares and is concerned.
Not overly involved, because that can be a drag too. I can
see from my sister's case how that can be pretty bad."

Rae Perls, an attractive, perky, good humored, intelligent woman, described one of Fritz's rare visits while
they were living in Chicago.

"Out of the blue we would get a telephone call. 'Hello.
I'm at the Palmer House. Come get me.' It was never
'What are your plans? What are you doing tonight? Would
you like to see me? I would like to see you.' It was 'Hello.
I'm here. Come get me.' That was so typical of the way he
would relate to Steve. And Steve would go get him.

"When Fritz came, he always wanted us to be his audience. It wasn't until Steve was into graduate school and I
was going ahead with my training that Fritz paid attention
to us—looked at us. It was only in the last few years that
Steve had something to stand on stage and show off about.
As Steve gained confidence, he forced Fritz to pay attention to him. 'Look at me. This is what I'm doing. This is
what I'm excited about.' He came to life a bit more and
Fritz had to look a bit more."

Alone, with Rae, I share my belief that her husband
must have wanted Fritz to say, 'Hey. I really like you. I
want to be close to you and around you without any strings
attached.' I told her that I was convinced that if Steve ever
asked for more closeness, Fritz would have given a lot.

"What you're saying he did say to Steve, but he said it
too late. We came to Albuquerque nine years ago. I'd
known Fritz maybe ten years by then. He brought Allison,
Ren's oldest daughter, out that first summer for a visit.

"We sat outside that first night and Fritz said to Steve:
'Why don't you tell me I'm a bastard? I would really ap-
preciate your getting angry at me. I've been a lousy father.
Say that to me. Let's have it out.'

"Steve wouldn't give him the satisfaction, I think.
Steve said, 'What good is it going to do me to call you a
bastard now? I've lived my own life all these years.'

"I felt that Fritz was frustrated. He attempted to have a real encounter with Steve that evening, and Steve wasn't having any. I just sat and listened and didn't get into that. But I remember feeling that somehow it was a victory for Steve. That Fritz seemed to be saying, 'This is the time and the place for me,' but it wasn't the time and the place for Steve.

"A lot of things happened those last few years that were really a shame. It was a year or two later that the letter from Steve—the one Fritz mentioned in his book—was sent.* It was funny, too, that he put so much meaning in that letter.

"Every Christmas I would bake things and gather together a box of stuff that I'd send off to Fritz from us all. And generally Steve would have no part of this. But I wanted to, for Fritz gave me what I needed from him, which was some attention and some training. But that particular Christmas I commented to Steve that 'it would be nice if you'd just write a note to put in there. It's up to you, but I feel funny, year after year, sending this stuff off and I sign *our* name. That's really phony.' And he said 'Okay,' and sat down and wrote Fritz the letter.

"I never read the letter, but part of the letter was 'please feel free to come and visit us whenever you want to.' It wasn't but three weeks later that Fritz called and said 'I'm coming for the weekend.' Which was a fantastic response to such a casual invitation.

"That weekend, I felt, was a tremendously important weekend because Fritz was really with us. We bought some land near the mountain and took him up and walked around the land. He liked that. And Steve took those three days off along with the kids—Nancy and Bob. I remember that they were with us because Fritz wore his little terry cloth jump suit and when we went into a restaurant, Bob said, 'Is he going to go to the restaurant like that?' For he

---

* Fritz referred, in *In and Out the Garbage Pail*, to the immense satifaction he got, at Esalen, upon receiving his first personal letter from Steve.

had his long hair and beard. And Nancy said, 'He looks neat that way.'

"I fed him breakfast one morning and gave him the newspaper. I sat at the table and read part of the paper, and he read part of the paper. A few hours later he said, 'I like this. This is a good visit. You've learned not to entertain me.' It was a very good weekend. When he left I felt there was some warmth and affection. He and Steve hugged each other. It was the first time I'd ever seen that happen. This was in January of 1968. The following fall was the A.P.A. [American Psychological Association] meeting in San Francisco, at which time Fritz had his seventy-fifth birthday party. That's when the whole thing blew up. I laugh, but it was sad.

"We knew we were going to San Francisco for the A.P.A. Fritz wanted us to be there for the big birthday party, but Steve didn't want to be *Fritz's son*, standing around. We arranged to be there a few days early to spend some time with Fritz but not as part of the mob that was celebrating his birthday. We told him that was the reason we didn't want to go. But Fritz didn't hear that.

"A week before San Francisco, Fritz called. There had been some letter writing where Fritz had said he was doing a Mill Valley workshop in which he wanted us both to participate. I was on the fence. I was involved in a therapy group at that point and had a lot of uneasy feelings about being in a group with Fritz and Steve. I'd had uncomfortable feelings over the years that Fritz, when he wanted to, used me in some way to get close to Steve. After that nice weekend we had, there was a little bit of letter writing back and forth. That's what did it. He kept writing, 'Come to Esalen and participate in some of my training sessions.'

"I was in group therapy as part of my training and in touch with some hostility toward Fritz as it related to my relationship with Steve. I was able to see how Fritz, because he was not a warm father, indirectly made it hard for Steve to be that. Now it seems like nonsense. But at that point I was feeling angry with Fritz. And he was sending these letters, 'Come participate in a workshop. I want you to experience my training. I have things to offer you both in training.'

"I was getting madder and madder, and wrote back on my own, 'I would love to come and visit you at Esalen to spend some time with you, but I don't want to be in your training workshop with Steve. If Steve chooses to go, fine. But I'm not going to.' He must have gotten the letter and immediately phoned. He was livid on the telephone. 'I'm sending someone to the airport to fetch you and bring you out to Mill Valley.'

"I said, 'Nobody's going to come and fetch me. I'm not coming to your workshop in Mill Valley. I'm tired. I've been working hard. I've been in a heavy group therapy thing. This is not what I need right now. I would very much like to see you and share some of the experiences I'm having and just visit with you. Where will you be staying so when we get into San Francisco we can contact you?'

"He wouldn't tell me. 'Well where are you staying?' I told him where. But he wouldn't accept it. He kept on with me on the phone. Then he said to me, 'Stop getting hysterical.' I said, 'I'm not hysterical. I just told you where I stand. I don't need this and I don't want it,' and I repeated my story very clearly as to why I wasn't going to participate. And he said, 'But Steve will come.' I said, 'I don't speak for Steve. The last Steve said was that he was tired and wanted to take those two days in San Francisco and just wander about the city and relax. But he's free to come.'

"Then he really laid it on me. 'You're really getting controlling and manipulating,' and he got very excited. I said, 'Cut it out. I'm not doing a damn thing except going to San Francisco for a few days and relax and wander about the city. Maybe you'd better talk to Steve later yourself, since we're not apparently communicating very well.'

'I'll call Steve later,' he said sternly. Clunk. And he did. He called Steve later in the evening and Steve said, 'No.' He really didn't want to do that. He didn't want to be in that Mill Valley training group where Fritz was the leader. He told him, 'I just don't feel comfortable about it. I want to see you and spend some time with you, but I don't want to be your son in your therapy group. I just don't want to do it.' Fritz was angry with him, too, but didn't get as nasty with him as he was with me. Steve asked again where he'd be staying so we could get a hold of him, and Fritz refused to tell him.

"We finally hit San Francisco, sat around, and did our thing. Fritz called on a Sunday night. He would not make any time available when he could get together with us and kept putting Steve off on the phone. This went on for the entire week we were there. He'd call and repeatedly ask, 'You will be there for the big session with Ellis and Bach [an A.P.A. panel that he was on with psychologists Albert Ellis and George Bach]? Each time Steve said, 'Yes. We'll be there.' And we were part of a mob of four hundred people squashed into this room. Afterwards we tried to get to him to say hello, but there were these mobs of people lined up to touch him and shake his hand. I went over to stand in line, but Steve got very angry. 'Damn if I'm going to stand in line to shake my father's hand. I'm going.' And I wasn't keen to stand in line to shake his hand either. So we left.

"I remember being sad about it, that this was the way we had to see him. I felt badly for Steve, too. That you had to fight the crowd to see your own Dad. Fritz called us the next night, right before we were leaving, and asked, 'Had you been there?' Steve said 'Sure we were there. We tried to get you but there were all those people. Can we get together tonight? We're due to leave tomorrow.' But, 'Oh . . . no.' Again, he put him off. That's when he mentioned again, 'You will be at the birthday party before you leave Saturday.' And Steve said 'No. We're leaving Saturday af-

ternoon. I told you that months ago. We're not staying for
the birthday party,' and explained why. And that was all.
'Good-bye.' "

"On his seventy-fifth birthday memorial dinner," Alan
Watts recalled, "we had this great, gorgeous gathering. He
was looking like the Lord God Almighty, Jehovah, and
wearing a beautiful colorful shirt with a necklace. I said,
when asked to make some remarks in his honor, that 'everybody knows that the idea of God, the Father, is a Jewish tradition. But we are finally very happy to note that he
has a twinkle in his eye."

There were no good feelings left between Fritz and his
son, however, who never again saw his father alive.

How was Steve to know that Fritz had gleefully told a
number of his friends that Steve would be attending a
group of his in Mill Valley; that this gruff autocrat delighted in thinking about showing off his skills to his son;
that being in a group with Steve would symbolize, to Fritz,
an ever-greater closeness?

How was Fritz to know that his apparently self-suf-
ficient, detached, undemanding son was hurt by not being
offered a more private manifestation of closeness?

And so, there was a Mexican standoff—each man too
proud to take the first or second step.

The similarities between Fritz's situation and that of
his despised father, Nathan Perls, went full circle. Each
achieved a reputation as a slob, a lech, a hater of children,
of being tight-fisted, of loving center stage, and of tooting
his own horn (Fritz would often describe himself as a "genius").

Each man was a wanderer who became progressively
alienated from his wife and children and reaped, for his
absences and unavailability, a harvest of scorn or indifference from his family.

Each, outside of his home, found willing admirers who
appreciated his charisma and Rabelaisian life style.

Steve, like Fritz, grew up on his own, independently of

both his parents. Like Fritz, he never talks about them and has truly carved out a life in which they have never figured. Ren, like Else, developed a very clinging relationship to her mother.

A Joni Mitchell song, "Clouds," contains a line which captures Fritz's existential dilemma: "Something's lost and something's gained from living every day."

What Fritz gained by living each day anew was the ability to extract whatever possibilities for people, excitement, or adventure that existed at the moment. What he lost was the continuity of experiences, of close family relationships and enduring friendships. This, too, was a need that he had and tried to satisfy, in wistful, small doses, with the Freys and the Simkins and, later, by creating his own family at Cowichan.

There is an anecdote permeated with loneliness and unexpressed desire that Laura tells regarding Fritz's father, whom Fritz avoided during the years that Laura knew the two men. Emotionally speaking, it appears to mirror Fritz's feelings for his children.

"When I was going out to take the baby, Ren, in the park, suddenly Nathan would turn up, look, for a moment into the pram, say something half embarrassed to the baby, and then go."

And how would his children like to see their father described in my book: Steve Perls echoed Renate when he put it this way: "I would like the world to think of him as a brilliant, creative, insightful person—a little crazy—who managed to work his way into many people's lives in a very constructive way. And that's fine. I think that's what's happening how. I would not want the world to get the feeling that he was an ideal person.

"The whole approach that he had of getting people to be liberated and free and open works, to a certain extent. But I still feel there is something about family, about commitment, about involvement. Without it, people just go drifting around. He did. He went drifting around. I don't think that's necessarily bad, but there are just lots of good feelings you can get from being with people and growing with each other and helping each other—not necessarily depending on each other, but sometimes that's okay, too."

10

Esalen, Continued . . .

As ill-tempered as Fritz appeared to many outsiders during his first two years at Esalen, he was deeply appreciative of the reception he was accorded—so much so that he invested $10,000 toward a building fund (to be matched, and later greatly exceeded, by the Institute) for the house he was shortly to live in. His investment was to constitute his "rent," with the building reverting to Esalen after his death.

"This is such a lovely place," he told Irma Lee Shepherd, another Gestaltist, protégée, and friend, when she took his Professional Workshop in 1964. "You can walk around emotionally naked and no one would do anything but respect you."

Or, as he confided to Ed "Barbarossa" Taylor, Esalen's baker, a chess partner, a fellow listener to music, and one of the few men "I completely trust": "How beautiful that people can live together and love each other and hate each other and still be together."

The recognition Fritz received here was certainly different from what he had known in New York, Los Angeles, or Miami. Although he had the usual chip on his shoulder at the beginning of his stay, none of the gentle Esalen folk were about to knock it off. What happened, in response, was that the chip diminished in size as the years passed.

If Fritz was grumpy during his first period at Esalen, the next year and a half—from 1966 through much of 1967—found him much mellower. What with his new home (". . . as you can see," he told Jim Simkin, "I have the most beautiful house imaginable"), his improved health, his burgeoning schedule, and a sense of community, the brazen rudeness disappeared to a large extent. Not only did he conduct groups at Esalen for staff and seminarians alike, but he began to attract more professionals in the periodic trips he made to San Francisco, Los Angeles, and the other cities on his circuit. The enormous distances he traveled to spread his Gestalt formulations were now paying off, for he was no longer simply Fritz Perls, but *Fritz Perls from Esalen.*

He would take his yearly cultural jaunts to Europe to take in museums, concerts, and especially opera. When he went abroad in 1968, he came back and gave Ed Taylor a list of fifty operas in a row he saw, "which must," said Ed, "be a world's record of some kind." Life was so satisfying, with Big Sur as its base, that Fritz on many occasions claimed the community as his family and vowed he would live out the rest of his life there.

His decision to build a house on the grounds thrilled him immensely. It was to be the first true home he had since his palace in South Africa. He was particularly delighted by its modernistic structure, its unrivaled view, and the prospect of sitting in an oversized sunken bathtub listening to the Pacific Ocean splash and crash against mountain cliffs. Fritz would carry the architect's blueprints with him on his travels and joyfully show them to old friends.

He was impatient to see the building completed, for it was a tangible representation of the roots he felt growing into that fertile soil. In the summer of 1966 he finally moved in, inviting Abe Levitsky, his latest in a series of protégé/assistants, to join him.

"We enjoyed each other in a lot of ways," recalled Abe, a big, smiling, bearded man whose face reminded me of the face of the French sailor that adorns the Zig-Zag cigarette paper package. "There were many aspects of music that I knew about that he didn't, so it was fun to introduce him to some things. Other music we enjoyed together, such as German Lieder. I would frequently go down to Carmel or Los Angeles and find something that I liked, and, with great glee, I would bring it back and we would listen to it together. They would be very moving scenes, because we would be overlooking this gorgeous expanse of the Pacific and listening to Bach and Brahms. At that time I had a great fondness for the Brahms Liebeslieder waltzes, and there were times that Fritz and I would waltz to them together."

Fritz's clinical skills were attracting more and more people to him, as was his refreshing candor; his willingness to allow all his creature attitudes to be on display without apology. Feeling more zestful and alive, now, he boldly let both "base" and "higher" motivations show. As he wrote in *Garbage Pail:*

> Right now quite a few people are crowding into this book, sneering at my leching, despising me for my lack of control, being shocked by my language, admiring me for my courage, confused by the multitude of contradictory features, desperate because they cannot pigeonhole me. I feel tempted to get into a dialogue, but . . .

Fritz took a certain pride in his excesses, a delight in his ability to shock and to do the unexpected. These engendered the stories—told and retold, true and exaggerated—that made Fritz a legend in his time.

Fritz, for instance, would contribute to his reputation for arrogance in a short film classic in which he appeared with the Maharishi Mahesh Yogi. The meeting between the guru of the East and the guru of the West was arranged while Fritz was at Esalen in the hope of illuminating a common path to emotional harmony. Instead, their discussion consisted of Fritz doing a great deal of one-up-manship and undercutting of the Maharishi's philosophy as he chain-smoked constantly while the Maharishi nervously tore the petals from a rose.

On another occasion, Diane Reifler remembers sitting on the side porch at Esalen with Fritz and two others. A woman wandered up to this foursome "who was pushy, cutesy, and unattuned to others' feelings about her behavior. She wanted to talk to Fritz about doing some publicity for him like she was doing with this one and that one. Fritz abruptly stopped her onslaught with, 'Go away. I'm not talking with you *ever!*'

"I have seen him do this with other pests—protect himself and his privacy."

As Fritz felt secure about his wisdom, maturation, and stature, he began to allow the small person within him to emerge. And so there are stories of Fritz, the Child.

One weekend he went to visit Bob Hall, a young psychiatrist and another of his former assistants. Several photographs of an Indian guru hung upon the walls of the house. This angered Fritz. He felt that the Indian mystique was an avoidance of recognizing your own power. And he couldn't take that sort of adulation for a Master.

On Sunday morning, the phone rang in Ann Halprin's house.

"Would you come and get me right away."

Ann and her husband, Larry, drove over to Bob's house and transported Fritz back to theirs.

"They didn't have breakfast ready for him and they weren't paying enough attention to him. They loved the guru more than they loved him, because obviously, there were all those pictures all over the walls. And they were meditating for three and a half hours instead of fixing his breakfast. It was no way to show your proper respect."

Fritz might tolerate the adulation of another Master, as long as the child in him had his breakfast prepared.

Diane Berghoff Reifler, a striking and voluptuous actress who towered over Fritz, came to know him as he entered his second phase at Esalen. Fritz was impressed not only by her ripeness as a woman but by her *presence*— her unique ability to stay in a moment to moment flow. Diane, who went on to train with him, was to become one of the most competent and creative Gestalt therapists I have ever. watched. Some of her fondest recollections of Fritz had to do with his willingness, now, to lay aside his austere mask and share, undefensively, the child within: "I remember the first time he walked into my house. He was going to hold a workshop there. I had it built in a canyon with lots of trees and glass and twenty-foot-high ceilings where you could see the trees and reflections all around. He walked in and said, 'A house to breathe in.' And he danced around and we both started to dance. He was a delight.

"When he would say something far out and brilliant he wanted people to say, 'Wow. That is really far out and brilliant.' He really needed that. I can picture his saying that and starting to dance and me walking into the other room and doing the dishes. That would just let his balloon out. Because he didn't just say these things for himself, but because Teddy Lyon, his secretary, heard him and I heard him. It was really important to him that he get heard and get all the attention.

"I loved the little kid in him. He was staying at my house once and he was going to do a Los Angeles television show. He had on a suit and he asked, 'Is this okay? What should I wear?'

"What was amazing to me about his not wanting to be around kids was that he was such a big kid. He was The Big Kid and didn't want to have any siblings around. He was really like a needy kid who didn't get fed. He wanted all the attention. I gave it to him because I was thrilled with him. When we were good together, he gave me all the attention and I gave it back. And he loved that.

"Fritz and I were actually intimate on two occasions. I think he wanted me to be his woman—I know he did. But I wasn't ready for that. I loved him, but not like that. I remember when I said goodbye to him one time. I had put him to bed and put the blanket over him and sang him a lullaby and he was a little boy. He was really delightful. He really enjoyed it, playing like he was two or three and I was the Mommy."

Aside from Fritz the child, there was often an adolescent on the make. Ilana and Frank Rubenfeld were young students of Fritz's whom he would frequently visit whenever he came to New York.

"We'd go to the movies together," recalls Ilana. "He was crazy for movies, a madman for movies. He'd call us up at ten o'clock at night and say, 'Let's go to a double feature.' Laura, Fritz, Frank, and I would go piling in a cab and go to a double feature until two in the morning. And the thing that just used to drive me batty is that in the movie house he'd make sure to sit next to me. Laura and Frank would sit next to us or behind us. And he'd try to smooch.

"He'd take his hand and grab mine and I'd say, 'Please, Fritz.' I'd take his hand and put it back on his lap again, not only because I didn't want him up there, but Laura's right behind me. Except that he'd do it again. For two hours this would go back and forth, back and forth, like a teenager in a dark movie trying to see what he could get. Slowly the hand would creep behind. Then my hand would take his off, and it would never stop him. He'd do it twenty times."

Well known for his theatrics, Fritz told a story about being at a party in Ein Hod, Israel. Several people had performed. He was envious and decided to outperform them all by pretending he was dying. The act came off very well. There was great worry and concern "until I took a bow and got them very angry."

Few things pleased Fritz as much as being noticed. Jane Levenberg, a social worker who sponsored workshops for Fritz, would often take him to the opera when he left Esalen to visit Chicago.

"His usual attire was his Nehru shirt. I remember one

Wednesday night, which is notoriously doctor's night at the opera here. He would stand in the lobby and preen like a peacock. And he was not an unnoticeable man. Anyone who would pass would turn to look at him. And he adored it. The more he got looked at, the more people I introduced him to, the better he liked it."

Fritz was a great show-off, for he always hungered for recognition. Many of his attempts to *show up* others were simultaneously intended to *show off* himself. He constantly attempted to expose others as misguided at best or frauds at worst. These others were not restricted to those of renown nor potential rivals for center stage.

Abe Levitsky met Fritz for the first time when he appeared on a program run by The American Psychological Association in Chicago.

"He was on a panel with Albert Ellis, Renee Nell, and some other psychologist. What interested and intrigued me at that time was the directness and vigor of his attack on Ellis. He made no bones about saying to Al, 'You're just making propaganda for yourself.' At other times he elaborately slept through other people's presentations, obviously not very moved or in agreement with what was going on. Pretending to be asleep."

Many people, like Diane Reifler, could enjoy his grandstanding. When the two of them were doing therapy with an uninvolved or unresponsive person, they might spice up the interaction and dramatize their own performances by hamming it up or making faces at one another. More conservative types, such as Jim Simkin, found such showboating antics distinctly unappealing.

"I was impressed," said Jim, "with his genius. I was impressed with his theoretical system. But I was appalled by his own personal life and his own personal values.

"He used to get up at meetings and make an ass of himself. In group therapy we sometimes speak of the one person who takes over the group—a type of prima donna who is apparently insensitive to the needs of others. Fritz was often that person. I'd feel ashamed that somebody I liked or identified with acted that way. I wanted to crawl away and hide like I didn't know that person. It was exhibitionistic, wanting center stage, not allowing for people who didn't have as much on the ball or are not as aggressive. And ruthless in that respect. I didn't like that about Fritz."

What Simkin considered Fritz's "making an ass of himself," Fritz considered exposing the asininity of others. Thus, for Fritz, his elaborate act of falling asleep on panel discussions was his way of making a statement about the boring pedantry of the participants. It was a form of street theater. The fact that it focused attention upon him added, naturally, to its desirability.

Once, in the middle of a seminar Abraham Maslow was conducting at Esalen, Fritz began to crawl on his belly and engage in other zany acts. He was obviously bored by the proceedings and hoped to inject some life and spontaneity into the program. Maslow, however, was unable to deal with Fritz in the way a less serious person such as Paul Frey might. Instead, the meeting was disrupted. Afterward, a sombre Maslow is reported to have said, "That man is crazy."

Fritz, during this time, achieved great renown as a sexual being. Here, too, the show-off element was in evidence. Much of the leching of his seventies stemmed from his desire to perpetuate his much enjoyed fame as a lusty and desirable man. Fritz wrote of his "reputation as being both a dirty old man and a guru. Unfortunately the first is on the wane and the second ascending.

"Once we had a party in the 'big house' at Esalen. A beautiful girl was lying seductively on a couch. I sat next to her and said something like this: 'Beware of me. I am a dirty old man.' 'And I,' she replied, 'am a dirty young girl.' We had a short and delightful affair after that."

Bernie Gunther, commenting on the Esalen years, had this to say: "He used to love to kiss. He would just walk up to girls. I was amazed at the incredible kind of nerve he had. Very few women would stand up and say, 'I don't

want to kiss you.' And a lot really enjoyed it. Many young
gals thought that Fritz was a great kisser."

"I don't know when I first met Fritz," said Alan Watts.
"I can't quite remember. But suddenly I ran into this
vastly patriarchal character with a big beard. And he was a
very affectionate man. He wasn't stand-offish. He was
warm. He would embrace you; he would touch you.

"Fritz amused me enormously. Because he was a wise
man, obviously. I mean he knew how to live. He knew
how to live in the present. And he was, like myself, a
lecherous man. He would sit around in those hot baths at
Esalen and keep his eyes on the girls.

"Once he saw a particularly beautiful girl sitting in the
baths at Esalen. He looked at her for a long time, and then
then went over to her and said, 'You vant to suck my
prick.' And, by God, she did. He was a terror!"

Then there is the well-documented story of how Fritz,
just prior to starting *In and Out the Garbage Pail*, spent a
weekend in bed sandwiched, nostalgically, between two lovely
young women.

Fritz's sexuality often stemmed from his sensitivity toward and affection for others and was part of a natural
flow. He wrote:

> My hands are strong and warm. A dirty old man's hands are
> cold and clammy. I have affection and love—too much of it.
> And if I comfort a girl in grief or distress and the sobbing sub-
> sides and she presses closer and the stroking gets out of
> rhythm and slides over the hips and breasts . . . where does
> the grief end and a perfume begin to turn your nostrils from
> dripping to smelling?

"Most men," claimed Wilson Van Dusen, "if they taper
off at sixty, celebrate that they lasted so long. But Fritz
wished to be fully active all the way."

"When Bill Schutz came here," said Esalen's Michael
Murphy, "he was sleeping with all the girls. That was a
little too much for Fritz and was related to his starting a
whole campaign against Bill, Bernie Gunther, and the
'turner-oners.'

"There was a macho element in Fritz. He'd preen and parade and challenge. But I think the bottom line was just an intensity to live. He was just a terribly alive guy.

"He had a rational, humanistic, bohemian scheme in which sex, I think, is way overrated, where it becomes a substitute for the ecstatic experiences that come more naturally. It becomes what he said it shouldn't become, a fantasy: a thing you live FOR. An impossible dream, this seeking perfect sex all the time.

"There was a particular kind of woman he loved. When they came to work at Esalen, I could just spot them. He usually liked big women, physically. He liked them with a lot of 'stuff'—*zoftick*—soft. He didn't like anyone who would challenge him. He nicknamed the waitresses 'The Floating Maidens.' They were the strong silent types. He liked a a certain amount of mind, too, bright, but a good listener."

Through his heavy sexual involvements, Fritz was able to achieve some comfort, warmth, and love. Playing the part of a Superpotent sexual being to the hilt, Fritz could experience *tit-in-mouth* without openly acknowledging his more profound need for nourishment. Yet he was keenly sensitive to this desire in others and often functioned, sexually, in a therapeutic way. Testimonials regarding Fritz's sensitivity and sexual prowess are common. Consider this one from Diane Reifler, the auburn-haired actress turned therapist with a lot of "stuff."

"He did a lot of therapy when he was intimate with me. I needed to do a lot of sucking, so he would put his hand in my mouth. He could connect to those kinds of needs. At that time I did a lot of crying. It was like reexperiencing being a baby. He could see that that's what I really needed rather than fucking. I wouldn't really consider it balling. A lot of time in bed allowed for anything that concerned contact. He eventually came. And he helped me a lot."

Marty Fromm recalls that "Fritz had a lot of ego involved in love making—in turning women on. So a refusal might whet his appetite, where he could show off and do his thing.

"His potency varied in the last few years. He gracefully withdrew from fucking and enjoyed kissing and playing in the baths. He always had a marvelous mouth and hands and always enjoyed producing orgasms for women. I really did enjoy *playing* after Fritz. I grew up, sexually. Everything I learned I learned from him and I'm grateful not only for what he did for me as a therapist but as a lover."

Fritz's capabilities as a jester also helped make him bigger than life, for his comic sense ranged far and wide. He could ham it up, slapstick style, for the entertainment of others by his parody of flamenco dancing, his satirical improvisations of other people, and his cutting one-liners.

As a phrase-maker his wit was razor sharp. Once, when asked his opinion on meditation, he responded with: "Meditation is neither shit nor get off the pot."

During his campaign to end mystical programs at Esalen, he referred to the Institite as "a spiritual Coney Island."

In putting down the Freudian's insistence on explaining all illness in terms of childhood traumata, he said: "Psychoanalysis is an illness that pretends to be a cure."

Fritz took great delight in twitting intellectuals who denied their animal instincts and their creature intuition.

"Intellect is the whore of intelligence," he wrote.

Since his Gestalt Therapy was grounded in immediate experience and awareness, Fritz had little patience with intellectual theoreticians—"mind-fuckers," as he caustically called them. His ability to satirize their endless quest for *explanations* was one of his chief weapons in countering their academic pretensions.

> *Why*, at best, leads to clever explanation, but never to an understanding. *Why* and *because* are dirty words in Gestalt Therapy. They lead only to rationalization, and belong to the second class ·of verbiage production. I distinguish three classes of verbiage production: chickenshit—this is "good morning," "how are you," and so on; bullshit—this is "be-

cause," rationalization, excuses; and elephantshit—this is when you talk about philosophy, existential Gestalt Therapy, etc.—which I am doing now. The *why* gives only unending inquiries into the cause of the cause of the cause of the cause of the cause of the cause.

Some of his most famous quips were directed toward other luminaries in the so-called *Human Potential Movement.* Abraham Maslow was known as the Founding Father of "Third Force Psychology." He preached a view of man that paid attention to ideals, values, choices, actualization, and spirituality. Although this was a more humanistic conception than that held by orthodox Freudians, it was equally rigid in its insistence upon a newer, liberal stereotype.

And what was Fritz's opinion of Maslow?

"A sugar-coated Nazi."

Rollo May, the preacher turned psychoanalyst, is another psychological Superstar who established a reputation for himself as an Existentialist. Fritz referred to him, while at Esalen, as "an Existentialist without an existence."

Bernie Gunther also recollects Fritz's ability to laugh at his own absurdity.

"In my position as the Masseur of Big Sur, I naturally found my way into the hearts and membranes of many a lovely and not so lovely woman. Those were the days when I was a Jewish boy in a pastry shop. It was hard to say 'No.' And I ran into this little girl who had the blackest raven hair you've ever seen—a little bit on the thin side but really buxom. Very lovely. Olive skin, attractive, young. The personification of the pretty, not particularly nourishing type of girl I used to go for.

"She and I had gotten together the night before and came down and went into the dining room. I had to go talk to somebody, so I left her in the dining room to wait for me. Well, Fritz was in the bar, and he apparently saw her standing there. I had said whatever I had to say and was coming back. But I saw him moving toward her and I thought I'd stay in the background and see what happened.

"He started moving toward her in this beautiful, leering, focused way that he had. And when he got within four or five feet of her, she said, 'Do you want something, Grandpa?' It's the only time I've ever seen Fritz totally freeze up. He just stopped, then laughed, and when he realized there was no way of moving forward, he turned and walked back."

During this time, Fritz gave many people the gift of *specialness*. Though countless souls felt they shared a rare moment with this man, the moments, in fact, were more common than they have assumed. At least they were for Fritz. One of his former assistants at Esalen put it this way: "People always wanted to be near him. And periodically he'd pick a fish out of the pond and it was very attractive. One day it was Marsha. She was the most important person in his life *right now*. And then, one day, he would drop her. Just as he dropped me.

"Everybody who worked with him thought that they were his favorite. And it surprised them to find out that there would soon be someone else. But it was great at the time.

"That was the nature of the man. And my reaction, like that of many others, was that of someone who wanted *more*."

The legion of people who felt that they had something extra special with this otherwise lonely and isolated man helped propagate the legend of Fritz Perls. Not only were there a string of ladies but also a host of "heirs apparent"—people who claimed the number two post in the Gestalt hierarchy after Fritz.

With the possible exception of Laura Perls, Jim Simkin has laid the longest lasting claim to Gestalt "leadership." One of his most impressive credentials is having worked *amicably* with Fritz since the Gestalt Institute of New York was founded. Few can match both his durability and longevity.

In his Esalen phase alone (and later, at Cowichan), Fritz asked a number of people to be his assistants. Aside from Jim, these have included Abe Levitsky, Bob Hall, Claudio Naranjo, Dick Price, Teddy Lyon, and Janet Lederman. A few he turned on, bitterly, as time went by. Others went their separate ways. Some remained his friends.

When Laura claims, "We never parted . . . I was still the one he was closest to," or when Marty Fromm states, "We never really left each other," both are in good company. Dozens of Fritz's other, briefer, more trifling intimacies report the same enduring and timeless quality of relationship.

"You're going to have a hard time with Fritz's relationships," Teddy Lyon told me when I interviewed her, "because Fritz had moments when he related to each one of us deeper or as deep as any of his human relationships. But to say 'he had a friend' is a hard thing to say. And I'm not sure that I'd say it."

Boredom had always been a problem for Fritz: what to do when he was not working. The stability and support he was now receiving enabled him to channel even this restlessness into ways that were to lead him to new heights of creativity.

Dick Price recalls seeing Fritz "restless for something to do when he wasn't conducting a group, wandering around wondering who's about to play chess with. And then, occasionally, he would get fascinated with something like the videotape. And then drop the tape suddenly as a child would drop a Christmas toy. 'Now I'm going to be on stage and do my own directing. . . . Now I'm going to be an author.' Almost like a very groovy child, completely into whatever he was doing."

This "groovy child" not only saw videotape as a way of giving people additional feedback, but recorded—both on tape and on film—a remarkable selection of his work with people, visual documents that would be widely shown and add, immeasurably, to both public and professional interest in Gestalt Therapy.

The quality and conciseness of his work also sharpened. Fritz felt that he was becoming better and better. Some of his work, taped in 1967 and 1968, was edited into his third book, *Gestalt Therapy Verbatim*, which was eventually published in 1969. The clarity and crispness of that work stand in sharp contrast to the ponderously coauthored *Gestalt Therapy*.

As his reputation spread, he launched what he called his "circus," where he gave demonstrations of Gestalt Therapy in front of a hundred people or more upon a stage that he had rigged. These demonstrations gave rise to his well-known "hot seat"—an empty chair beside him that members of the audience could occupy if they wished to work with him. The beckoning quality of this empty chair and the dramatic tensions that ensued from people working alongside him led him to bring the hot seat technique back from the circuses and into the smaller workshops that he ran.

Fritz also discovered the Good Mommy he never had in the person of Teddy Lyon, a woman in her mid-forties, who evolved from patient, to maid, to lover, to secretary, to disciple, to assistant. She was in daily contact with him for the last three years of his life both at Esalen and Cowichan (the Gestalt "kibbutz" Fritz subsequently founded in Canada). Teddy was privy to Fritz's personal affairs in a way few others had been, for he came to trust her implicitly. Unlike any woman he had previously known, she was loyal, undemanding, and willing to quietly "be there" for Fritz. And, aside from some initial sexual possessiveness on his part, he was never to foul up their relationship by becoming romantically involved with her.

An ascetic-looking, slim, gaminish, older Audrey Hepburn type, Teddy, with short grey page boy hair, deep eyes, and a soft manner, first met Fritz in January 1965, at a workshop he was giving at Esalen. Her life had centered around her children; the "mothering" role was a very essential one for her to play in order to validate and give meaning to her existence. Two years before signing up for Fritz's workshop, her son had been killed in an automobile accident and her younger daughter went off to college. So at the time she was undergoing a process of great despair/unhappiness/transition.

Although she saw Fritz and Jim Simkin on and off during the next two years, she failed to make much headway in finding new meaning and involvement in her life. Then, in the summer of 1967, she signed up for a month-long program that Fritz was giving.

"At the end of that month I didn't know what I wanted to do. I didn't feel like leaving Esalen and I didn't want to go home. Fritz had, in the interim, built the round house and moved into it. It was very dirty because there wasn't anybody cleaning. I said to him that I would like to stay there for a few days and that I would be glad to clean his house in exchange. It needed it. I said that the only thing worse than a Jewish mother was a Presbyterian mother—which I was. And he said, 'Fine.' I asked how long did he think he could stand me, and he said 'Maybe five days.' So we had an utterly loose agreement.

"The first day I started out I cleaned really hard. The place was absolutely filthy. Fritz had gone to rest in the guest room, where I was staying. Just about the time I was finishing, he got up and came into his room. I asked him one of those things that you ask when you've been cleaning for hours, like 'Where does this go?' And he said, 'Please. I've just had a nightmare that women are putting order in my life.' I answered that 'If that's the worst trouble you're in, you're not in real trouble.' And he laughed. From then on, except for one brief fight we had with each other, I worked for him until he died.

"I lived in the round house for about a month and a half. Then we had a terrible fight and both decided that we hated living with each other, that it was an enormous relief not to anymore and we stopped it. The trouble began when he want away for a trip. In leaving he had said to me, 'Misbehave.' I took him very literally, being very dumb and stupid. So I went out and had an affair with a much younger man. Fritz comes back, finds out about that, and claims there's something I'm supposed to have done that I haven't done because I'm playing around. Something I'm supposed to get in the mail. And he seemed mad about that."

The old anger was rising up once more—the same anger he felt when Marty shared her favors with someone else in Miami, the hurt and resentment he must have experienced as a child when his mother showed greater involvement with another rival, his sister Else. His resentfulness erupted at his seminar that evening and carried over for a few more days until he put the pieces back in perspective so that he and Teddy might establish a more platonic, respectable, and enduring relationship. Teddy continues: "That night there was a group. I attended all of his groups at that point. Everyone was saying where they're at. They get around to me and I'm sitting, rocking back and forth on this chair. I'm feeling very hot. And Fritz asks, 'What do you resent?' I answer that I don't resent anything. Fritz says, 'You're such a liar.' And then, of course, I did resent something. I instantly resented him telling me I'm a liar.

"He said, 'Rocking is always a sign of resentment.' And I was confused. I wasn't aware of it, but if I look for something I can always find it. Yet I wondered if rocking was *always* a sign of resentment. That was all in public.

"When the group finished that evening, I went up to Fritz and said, 'I want to talk to you.' He's tired and exhausted and doesn't want to get this straight, but I did. I remember sitting on the bed in his bedroom, and his telling me that all he could hear in my voice was 'righteous indignation.' And that made me mad, too. The next morning he looked at me with this terrible look and said, 'Finished.' It was the first time he had looked at me that way, though I saw him look at others like that. It was awful.

That's how I initially lost my job with him and permanently left his house."

It was not long before Fritz asked Teddy to resume working for him as his secretary. She would help him with "the kinds of things he always hated—which was opening mail," answering it, paying bills, and making arrangements." Teddy would type his manuscripts, share his excitement as he wrote sections of *In and Out the Garbage Pail*, and never begrudge him his involvement with other people.

"Much later on, when he moved to Canada, Fritz asked me if I'd live with him and keep house for him. I said 'No.' I would not do that for him but I was willing to go to Cowichan with him as his assistant."

Teddy found new involvement through her relationship with Fritz. At Esalen she served as his chief cook and bottle washer—someone he could bounce ideas off, someone who approved of him wholeheartedly, someone who could disagree with him in a loving way. And, by being a quietly accepting and faithful Supermother toward him, Teddy could reclaim a role she had been unable to play since her children departed.

What with his house, his work, his growing fame, and the love that many of those at Esalen felt for him—from Dick Price, to Teddy Lyon, to staffers such as Ed Taylor and Selig, the gardener, to fellow group leaders such as Janet Lederman and Julian Silverman—one might have expected that Fritz would live harmoniously, at Esalen, ever after. Such speculation failed to take account of his growing jealousy of coresidents Bill Schutz and Bernie Gunther. Although Fritz was impatient to establish further refinements relating to Gestalt Therapy, refinements that could be instituted only at a place he was fully in charge of, it was his own destructive envy and rage, more than anything else, that ruined the paradise Esalen had been for him.

11

Esalen, Concluded

All great teachers teach what they themselves have learned and need to remind themselves of. If Alfred Adler taught others to appreciate the inferiority/superiority axis, it was because he was deeply enmeshed in this situation himself. Sigmund Freud's helping people to recognize the strength of their sexual instincts stemmed from the power of his own sexual repressions. Similarly, Fritz's lessons of "be true to yourself," "live in the present," and "reown your projections" flowed directly from his own difficulties in achieving these same ends. Never was this discrepancy clearer than during Fritz's final period at Big Sur.

When I confine myself to thinking of *process*—the "how" as it occurs in the "now" (the Gestalt-Existential-Phenomenological viewpoint)—I discover that my understanding of Fritz improves to the degree that I can suspend trying to understand him. If, on the other hand, I try to explain him in terms of some irreducible theory, he becomes unexplainable. Fritz, more than most people, was both simpler and more complex than any theoretical system would have us believe. That is why he is best understood in terms of paradox.

For example, Fritz preached, "I do my thing and you do your thing." Yet the most painful contradiction Mike

Murphy had to deal with during Fritz's six years at Esalen was the conflict between his philosophy of encouraging others to be autonomous and then rewarding the sort of behavior that he desired.

"He wanted Esalen to be a certain way. At the same time he was saying 'Do your own thing.' Whenever there were changes made in the schedule, he'd come and compliment me or scold me, depending on how it was going. He was intent upon getting the religious, mystical, occult, and Eastern programs out.

"Once we had a workshop with Peter Hurkos, the famous clairvoyant who solved the Boston Strangler murder case. He and Charles Tart, the psychologist, were running psychometry experiments in which you feel an object—in this case a hair—and describe the person. But it didn't work out. And Fritz was outrageous this weekend in putting down Hurkos.

"Finally, when Hurkos was obviously failing, the dramatic moment occurred where Fritz stood up, faced some of the audience, and with a sweeping gesture said, 'You see vat a fake zis man is.' He knew just when to get Hurkos, and you could see Hurkos collapse. Because people like him represented the kind of thing Fritz was against."

Did this mean that Fritz was oblivious of his tyrannical instincts? Not at all.

"Once, when I was on good terms with him," remembers Dick Price, "and he was trying to get something from me, I said, 'Hey Fritz. I'm not in this world to live up to your expectations.'

"He turned to me and said, with good humor 'Oh yes you are.'"

Was he, then, a hypocrite in not practicing what he preached? I think not. Fritz's authoritarianism was simply a matter of his "doing his thing." If you didn't like it, "your thing" ought to be to resist him. He was not out to protect you or make it easier for you to take a stand by blunting his own desires. Indeed, some part of his telling others to do their own thing was, I am sure, done in order to help them resist his persuasiveness. He often, both at work and at play, respected people who openly stood up to him.

"I know what a *satori* experience is," wrote Fritz, "though I have not made the total enlightenment grade, in case such a thing exists."

That bit of double-talk lies at the heart of Fritz's contradictory attitude toward the mystical, for satori *is* the total enlightenment grade. Not that it lasts forever. Nothing does.

Fritz's antagonisms toward Peter Hurkos, the Maharishi, Baba Ram Dass (who he was proud of having "bested" in a joint television appearance), and the mystical was, I believe, the attitude of a man who comes in fighting but hopes to be convinced. Unfortunately, he was such a good battler that no one could overcome his defenses.

Fritz didn't believe in the mystical simply because he had never experienced it. That is what he would have required in order to Believe. Still, he was intrigued. Otherwise why go listen to Hurkos in the first place?

The thing Fritz found most difficult to accept about himself was his lack of perfection. Thus, in spite of his writing, "Friend, don't be a perfectionist . . . be proud of your mistakes," he always strove for perfection. When he wrote *Garbage Pail,* he would repeatedly ask his friends, "Do you like it? . . . Do you really like it?" When the answer was affirmative, he glowed. When old friends such as Erv Kempner, a Cleveland Gestaltist, and New York's Isadore From said that they thought it needed substantial editing and wasn't really worthy of him, he was insulted and furious. At other times, after a good demonstration, he would ask: "How's that? Good? Good? I'm still the best therapist around."

The very last Gestalt demonstration that he gave at Esalen was one before a hundred people. It went quite well. When it was over, Fritz went up to Dick Price and said: "Dick, I was finally perfect."

Anyone who spent some time with Fritz or has read all

that he has written realizes that he was fully cognizant of all these discrepancies within himself. It was, in fact, his own success and his own discoveries in partially resolving these dilemmas in his own life that he passed on to others in both his theories and his clinical parctice. Yet, understanding the contradictions did not make them disappear.

He would, for instance, make snide references to Will Schutz as being merely an "integrator" of other people's ideas, as someone who offered "instant joy." One would think, by comparison, that Fritz was against quick cures and respected only originality. And he did.

But this is the same Fritz Perls who offered "three-month cures" in Canada, who showed films depicting "instant breakthroughs," who knew, according to Jim Simkin, that "there weren't any quick cures, yet looked for them and kept putting others down for looking for them."

And who was a better integrator and synthesizer of other people's ideas than Fritz Perls himself? And what is wrong with integrating other people's ideas? Nothing, I submit, unless you feel you have to do something better, unless you feel you are not an original article yourself, unless you are a perfectionist.

In truth, there is no such thing as an original idea. All our concepts and discoveries have been made by and/or shared by others. Freud was not the first to recognize infantile sexuality. Native women on Caribbean islands realized that crying infant boys could be pacified by playing with their penises long before Freud made his "discoveries." And as far as dream interpretations were concerned, Joseph worked with Pharaoh's dreams thousands of years before the publication of *The Interpretation of Dreams.*

What originality any of us have stems from the selection and blending we make of the ideas of others. Part of Fritz knew this. That's why he called himself the "finder or refinder" of Gestalt and not a founder or an original discoverer.

An idea is no less great because it lacks originality. The great messages have always been simple ones: Love.

Peace. Harmony. Living in the present. They have been taught by different teachers throughout the ages, be they Christ, Moses, Lao Tse, Buddha, Freud, Fritz, or the neighborhood hippie.

Fritz had an antipathy toward people who attended groups simply for the fun of it. This was one of his criticisms of Schutz and Gunther, the "instant turner-oners." When he conducted a group it was for the more serious purpose of "work"—just as he would perpetually work on his own problems. In his preference for work over play he betrayed not only his perfectionism, this treadmill of always striving to be better and therefore never arriving, but a Calvinistic streak as strong as his Jewish Buddhism.

This philosophical bias toward *not accepting yourself as you are but as you hope to be* is inherent in nearly all psychotherapeutic systems. Exponents of Eastern thought, such as Alan Watts and Baba Ram Dass, teach that *you are already there,* that perfection needn't come tomorrow, but it exists right now. Fritz and the Gestaltists who followed him not only span Eastern and Western psychotherapeutic thinking but are caught up in the dilemma of the middle: proclaiming the validity of the here and now but implying that you must work on yourself for a better tomorrow.

"I am not responsible for anyone but myself. I take none for you. I am available to work with you if you desire it. If you wish to go crazy or kill yourself, that is up to you." This was the message that Fritz frequently broadcast upon starting a workshop or a demonstration.

But again, we have a paradox. Why would he have struggled so long and so hard to present a new psychology to the world unless he hoped in some way to save it? He obviously believed that Gestalt thinking would ease the self-torture and self-doubts of many people and contribute to more harmonious and less blaming interpersonal relations among people.

Ann Halprin's observations about Fritz during the last months of his life have, I think, much validity.

"In spite of the fact that he said, 'You take care of your-

self' and 'everybody's responsible for themselves,' I fel
that part of his sense of being tired and exhausted with the
world and man's inhumanity to man was that he imagined
or in some Jewish way, felt responsible. No matter how
much he did, it wasn't going to change things. And he
wanted to. That was the whole anachronism of this man.

"There were very trying times just before he died, both
politically and socially. Our leaders were all being shot
off. He was absolutely sure we were going to have another
Nazi Germany here. That's why he went off to Canada.

"He was sarcastic and flippant, true. But underneath
that all he cared so desperately."

And underneath all that there were Bernie Gunther
and Will Schutz.

"If I knew then what I know today," said Bernie, "I
would never have hung around him as much as I had.
Because there were times when he really put out bad
vibes. I was very admiring of him. And I don't think he
dug that very much. He knew I was there to get what I
could from him. But my trip has always been to try, if I
could, to give and take. In a lot of ways, in my relationship
to Fritz, I think I gave him a lot."

Fritz's disrespectful attitude must have been based, in
some measure, on disbelief. He could not accept Bernie's
true admiration in the face of his repeated rebuffs. Ber
nie's friendliness made Fritz increasingly uncomfortable
and led Fritz to view him with even greater contempt as a
"patsy."

"Our second falling out occurred at a workshop he was
giving at Esalen in which we started out very close. The
people in it wanted to learn massage, so he asked me to
teach it. And he offered to pay me a certain amount. It was
less than I was already getting from anybody else. I de
cided that I didn't want to work for the price he was offer
ing me, mainly because he was only going to pay me for
one hour and I was going to wind up working an hour and
a half or two hours in these sessions. I didn't want to do it
for less. He wanted to pay me $15 an hour and I was get

ing $25 from everybody else. So I said, 'Look. I want
twenty-five bucks for each massage session.' And he said,
'Well, I don't want to give you that much.'

" 'Okay. But I don't want to do it then. And that shut
him off totally. He looked at me and he said, 'Fuck you.
You're already getting three times as much as a major
craftsman would get—a carpenter or some kind of artisan.'
And I said, 'Fritz. I'm an artist. A therapist. Not a craftsman. And that's what I want.' And so he said, 'Forget it.'

"But there were very bad vibes that came from all that.
The people in the workshop were all disappointed. And I
put myself in a very bad emotional place because of it. I
was bothered that those vibrations were coming from him.
So I thought it over and I went up to him the next day and
I said, 'Look Fritz. In the interest of harmony and Esalen
and all that I'm willing to do it for the price you offered
me.' He looked at me and said, 'I thought you'd do that.
You always make compromises.'

"He was just very shitty about it. I really felt like saying 'Fuck you and forget the whole thing.' He and I were
never particularly close after that."

It must have galled Fritz all the more to find that by
1968 Bernie Gunther, his erstwhile lackey, was becoming more of a Superstar than Fritz. Bernie's book, *Sense
Relaxation*—a photographic guide to touching/feeling/mas-
saging—was running just behind Bill Schutz's book, *Joy*,
in terms of attracting people to Esalen. Was it right that
two brief books should give these men instant acclaim and
influence that Fritz, after decades of effort, had only begun
to achieve? And hadn't Schutz himself sat in on Fritz's
groups? And didn't he use many Gestalt techniques in his
encounter sessions?

The more popularity that befell Bill and Bernie, the
more Fritz resented them. What sort of cosmic injustice was
this that these people, thirty years his junior, should
garner such recognition for work which was so "superfi-
cial" and inferior to his own; that they would *upstage* him
in his hour of triumph?

"For a while," said Dick Price, "there was a publicit
sweepstakes. The main entries were Bill, Bernie, an
Fritz. And when they were off and running, Fritz came i
third."

Fritz's response was immediate, despite the fact tha
Bill and Bernie were among his top boosters (indeed, i
was Schutz who—even after his falling out with Fritz–
suggested that I work with the old Gestalt master). Frit
redirected his most caustic comments from Freud to th
"turner-oners" and tried to lessen their influence at the In
stitute. When it was clear that his campaign was making n
headway, he decided to establish his own center in Britis
Columbia.

Will Schutz is a soft spoken articulate man with brigh
eyes. His premature baldness, smooth-shaven skin, an
firm jaw make him appear cherubic and stern at one an
the same time. Bill's account of his relationship with Frit
was given with great thoughtfulness and, if anything, un
derstatement.

"I came to Esalen in sixty-seven. In preparing to come
here I asked all the people who were here who I woul
have something to do with—Virginia Satir, Berni
Gunther, Mike, Dick, and Fritz—how they'd feel about m
coming. Fritz was very warm and supportive. He said h
would like the idea very much, and he had told som
friends of mine how I was the most authentic person h
knew. It was a very good feeling that I had toward Fritz
And the first year was a very good year with him. We go
along well and more or less were allies against the es
tablishment. We would share a good deal of what woul
happen when we went out. He'd show me his newspape
clippings—how he was successful here and there. W
more or less amalgamated ourselves without differentia
tion as people who were more into *Here and Now* feel
ings, body oriented, and so forth—as opposed to 'Them.
There was a close alliance and that was nice. Not per
sonally close—I don't think Fritz had such relationships—
and ours wasn't intimate.

"Still, he would tell me about his life and loves sometimes, and I would tell him of some of mine. I never had
the feeling he was interested in my personal life, but we
would talk a great deal about professional matters. I would
invite him to my house for parties frequently, and my
image of him was always sitting in a corner while a party
was going on, hoping that somebody would come over and
talk to him and feeling quite uncomfortable at a party. And
really needing someone to pull him out and help him.

"But that was the first year. We essentially had two
years together. The first year was a good one and the second was pretty difficult. And mostly from his side. I didn't
feel that I wanted to be alienated from him. I wanted to be
closer and he wanted to push me aside.

"There was a television program—I think it was *California Girl*—that wanted to make a documentary of Esalen. They were out on deck over by the lodge and asked
me to run a group. So we just picked a few people who
were out on the deck. The edited tape would run on television for about three minutes. Fritz was there. He said
he'd like to be in my group. So after a few minutes we obviously had to confront each other, and we sat down in
front of the cameras and had about a ten-minute encounter, which essentially consisted of 'I would like to be
closer to you Fritz,' and he would push me away with 'No,'
or 'Not yet,' or something like that.

"I did that for six or eight months and finally got tired
of the whole thing and just wrote him off. I assumed it
would never happen between us and so I just became
civilized. I didn't try, any more, to get closer. It coincided
with the success of *Joy* and the fact that I was getting
more prominence. I can't say that's the reason, but the two
things did happen at about the same time."

In 1968, at the age of seventy-five, Fritz gave up both
'compulsive masturbation" and women. Spare hours that
were previously spent in sexual pleasure were now available for other pursuits, and one of these was the writing of
his own reflections, *In and Out the Garbage Pail*—a

book that might, hopefully, outrank those of his rivals
Fritz wrote the first few pages during a "workshop" visi
he made to Atlanta, at the home of Irma Lee Shepherd and
Joen Fagan, and, according to Irma, "He was just ecstatic
with his creation."

"He was writing *In and Out the Garbage Pail*," con
firms Ilana Rubenfeld, "during the second summer I wa
at Esalen. He'd come over with every chapter, like a kic
that had just made the biggest toy you had ever seen. He'
go from person to person, asking 'Would you read it and
tell me what you think?' And each one of us would g
through reading it.

"He'd sit at the table and read us the poems that he
was writing. He was just elated. We'd be very patient
After each one he'd read, you would say, 'Fritz, that really
sounds good.' And he'd say, 'You really like it?'

"One day he sat across from me and he grabbed a table
napkin and wrote the first poem that appears on the from
page of the book. I said, 'When you get that typed up, wil
you give me the napkin?' And he said 'Sure.' And he did
He signed the napkin and he gave it to me. He was really
into that book. It was quite a thing."

Mike Murphy, an articulate, clean-shaven, reflective
man in his mid-thirties, reminds one—in physical appear
ance—of the wholesome, amicable boy next door. How
does he remember Fritz's years at Big Sur?

"We had a distant relationship, and, frankly, I was re
lieved when he decided to go up to Canada and start his
Gestalt Center there. For he was a difficult guy for me to
be with.

"He saw me as the 'President' of Esalen and had a
campaign on to turn the place into his vision of what a
center should be. He was against mysticism and lobbied to
get those programs off our calendar. At the end he also
lobbied against Schutz and Gunther.

"He was one of the great phrase-makers and was so
very forceful that I had to sit through powerfully rendered

and creative prejudice whenever we met. So I tried to avoid him as best I could.

"He had this incredible gift of seeing into people and also had a strong sense of *how people should be*. One great game at Esalen is *Capture the Flag* (influence the program). And Fritz played it harder and better than anyone else. But his campaign against the 'turner-oners' made no headway with Dick [Price] and me.

"That was one of the reasons he decided to go to Canada. He wanted a place where he could make his own statement more fully. That, plus his fear of the coming repression. He was shaken by Nixon's election as President and Reagan's as the Governor of California—felt an indigenous American fascism on the rise. And then there was always his gypsy quality, his restlessness.

"There was a 'too muchness' quality to Fritz, at least for me. In the last year, after he decided to go to Cowichan, he was mellower, clear, and easy to be with."

Given rivals he couldn't come to terms with and an administration that he couldn't influence, Fritz had been casting about for a center of his own that he might direct—a Gestalt "kibbutz"—where participants would share *work* as well as stories and *labor* as well as receive therapy. By mirroring life more fully, whatever therapeutic feedback occurred ought to be more accurate for those who took part. He also saw it as a great training center for Gestalt Therapists, who might immerse themselves in Gestalt concepts for months at a time.

One property he considered was just outside of Albuquerque, New Mexico, where his son Steve lived, but for some reason or other it never materialized. After the elections of 1968 and his fear for our evolving body politic, Fritz opted for Canada. He bought an old motel on Lake Cowichan, Vancouver Island, British Columbia, at the end of 1968, and in late 1969—at the age of seventy-six—along with a nucleus of his coterie at Esalen, founded *The Gestalt Institute of Canada*.

12

Cowichan

With the establishment of Cowichan in June 1969, Fritz Perls had come full circle from lone wolf to kibbutznik Fritz, who was so insistent upon having people "do their own thing," established a center in which interdependence was essential and in which he, the prototypical Ayn Rand solitary hero, played paterfamilias to a community of others.

Although The Gestalt Institute of Canada ranked as the fulfillment and culmination of his life's work, he was not around very long to enjoy it. In December, six months after its founding, he was off on his annual European junket. He died the following March, before returning to his commune.

Cowichan itself is a small hamlet, not more than a block or two long but sporting its own gasoline station. A couple of motels and hotels constitute its main attractions. One of these was purchased by Fritz for a down payment of $12,000. Although not exactly in the wilderness, it was nonetheless distinctly off the beaten track.

To get there from San Francisco, you fly to Vancouver, on Canada's West Coast, take a ferry to Victoria (on Vancouver Island), a half-hour bus ride from Victoria to Duncan, and are met in Duncan by a car from the Institute.

which takes you on your final automobile and ferry jaunt to Cowichan. Down the road, a large sign announces "The Gestalt Institute of Canada."

The Institute had been an old fishing motel on Lake Cowichan and was best described as "ratty," "charming," "run-down," or "funky"—depending on one's attitude toward such places. There was the main house, which contained the dining room (which featured two long tables that the residents ate at), a kitchen, a living room, and a small vestibule where the one telephone was placed. The furniture was ancient, worn, and comfortable.

There were two rows of clapboard living units equally as old as the main house, each unit containing a room or two with toilets. A new building that quickly went up between them served as the community meeting place. From the main house, one could view the lake and watch the barges go by, carrying the logs cut by neighboring lumbermen. Upon its two and a half acres were a woodshed, trees, and lawn. A couple of pigs being raised on the property kept getting loose and had to be chased and repenned.

Fritz lived in one of the units beyond the new building, the Lord and Master of this rustic paradise.

At Esalen, many observers picked up a mood of pathos and loneliness surrounding Fritz. Will Schutz was not the only person to observe his lack of ease at social gatherings. John Brinley, for instance, noticed that on New Year's Eve, 1967, "when everybody else was celebrating, Fritz sat alone without a soul—not even staff—to keep him company." No such signals were picked up in Cowichan, for this was Fritz's turf—space in which he was surrounded by friends and admirers. No rivals existed who might divert the attention of those about.

"When my husband and I went to see him in Canada," said Ilana Rubenfeld, "and he walked down the lawn and saw us, he was like a King presiding over his Kingdom. He walked up to us smiling from ear to ear and said, 'This is my place.' And he looked it. He looked so happy, for this was his place. He was the big boss. And although he encouraged community voting and letting people decide what they were to do, he had the last word. He really did.

"That evening he took ten of us out for a big Chinese dinner and *he* asked for the check and he paid for it. We were all sitting there dumbfounded, our mouths agape. But he was in such a good space at the time that he just treated everybody to dinner."

Dick Price picked up the same regal impressions of Fritz at Cowichan: "I would see him walking in the morning at Cowichan like a King. He couldn't do it at Esalen. He had other people to contend with. But here there was no question of having to compete with Virginia Satir or Bernie Gunther or Bill Schutz or anybody else coming down the pike. And he had great satisfaction in being able to do what he felt was right."

Stella Resnick, a strikingly attractive, dark-haired young psychologist, came to Cowichan to study with Fritz shortly after the Institute started. Half coquette and half Jewish mother, she was attracted by Fritz's "commitment to himself rather than to anybody else, the sense that I'm more important to me than you are." For her, it was important to learn to satisfy herself, in Fritz's fashion, before she provided for others. Stella describes other facets of Fritz that were much in evidence at his new home: "Fritz was very happy at Cowichan and said that this was the happiest time of his life. He clowned around a lot. He used to enjoy sitting around, talking or playing chess, or pouring over his stamp collection in his room at night. He was very comfortable and felt loved and was very much in touch with his own love and caringness. He was so much less brittle than I had seen him before, at Esalen, and less lonely. He was being nourished and he was nourishing himself. This was very definitely his family."

The closest members of Fritz's "family" consisted of Teddy Lyon, Barry Stevens, and Janet Lederman. Others contributed their share. There was John Stonefield, a young psychiatrist who helped Fritz out, and Gerry Rothstein, who came to Canada two months before Fritz left for Europe and became a Director of the Institute after Fritz died. Along with these stalwarts, a bevy of credentialed people taking programs brought the resident population up to twenty-five to thirty-five at any given time.

All the communitarians, except for Fritz and Teddy Lyon, paid a fee while they were in residence. Part was allocated for tuition, part for board, part for room, and part for miscellaneous projects and various shares of the maintenance. If the community decided that they wanted to allocate more money for some particular project or other, they might, for instance, decide to save money on food. Those who shopped and those who cooked would then meet and see how they might prepare meals more inexpensively. Responsibility for running the Institute was thus turned back to its participants, fostering self-respect and creative grappling with options and dilemmas rather than getting into blaming some authority when things didn't satisfy them.

To say that Fritz was at Cowichan for six months is misleading, for he lived in Canada as he lived elsewhere, taking periodic weekend or weekly trips to other places, spreading the Gestalt word and hyping his new center. He planned to continue his association with Esalen. Dick Price was to lead preliminary month-long workshops in Gesalt Therapy there Fritz would come in during the final week and invite the most promising candidates back to Cowichan for more intensive training. The actual day-to-day management of the place was left to Teddy and Barry Stevens, his new secretary and a contemporary of Fritz's, in consultation with the rest of the participants.

I recall hearing Fritz at a lecture/demonstration he gave in New York, doing his best to arouse interest in the Institute.

"Come to Cowichan for three months," he said with the utmost belief and conviction. "In three months there I can cure any neurosis."

Cowichan revolved about shared work, Gestalt Therapy training sessions, and free-floating evening encounters in which appreciations and resentments were expressed. Fritz, Teddy, Barry, or week-long visitors like Esalen's Janet Lederman, author of *Anger and the Rocking Chair*, led the Gestalt sessions along with those participating in the training program. And everything that happened there was grist for the therapeutic mill.

"Fritz never believed in his therapeutic genius," according to Janet. "That's why he hungered for the recognition of others, why he wanted support. He found that support in the last few years and even gave up control of Cowichan. He felt it as too great a responsibility and left the management of it to others."

The contrast between Esalen Fritz, insisting upon imposing *his* philosophy at Big Sur, and Cowichan Fritz, allowing *others* to take over and mold the program, is not entirely accurate.

Granted, Fritz was mellower by far at Cowichan than he ever was elsewhere. But at Cowichan he surrounded himself with and attracted people who basically shared all his ideas. Thus, when he left the managing to others, these *others* were "spontaneously" running the place along the lines he might have dictated himself. He gave up detail control but retained veto power. He was in a position, by fiat, to make whatever rules he wished, like the stated rule of "No children; no dogs" and the unstated rule of "No rivals."

Cowichan is a spot that evokes universally gentle reminiscences of Fritz. Janet recalls his little boy excitement and glee as he anticipated a visit from Julian Silverman, an Esalen staffer and a beloved companion.

"Is he here yet? . . . Is he here?" Fritz would ask every ten minutes. When Julian finally did arrive, he stopped his group so as to fondly embrace and greet him.

Ilana remembers his childlike embarrassment.

"We once got him a chess set. I'll never forget when we handed it to him. He was like a kid. He tore open the wrapping and he went through the whole thing: 'Aw, you shouldn't have. You shouldn't have spent the money'—a whole trip. There were moments when he was just so simply human."

Stella Resnick recalled the affectionateness that radiated from this huggy, kissy, no longer sexual but "accepting" Ancient: "I wanted to be appreciated in a way my father never appreciated me. So Fritz was very important to me. He was the father that appreciated me. And what an impressive father to do so, both verbally and physically. He was constantly saying things to people about me, like how smart I was, how good I was, and what a jewel I was. And I loved that. I felt very nourished by his affectionateness."

Barry Stevens wrote her autobiographical *Don't Push the River* during the time she spent at Cowichan. It is written in the same free flowing stream of awareness *whatever-wants-to-be-written-will-be-written* style that characterized *Garbage Pail*.

She recalls how he decided, one day, to learn to fix his own breakfast and told her, "with humility and awe—that he had boiled his eggs perfectly that morning, without a clock."

She noticed how he had cut down, enormously, on his restless and constant smoking, how he ceased courting approval outside of groups, how he trusted others more and allowed them to handle the financial matters that concerned the Institute.

"Fritz is almost always a very warm and gentle old gentleman now. He spends more time chatting with people than he used to. He's much more patient."

When she told Fritz what she noticed of the changes in his work—of the increased softness, the increased compassion, and the absence of bitterness and spite—he said, "without pride or boasting, simply as a fact: 'Finally I am perfect. I have arrived. I can't do any better.' "

"For the first time in my life," he confided in her, "I am at peace. Not fighting with the world."

Fritz, in his travels, always went "tourist" or "second

class." But when he embarked on his final visit to Europe that winter he traveled, as befits a King, "first class." He seemed extremely tired as he prepared for that journey. Some attributed it to the energy he had expanded in founding Cowichan. Others thought he was somewhat under the weather or believed that at seventy-six, old age was finally catching up to him. Teddy had a premonition that he might never return.

He didn't.

13

The Journey's End

So let me be and die my way
A clearing house for people
A lonely bum who loves to joke
And think and play, and is all there.
Fritz

In the winter of 1969, a fatigued Fritz Perls went to Europe on what would be a farewell voyage to his usual haunts: the museums and opera houses of Vienna and Salzburg, Paris and Berlin.

Fritz had little faith in the ability of his medical cohorts and was not one to visit them. Yet in London, prior to his reembarkation for America, he decided to have a consultation for not only was he feeling weaker, he was running a fever as well. The diagnosis was Hong Kong flu, and Fritz was advised to drink plenty of fluids.

On returning to the United States in late February 1970, Fritz did a workshop for Cumbres, a New Hampshire growth center, another four-day program for The Associates for Human Resources in Concord, Massachusetts, and began a third one at Frank and Ilana Rubenfeld's home in New York. He planned to work his way across the country back to the Cowichan commune.

It did not happen that way, for his "flu" worsened.

By the time he got to Massachusetts, he was having bouts of nausea and diarrhea and was reduced to taking naps between sessions. In New York, he continued to deteriorate.

"Here at the house something strange happened," Ilana recalled. "All the lights went out during his work. And two hours later it happened again. Somehow, the lights just going out and seeing the way he looked gave me the feeling 'that was it,' that I'd never see him again. Lights just don't go on and off like that."

By the second day, the Rubenfelds were forced to cancel the remainder of the program, for Fritz felt too weak to continue. Laura was out on the West Coast doing workshops. Fritz went up to her empty apartment to rest, attended and visited by Frank, Ilana, and a few friends.

After a few days he determined to fly on to Chicago, where Bob Shapiro and Jane Levenberg, two charter members of another human potential center, Oasis, had arranged for him to give a public lecture and demonstration at the University of Illinois Medical School on Friday evening, March 6. It was another manifestation of the professional recognition that Fritz and Gestalt Therapy had started to receive, and he would not have willingly passed it up.

He was met at O'Hare Airport, in Chicago, by Jane at three in the afternoon. Noticeably jaundiced, he immediately and uncharacteristically asked to see a doctor. Jane transported him to Bob Shapiro's apartment, where he was to stay, and had a doctor friend come right up to see him.

After the examination, as the physician started to give his diagnosis, Fritz interrupted.

"I'll tell you what it is. I have cancer of the pancreas."

"You might be right," the doctor answered. "But it could also be hepatitis. That's still possible. Rather than guess, I'd prefer to put you in the hospital."

"Okay," said Fritz.

A call was made and a room reserved at Weiss Memorial Hospital.

Before leaving Bob's place, Fritz said: "I think I want to talk to Laura."

Bob phoned her at Elaine Kempner's home, where her

workshop was being held, introduced himself, and put Fritz on the phone.

"Laura, this is Fritz. I don't have good news. I am sick."

Her unspoken assumption must have been: "Why are you calling me? You must want me to come."

She answered: "Well I can't come right now. I'm doing a workshop. Where are you?"

"Shapiro's. But that's all right. I just wanted you to know."

"Well, I'll come Monday."

"I just wanted you to know," he repeated and hung up.

"I don't vant her to come," he shouted at no one in particular.

"So what the hell did you call her for?" asked Bob.

"I don't know."

"You're crazy. But you're entitled to be crazy. You're sick."

At 6:40, Jane Levenberg and another acquaintance, Bill Swartley, drove Fritz to the hospital. Bob Shapiro went over to the university to tell the seven hundred people assembled that Fritz was not well, had to go to the hospital, and would not be there that evening. Following the cancellation, he picked up a number of messages for Fritz and returned to the hospital in order to deliver them. His account of those last seven days follows:

> When I went back to Weiss Memorial Hospital that night he was still sitting up. He wouldn't lay down. He was quite a character in a hospital gown, smoking away. And he didn't want Jane and me to leave. So we stayed there until about ten or eleven o'clock. There was no testing that they could start, except that they started feeding him intravenously because he was completely dehydrated.
>
> The next day they started conducting a lot of tests. They continued to feed him intravenously and started giving him some plasma. Jane and I decided that we would have private nurses put on, which he didn't want, so he just kept firing them. At the end of two days we induced the night supervisor

of nursing, a beautiful woman, to attend him. We gave her a copy of the *Garbage Pail* and said, "Read this and you'll know who this guy is." She got into an instant appreciation and nobody could give him more tender, loving care.

Laura came flying in Monday night. By Wednesday, nothing was happening, in that his fever was still elevated. We called in a couple of more internists and a surgeon. Obviously something was going on beyond their ability to diagnose. They came to the conclusion that they would have to go into the abdomen and see what was occurring. None of the tests told them anything definitive and he was not responding to any of the drugs. So the three doctors, Fritz, Laura, Jane, and myself met. The one commitment we made to Fritz was that he wanted to know about everything that was going to happen. And that certainly was a commitment that I insisted on being respected.

The exciting thing is that even though he was given various kinds of sedation, he would move in and out of that stage of clouded consciousness anytime anything of significance occurred. Like in a good marijuana trip, he would come right up to his most astute sense of awareness and then he'd go back. So he came in and out at will.

Anyway, Wednesday, the doctor said, "The only thing we can suggest is to operate. And as soon as possible." Fritz said, "That's all right." So we set the operation up for Friday. By Thursday, his temperature went up and his respiration wasn't too good. There was the typical discussion between the surgeon and the internist as to whether you operate under these conditions. I said to them, "The man to make that decision is Fritz."

"Oh, well, he's in no condition to make the decision."

"Let's find out," I suggested.

And sure enough, he came back as lucid as you are. At that time he was very uncomfortable because they were feeding him medicines in one intravenous and fluids in another. They very carefully explained that "it was very possible to die during the operation and that you don't ordinarily operate. What we really should do is fight for the next two weeks to get your strength and lower your temperature. On the other hand, you're going downhill. If we ever operate and don't turn the tide, medically, you're never going to have as much strength as you're going to have right now."

He didn't hesitate a minute. He said, "We go tomorrow."

Tomorrow came. It was a long operation. The two biopsies they took during the operation both came back as negative.* Among other things he actually had stones in his gall bladder. They took him up at about eight o'clock in the morning and he came down about two o'clock. They also arranged—instead of sending him to intensive care—to make an intensive care unit in his room and thus preserve his privacy.

He had a tube in his nostrils and they opened his throat and he had a tube there and a glass tube up his ass and he was confined at that time by these two boards under his arms with all sorts of intravenous fluids running into him. He finally came awake and he said, "I'm nutin but a pincushion, and I don't vant to be here."

"Fritz," I said, "you know they're doing all this because they're trying to help you."

"Nah," he answered and then drifted back off.

His language was not easy to understand if you knew him, and the nurses had a terrible time understanding him. On Saturday morning, about ten o'clock, he said "I vant a bed pan." At that time they had the senior nurse of intensive care taking care of him. The girl leaned over and asked, "What did you say?"

"I vant a bed pan."

She apparently didn't hear or understand him. If you knew Fritz, you knew that he *never*, but never repeated. His basic principle was "People do hear," and that they hear even without the words if it's significant. So he lay there for about two minutes, then he kind of half sat up, and shouted: "I vant to shit!"

And she said, "Oh . . . just a minute."

We really cracked up. There was a lot of that going on. The day before, Laura, when they decided to operate, said: "Fritz. If they operate you should tell them about when you were in Miami and they gave you that anesthesia, and you had a very bad reaction. And they shouldn't give you that type of anesthesia."

And again, he came back into full bloom and he said "Laura. If . . . If . . . Should . . . Should! Mind-fucking. Won't you every learn? Stop this self-torture," and then he lapsed.

---

* An autopsy disclosed that Fritz did, indeed, have cancer of the pancreas, in a most advanced stage.

Anyway, at three o'clock that afternoon he fired another nurse. He said to me, "I don't vant her." So we switched nurses once more.

At about nine o'clock that evening, he kind of half got up with all this paraphernalia attached. The nurse said, "Dr. Perls. You'll have to lie down." He sort of went back down and then almost sat up and swung his legs out a bit. Again she said, "You must lie down."

He looked her right in the eye and he said, "Don't tell me what to do," fell back, and died.

I'm sure that he decided to leave his body, and he did. Very peacefully.

If Fritz died as he lived—teaching, joking, irritating, risk-taking—so did those who survived him continue true to their interrelationship with him.

For Paul Frey it was with love and mysticism.

On Saturday night, March 14, Paul, who hardly ever wrote letters, experienced the most uncanny, "far out thing in my whole life." He didn't know that Fritz was sick, let alone in Chicago, yet felt overwhelmingly compelled to write to him. "I was obsessed . . . forced to do it," and with a green felt-tipped pen he began:

Leibster [Dearest] Fritz—
Thank you for the fond *eriturum* [remembrance] in your book. I remember the times you used to visit . . .

He reminisced about the hours they had shared and closed by reminding Fritz

about the time you said "I'm just another Jew charlatan" and I said, "Yes. But you disarmed me with your cigarette smoke and your German accent and the fact that you come out of my soul, somehow."

He mailed the letter to Cowichan, whose address he had gotten from Ralph Metzner, a mutual friend. Shortly afterward he was to discover that the letter was penned within an hour or two of Fritz's demise.

For myself it was as a respected teacher.

During that final workshop Fritz gave in Concord, he had a bad case of the shivers. It was winter, the house was drafty, and Fritz thought he had the flu. I lent him my winter coat to wear indoors to keep him warm.

As the workshop drew to a close, I told him that I wished to give him a gift, a token of my esteem for what he taught. I offered him my "magic coin," but he told me he didn't believe in magic."

"I like your coat, though."

"I want to give you something," I said. "Take the coin or the coat."

"If you mean it," he answered, "I'll take the coat."

I returned to New York in my shirtsleeves.

After he died, I wanted the coat back in order to wear Fritz's mantle and to have something of his. The possessions he took to Chicago were sent back to Laura, yet I was reluctant to speak to her about it, fearing she'd feel my act was tasteless, like a scavenger bird who can't wait to tear the flesh from a dead carcass. I wondered what to do and I felt stuck. Then I decided to play it out Gestalt-wise. I set up an exercise in which I played myself and Fritz. First I told "Fritz" of my dilemma. Then, as Fritz, told myself: "Do what you feel like doing. It doesn't offend me. What do you care what Laura thinks?"

I spoke to Laura and got the coat.

For the Cowichan communitarians it was their desire to preserve their community as well as to accept their personal motivations.

"When Fritz died," reported Teddy Lyon, "there were all kinds of hassles at Lake Cowichan. People were willing to dip their fingers in the Fritz bank account and get what they thought they could for the institution. I very much disapproved of that and said I was going to tell if they did that. Someone said that Fritz was looking down and would approve of their using their wits to keep as much together for The Gestalt Institute of Canada as they could.

"I believe that what happened to the money would not have been foreground for Fritz. He wanted people to carry on his work and that was what he was training them for in the last year. And as far as I was concerned, being true to my own reality involves telling the truth, or at least not getting involved in that stupidity."

Laura wound up short-changed, as usual.

She did, of course, have Fritz back again, his ashes residing in a closet in her apartment. But it was a hollow homecoming.

Fritz died with over $300,000 squirreled away in dozens of banks in the United States and Canada, in sums ranging from a few hundred on up to $40,000 in each account. Earlier in their lives, while they lived together, he and Laura worked out an arrangement whereby she took care of day-to-day expenses and he was to put money aside for the future. Laura always assumed that this agreement was still in force, that when he died or they chose to work less, money would be available.

Except that Fritz stopped paying taxes in the late 1960s, refusing to support what he saw as the coming fascist state. Also, he left no will. Consequently, over 50 percent of his hoardings would be lost paying back taxes and penalties. Add to that attorney fees for dying intestate and for handling tax matters, further divisions of the estate among other claimants, and Laura was unable to look forward to the leisurely life she anticipated.

The New York Gestaltists continued to affirm that Fritz was not all that hot.

Laura asked her friend and confidant, Paul Goodman, to deliver the oration at funeral services held for Fritz in Manhattan. Paul repeated the comparatively belittling arguments that drove Fritz from New York in the first place. He began by indicating some measure of respect for Fritz's contributions but went on to say that Laura and Paul Weisz were the best therapists in the New York Gestalt group, that Fritz had deficiencies. And where the lack came, he felt, was that Fritz wasn't sufficiently intellectual. If anybody was the intellectual it was Laura.

Many in attendance, particularly those who knew Fritz from the West Coast, were outraged and felt that his testimony was in poor taste. Laura felt that such a reaction was typical of the "Fritzers."

Those in California who gave him appreciation in the last years of his life also gave him a most appreciative send-off.

At Esalen's San Francisco headquarters, over a hundred people who knew him divided themselves in groups of four or five, sat on the floor, and shared their personal experiences of Fritz.

Ann Halprin was asked to dance at his West Coast funeral services. She knew that she couldn't plan a score, because Fritz was against rehearsing. Instead, she stayed by herself for the three days preceding the funeral and thought about Fritz.

She selected a piece by Mahler, Fritz's favorite composer. When it came time to dance, she found herself asking for a minion—ten people who, among Jews, form a religious congregation and make a place sacred. Ann was very much in touch with Fritz's Jewishness.

She had the minion disorient her through a type of levitation and spinning around, following Fritz's dictum of "loose your mind and come to your senses." After loosing control through the tumbling, she had the image of being a bird on fire and danced the burning bird. It was, at one moment, a repeat of their initial meeting where she became the burning bush and the guardian angel together, where she and Fritz became one.

Then the dance changed. Out of her trance state, now, she looked at all the people in the room and danced with each separately, picking up their rhythms and integrating each with her own, starting with the members of the minion and extending to all the rest in attendance.

This, too, flowed from Fritz's emphasis, in life, that *balance* depended upon being able to go from contact with internal states to contact with the outside world. "So the dance that I did at his funeral reflected the most important experiences that I had with Fritz."

On March 28, two weeks after Fritz's passing, a reluctant Abe Levitsky was drafted to give a final oration for services held at The San Francisco Gestalt Institute:

> It's customary on such occasions to wish for the departed that he have eternal peace, that he rest in peace. But Fritz, that's the last thing I would ever pray for you. Eternal peace, resting in peace—that is for the dead.
>
> Let's face it, Fritz, we all have our shortcomings and playing dead is not your great virtue. For there was far too much life in you to be dead. So very much life, so much love, so much anger at phoniness and pretense, so much eagerness for battle, so much daring, so much shrewdness—and above all—how can we ever thank you enough for your courage and tenacity.
>
> Fritz, you were very definitely not a good boy, and frankly, it's a bit puzzling to know exactly where to send this farewell note. You could be most anywhere. I imagine that typically you are shuttling back and forth between both polarities. You wouldn't want to get stuck in either place.
>
> In any case, don't rest in peace. Make trouble; stir up a fuss. Make as big a fuss as you made with us. Of course, you'll hear a lot of squawks, but then as you yourself would say: when everyone truly does his own thing, the sparks are sure to fly. I bet you'll see a brand of sparks that you can really respect.
>
> Let's see now, this is Saturday night. Is it possible that tomorrow you start a new workshop—for superprofessionals only? The gossip is that some amazing people have signed up: Sigmund and Carl and Kurt and Wilhelm and Karen. Now there's a workshop for you. The kind no one has to lead. The kind in which it's an honor to take your rightful place among your gifted peers and enjoy. They'll listen with keen attention and respect to the new inventions, the new developments you bring them.
>
> How you thirsted for your place, your chapter in history. You have it now.
>
> We, gathered here tonight, appreciate that you were with us, that we met and touched each other. And we say to you, farewell, Fritz, and thank you for being.

14

Epilogue: The Work

I first met Fritz Perls in 1968, less than two years before his death, when I attended a demonstration that he gave of Gestalt Therapy in New York City. Like many others before me, I was dazzled by his clinical skills, impressed by his outspoken candor, appreciative of both his originality and his theoretical base, and intrigued by his "I don't give a damn what you think of me" attitude. Fritz performed his psychotherapeutic magic, in those days, in either one-day demonstrations or weekend, week-long, or month-long group workshops. I attended several of these programs before he died.

By then Fritz's reputation for extraordinary therapeutic skills preceded him wherever he went. If you can imagine the thrill of a groupie waiting to meet Mick Jagger or a commoner the Queen, of Woody Allen waking up in Sophia Loren's bed, you might just begin to appreciate the attraction that Fritz's hot seat had. To work with this bearded, brilliant, unpredictable, rascally old marvel offered the hope of nirvana, of cure, of coming to Lourdes on a stretcher and being able to leave by foot. It was akin to being touched by the blessed spirit.

It is a testimonial to Fritz's openmindedness that so many people in other disciplines deny him his originality and see him as merely imitating them. That is simply the result of his success in incorporating so many varied approaches. In the theater there was Max Reinhardt. In psychoanalysis there were Freud and Reich. In philosophy there were Smuts and Friedlander.

There was Arthur Ceppos, who taught him Dianetics; J. L. Moreno, who founded Psychodrama; Charlotte Selver and F. M. Alexander, who contributed to his knowledge of body awareness and body language; Lao Tse, the Chinese mystical poet whose works form the tenets of Taoism; Paul Weisz, who introduced him to Zen; Paul Goodman, who stood for honesty and the integration of one's personal and professional life. Traditional Gestaltists claim him because of his studying classical Gestalt Psychology in Frankfurt, with its appreciation of figure/ground relationships and its academic preoccupation with how things are perceived; because he married an academically trained Gestaltist; and because he called his new Concentration Therapy, Gestalt. As Fritz's Gestalt Therapy grew from a relatively unknown therapeutic school to one which now ranks second, perhaps, to the Freudian approach, and as psychoanalysts slowly begin to abandon their annonymity, even some Freudians have begun to declare Fritz in the mainstream of the psychoanalytic movement.

Fritz was willing to learn from anybody and anything. He claimed his cat, Mitzie, as one of his gurus. He learned from and adopted the technology of tape recordings and video tape, not only to record his work with others, but to play back these devices to see what he and others could learn from them.

Fritz once disrupted a lecture by the renowned psychologist Abraham Maslow by crawling on his belly, but he was there to check him out. Just as he checked out drugs, mystics, and wise men of all persuasions who crossed his path. He was psychoanalyzed, bio-energeticized, dianeticized, Alexanderized, Rolfed, psychedelicized, and spent several months in a Japanese Zen monastery. If he came away disillusioned much of the time, this might readily be seen to be the mark of a student who has pursued and experienced most of the areas of his interest and, in the process, rid himself of the illusion that any one particular program would lead to Salvation.

Fritz learned from life as well. From the school of life he learned what it meant when a parent doesn't love you and how people tend to perpetuate antagonistic relationships. He learned what it felt like to be an outsider and to be discriminated against. He learned heroism and pain in the trenches during World War I. And how to endure loneliness and isolation. From his mother he acquired an appreciation of art, beauty, and drama—an appreciation so strong that he perpetually strove to make living simultaneously artistic, dramatic, and exciting. If you take Fritz's childlike curiosity, add a great capacity to synthesize and integrate the ideas and techniques of others with his intuitive sense of life, and mix thoroughly, you will have discovered the recipe for Fritz's abilities as both a student and a teacher, for whatever he learned of value, he immediately passed on to others.

Paul Frey introduced Fritz to Hans Vaihinger. Fritz, in turn, passed on this knowledge in *Garbage Pail.*

Paul presented Fritz with a paper he wrote on this German philosopher, in which Paul discussed Vaihinger's idea that the curse of self-consciousness stems from the brain's having solved the basic problems of existence. Having little remaining biological function, it now ponders the imponderable *meanings* of life and the ineffable relationship between mind and matter.

"Naturally," wrote Vaihinger, "the human mind is tormented by this insoluble contradiction. But in intuition and in experience, all of this distress fades into nothingness. Experience and intuition are higher than all human reason.

"When I see a deer feeding in the forest, when I see a child at play, when I see a man at work, but above all, when I myself am working or playing, where are all the problems with which I had been torturing myself unnecessarily? We do not understand the world when we are pondering over its problems, but when we are doing the world's work."

Elaine Kempner and Lois Brean wrote a paper on "Phenomenological Behaviorism" for Irma Shepherd's book, *Gestalt Therapy Now.* They brought a copy of it to Fritz to read. Their argument was that internal events can also be considered behavior and that Gestalt Therapy consisted, essentially, of making the implicit (internal) behavior explicit. The next day Fritz delivered a paper in which he explained that Gestalt Therapy was actually "phenomenological behaviorism."

Just as Fritz learned from many people, he taught in a variety of ways.

He taught by perpetually analyzing people's roles and reactions—from the beaches of Provincetown, to the parties in New York, to Marjorie Van Dusen's living room in California.

He taught by proselytizing Gestalt: by trying to persuade Wilson Van Dusen to write a book for him; by attempting to get son Steve, daughter-in-law Rae, lover Marty Fromm, and rival Will Schutz to become Gestalt therapists; and by proclaiming a "three-month cure of neurosis" at Cowichan.

Yet, for all his hard sell, he encouraged people to find the answer within. There are no Perlsians, as there are Freudians. Although a very vivid personality, he abhorred the cult of personality. If you asked him too many questions he'd ask you to write a dialogue with your own "Fritz." And he'd warn you against healers, including himself.

"Beware of any helpers. Helpers are con men who promise something for nothing. They spoil you and keep you dependent and immature."

For Julian Beck, Judith Malina, and many, many others experimenting with different life and work styles, Fritz taught by "giving our experimentation a certain kind of license, a certain kind of leave, a certain kind of ground for playing that was very solid ground." He did this simply by appearing as an eminent man, a psychoanalyst who appreciated innovation and novel statements, thus allowing others to truly find their own way.

His remarkable gift for phrase-making also helped him as a teacher, for he could pungently remind us of certain universal truths. Among those that have hit home for me were the following:

On trying to get one-up on life:

> Actually we have it all wrong when we say we look forward to the future. The future is a void and we walk, so to say, blindly with our *backs* toward it. At best we see what we left behind.

On anxiety:

> Discomfort is always a symptom of dishonesty. If you don't express yourself honestly, you feel uncomfortable. The very moment you express yourself adequately, the discomfort goes.

On perfectionism:

> Friend, don't be a perfectionist. Perfectionism is a curse, and a strain. For you tremble lest you miss the bulls-eye. You are perfect if you let be.
>
> Friend, don't be afraid of mistakes. Mistakes are not sins. Mistakes are ways of doing something different, perhaps creatively new.
>
> Friend, don't be sorry for your mistakes. Be proud of them. You had the courage to give something of yourself.

On questions:

> You know the proverb, "One fool can ask more questions than a thousand wise men can answer." All the answers are given. Most questions are simply inventions to torture ourselves and other people. The way to develop your own intelligence is by changing every question into a statement. If you change your question into a statement, the background out of which the question arose opens up and the possibilities are found by the questioner himself.

Fritz taught by using his considerable intellect to demolish the glib explanations of the academic intellectuals.

In the early 1940s, he wrote in *Ego, Hunger and Aggression:*

> Intellectualism is a mental hypertrophy and by no means identical with intelligence, a fact which many people dislike admitting. It is an attitude designed to avoid being deeply moved.

Later, he would more pungently state that "Intellect is the whore of intelligence," or describe "the three classses of verbiage production as chickenshit . . . bullshit . . . and elephant shit."

Through his training groups, clinical work, and publications, his teachings were finally recognized by his peers. In the last two years of his life, the Outcast, along with Jim Simkin, were asked to talk on Gestalt Therapy before The American Psychiatric Association's annual meeting in Boston. Jim has heard Fritz describe this recognition, in glowing terms, as one of the biggest thrills in his life.

Ilana Rubenfeld was, to Fritz Perls, what Viva was for Andy Warhol. She was Fritz's Superstar—a participant in a workshop he gave at Esalen in the summer of 1967 that was recorded on video tape and later transferred to film.

The sequence with Ilana, edited into a short movie, showed Fritz and his Gestalt Therapy at their very best. Ilana performed the "patient's" role perfectly, profiting from the parts of her dream that she acted out. Fritz demonstrated his uncanny knack of directing her to role play just those elements that would help her grow and discover a fuller psychological self. And both of them had an interaction that was alternately wise, respectful, humorous, serious, tender, moving, and very, very real.

Fritz frequently showed this film at workshops and demonstrations that he conducted during the last years of his life. It invariably brought the house down and interested many a young psychotherapist to learn Gestalt technique. Ilana went on to become not only a friend of Fritz but a most competent Gestalt therapist in her own right. Concerning other Gestaltist's who have trained with Fritz, she had this to say: "It's interesting for me to see people who met him. I can tell when they met him—at what stage of his life he was at—because they latch on to a certain period of his life and they work like that. I feel lucky that I met him in the last four years because those four years were like a melting pot of many, many things. People of twenty years ago will say that he wasn't doing Gestalt in the last few years. Or that he was doing a different Gestalt. *He was a different Gestalt.* That was Gestalt.

"One workshop he was into contact/withdrawal. Everyone went up to the hot seat for contact/withdrawal. 'Okay. Close your eyes. Let yourself withdraw. . . . Open your eyes again and let yourself come back to the present.' At another workshop he was into body movement. So everybody exaggerated their body movement. It all depended on what thing he was experimenting with, what he was excited about, what was in the foreground for him. *That* was what was so beautiful about him. I never knew what he was going to do. I could go to one workshop after another with him. Yet, when you watched this man work, you saw that *he worked with every person from where they were.* That was the beauty of it. Other people pick up techniques and forget the essence. And the essence is to be aware of where the person is while you work with them."

Indeed, the most accurate statement that one can make about Fritz as a clinician is that his style continuously changed as he became fascinated by and integrated new techniques, which one must do if one lives in the Now. Fritz, echoing Marcus Aurelius, often said, "You never step into the same stream twice."

Most people interested in psychology came to know Fritz, as Ilana did, during his last four years, after he had achieved his fame and influence. In this final phase as a therapist, Fritz managed to find that halfway point between psychotherapy and theater. He had often talked about wanting to write, direct, and produce a play. Just as he told Ilana, an exconductor turned therapist, "You don't need an orchestra to be a conductor. You can make your own music," so did Fritz create his own theater. Fritz's brand of Gestalt Therapy could be seen as a drama where he, as director, would have the individual he worked with play all sorts of roles and parts, often building up to emotion-packed climaxes. It was, if nothing else, good theater. And, more often than not, good therapy, too.

His style of working at that time utilized two empty chairs. One was the *hot seat*, which you approached and sat in when you wished to work with him. The other chair was there to help you switch roles; the person on the hot seat moved over to it whenever he or she enacted different parts. Fritz sat alongside the hot seat. Had he lived longer, it is likely that there would have been a change in that style of work too. For *change* was Fritz's style.

In his work with others, Fritz focused on three things. These were *owning projections,* the *awareness continuum,* and *emotional involvement and interaction.*

Rashomon was one of his favorite films because it expressed, with great artisty, his knowledge of how much men project—how they see only what they wish to see, what is denied in themselves, or what their needs are. As Hari Dass Baba, an Indian sage wrote, "If a pickpocket meets a saint, he sees only his pockets."

Fritz had a theory that he invariably wished others to try on for size, namely, that whatever we believe about or see in another person or the world at large is invariably a projection. Thus, a statement such as "Nancy is a gossip" was to be rephrased as "I am a gossip." A complaint that "my shoulder is tense" might lead to a request that you *be* your shoulder, say "I am tense," and see if you might not explore the causes of and take responsibility for your tenseness. When one is playacting the people, things, or events they complain about, they have the possibility of having an "Aha!" experience, in which there is the recognition "This is me!" This is what is referred to as *owning projections.*

To be a whole person meant, to Fritz, that you had to reown all these fragmented, split off, denied parts of your personality. He was particularly fond of working toward this end by using dream material. With dreams it was harder for the person working with him to deny his or her projections. If a timid woman complains that her husband is a bully and *if he happens to be one*, she is not as likely to recognize a similar power within herself as she might by playing the Nazi that she dreamed about last night. Since the dreamer has clearly authored her own dream, Reality is not there to distract her from emotional truths.

In *Gestalt Therapy Verbatim*, he put it this way:

> I believe that every part of the dream is a part of your-self—not just the person, but every item, every mood, any-thing that comes across. My favorite example is this: A patient dreams he is leaving my office and goes to Central Park. And he goes across the bridle path, into the Park. So I ask him, "Now play the bridle path." He answers indignantly, "*What?* And let everybody shit and crap on me?" You see, he really got the identification. I let the patient play all these parts, because only by really playing can you get the full identifica-tion, and the identification is the counteraction to the *alien-ation. Alienation* means "That's not me, that's something else, something strange, something not belonging to me."

Fritz was also acutely aware of how people project their power onto the therapist, how they see him as wise, all-knowing, and competent to solve their problems. Un-like the classical psychoanalyst, who is content to sit in silence and allow his patients this illusion, Fritz did all in his power to discourage it, for he knew that self-con-fidence grew only out of self-directed actions. Again, he used his projection technique.

In this instance, Max, a participant in one of Fritz's groups, began to work on a dream. Before he got to it, however, Fritz had him identify with the tenseness in his body. After some minutes of this, Max asked: "Could I go ahead with the dream?"

"Ask Fritz," Fritz responded. "Put Fritz in that empty chair and ask him."

Max (talking to an empty chair): "Fritz, could I go

ahead with the dream? . . ." (He switches to the empty chair and answers back as Fritz): "You decide for yourself."

After doing some useful work on his dream, in which Max is asked to continue to direct the inquiry by playacting the therapist, Fritz closed with these remarks:

> Well you see this is what I'm concerned with. I, *this* Fritz can't go home with you. You can't have me as a permanent therapist. But you can get your own personalized Fritz and take *this* along with you. And he knows *much* more than I do because he's your creation. I can only guess or theorize or interpret what you're experiencing. I can see the scratch, but I cannot feel the itch. I'm not in you and I'm not arrogant enough to be a psychoanalyst and say that I know what you experience, what you feel. But if you understand the idea of this purely personal Fritz, you can get yourself a chair, couch or whatever you have, and whenever you're in trouble go and talk to this imaginary Fritz.

A fuller example of his work with projections may be seen in this excerpt (which, like the others in this chapter, are taken from a Dream Work Seminar he gave at the Esalen Institute and are recorded in the book *Gestalt Therapy Verbatim*). Meg is a woman who reports a nightmare in which there are a number of rattlesnakes—one on a platform she is sitting on and another near a dog that lies below. As in all his work with dreams, Fritz asks her to recall the dream not as a past event, but as something that is occuring in the *here and now*, so that she might experience it anew, with all its attendant fears, in present time.

> F: So, up here is one rattlesnake and down below is another rattlesnake and the dog.
> M. And the dog is sort of sniffing at the rattlesnake. He's—ah—getting very close to the rattlesnake, sort of playing with it, and I wanna stop—stop him from doing that.
> F: Tell him.
> M: Dog, stop! /F: Louder./
> *Stop!* /F: Louder./
> (shouts) STOP! /F: Louder./
> (screams) *STOP!*

F: Does the dog stop?

M: He's looking at me. Now he's gone back to the snake. Now—now, the snake's sort of coiling up around the dog, and the dog's lying down, and—and the snake's coiling around the dog, and the dog looks very happy.

F: Ah! Now have an encounter between the dog and the rattlesnake.

M: You want me to play them?

F: Both. Sure. This is your dream. Every part is a part of yourself.

M: I'm the dog. (hesitantly) Huh. Hello, rattlesnake. It sort of feels good with you wrapped around me.

F: Look at the audience. Say this to somebody in the audience.

M: (laughs gently) Hello, snake. It feels good to have you wrapped around me.

F: Close your eyes. Enter your body. What do you experience physically?

M: I'm trembling. Tensing.

F: Let this develop. Allow yourself to tremble and get your feelings . . . (her whole body begins to move a little) Yah. Let it happen. Can you dance it? Get up and dance it. Let your eyes open, just so that you stay in touch with your body, with what you want to express physically . . . Yah . . . (she walks, trembling and jerkily, almost staggering) Now dance, rattlesnake . . . (she moves slowly and sinuously graceful) . . . How does it feel to be a rattlesnake now? . . .

M: It's—sort of—slowly—quite—quite aware, of anything getting too close.

F: Hm?

M: Quite aware of not letting anything get too close, ready to strike.

F: Say this to us. "If you come too close, I—"

M: If you come too close, I will *strike back!*

F: Say this with your whole body.

M: If you come too close, I will *strike back!*

F: How are your legs? I experience you as being somewhat wobbly.

M: Yeah.

F: That you don't really take a stand.

M: Yes. I feel I'm . . . kind of, in between being very strong and—if I let go, they're going to turn to rubber.

F: Okeh, let them turn to rubber. (her knees bend and wobble) Again . . . Now try out how strong they are. Try out—hit the floor. Do anything. (she stamps several times with one foot) Yah, now the other. (stamps other foot) Now let them turn to rubber again. (she lets knees bend again) More difficult now, isn't it?

M: Yeah.

F: Now say again the sentence, "If you come too close—" . . . (she makes an effort) . . . (laughter) . . .

M: If—if you . . .

F: Okeh, change. Say "Come close." (laughter)

M: Come close.

F: How do you feel now?

M: Warm.

F: You feel somewhat more real?

M: Yeah.

F: Okeh . . . So what we did is we took away some of the fear of being in touch. So, from now on, she'll be a bit more in touch.

You see how you can use *everything* in a dream. If you are pursued by an ogre in a dream, and you *become* the ogre, the nightmare disappears. You re-own the energy that is invested in the demon. Then the power of the ogre is no longer outside, alienated, but inside where you can use it.

This excerpt with Meg also illustrates the *awareness continuum* aspect of Fritz's work. On at least seven occasions, Fritz directs her attention to what is going on either inside or outside of her.

"Look at the audience. . . . Enter your body. What do you experience physically? . . . Allow yourself to tremble and get your feelings. . . . Now dance, rattlesnake. . . . How does it feel to be a rattlesnake now? . . . How are your legs? I experience you as being somewhat wobbly. . . . Okeh, let them turn to rubber. . . . How do you feel now?"

Such directed attention is not meant to serve any end nor intended to produce any insight. It is, instead, an end in itself, for it produces a fuller awareness of the present moment. At times, in his groups, Fritz would suggest endless go-arounds, where participants would fill in the blanks to statements such as "Now I am aware of _____," "Now I see _____," or "Now I feel _____."

There is much in this that is akin to training in Zen meditation and similar, as well, to the experience of the Eternal Present that some people first arrive at through the use of psychedelic drugs. In either state, one is not only fully aware of the moment, but aware, as well, that it changes and flows from moment to moment as surely as the water in a brook. This is a unique experience for people who have trouble living in the *Now* or who foolishly seek to hang on to one moment, pinning it, like a butterfly, instead of letting go and flowing to the next event.

The third quality that Fritz brought to his work with others was *emotional involvement and interaction.*

In the spring of 1968, Fritz came to New York to lead a workshop for professionals. At one point, he put down a well-known psychologist by making a motion with his hands to indicate that she was chattering without making any sense. Being treated so disdainfully in front of her peers apparently got to her, although she said nothing at the time. John Brinley, another therapist who participated in that session recalls it in this way: "She was furious. She was going to get back at him and she did. At the end of the session she sat next to him, was teasing him and, inadvertently at some point, began to pull his beard rather roughly. So he lashed out and really smacked her. Left and right. Everybody was completely paralyzed. Finally, someone screamed 'Stop,' and jumped in. But it seemed an eternity."

Involvement was not, however, always so harsh. I recall another professional group that I attended in New York, in the spring of 1969. Asya Kadis, an elderly psychologist, was working with Fritz. Her mood was depressed, her foot in a cast, and she resented not being able to get up and around. She was not accepting her great age and infirmity. Her "should" system was operating full force, and her hurt and futility resulted from her not fulfilling her expectations.

"I can't get it up," she said, referring to her broken leg.

"I know just how you feel," said Fritz, one septuagenarian to another, his arm reaching out tenderly to make contact. "That's the price of old age. Lately, when I find myself in bed with a willing woman, I feel the same thing. I can't get it up either."

It was enough to lighten her mood for the moment.

Often, the emotionality came from Fritz's no-nonsense approach and his great candor. Lloyd Aleksandr, who runs a center in Syria, Virginia, tells of attending The Association for Humanistic Psychology's annual convention in Washington, D.C., in 1969. Fritz was giving a demonstration of Gestalt Therapy before, perhaps, some 5,000 people. A woman walked on stage, sat in the hot seat, and was engaged, rather informally and kindly, by Fritz.

He asked her name, where she was from, and her age. She disregarded the last question.

"Oh, so you're going to play that game, eh?" he retorted.

"I'm sorry. I didn't hear you. Will you repeat what you asked?"

"You repeat it," Fritz said.

"I didn't hear you," she answered.

"Either stop playing games with me or get off the stage," he retorted angrily.

The woman broke into tears. She protested her innocence and talked about illnesses she had suffered as a child, hearing problems that she had, and operations on her ears. People in the audience was aghast at the apparent cruelty and insensitivity of the fabled Fritz.

"I have heard nothing but lies for the last several minutes. Now either repeat what I asked of you or get out of here," he added, glaring at her all the while. "I don't work with liars."

The sobs stopped, there was a pause, and the woman, in a soft voice, repeated word for word Fritz's original question.

As with the coy lady, the following work with Beverly packs emotional wallop through Fritz's simply giving feedback—reflecting the person back to herself and telling her things that her psychoanalyst wouldn't. Here it is done with playful humor. Again, one can see how he works with the awareness continuum, trying to make Beverly aware not only of the role she plays in the moment but aware of those about her and of her own inner experiences:

Beverly: I guess I'm supposed to say something. I don't have any interesting dreams. Mine are sort of patent.

Fritz: Are you aware that you're defensive? . . . I didn't ask you in only to bring dreams.

B: You asked for them last night and I was afraid that would disqualify me. If I could manufacture a few . . .

F: Now you have a very interesting posture. The left leg supports the right leg, the right leg supports the right hand, the right hand supports the left hand.

B: Yeah. It gives me something to hang onto. And with a lot of people out there you kind of get some stage fright. There are so many of them.

F: You have stage fright and there are people outside. In other words you're on stage.

B: Yeah, I suppose I feel that way.

F: Well, what about getting in touch with your audience . .

B: Well they look very good. They have wonderful faces.

F: Tell this to them.

B: You have very warm faces, very interested, very interesting . . . with—with a lot of warmth.

F: So then shuttle back to your stage fright. What do you experience now?

B: I don't have any more stage fright. But my husband doesn't look at me.

F: So go back to your husband.

B: You're the only one that looks self-conscious. Nobody else looks self-conscious at me. (laughter) You sort of feel like you're up here, don't you? Or sort of like your youngster's up here? . . . No?

X: (from audience, yells) Answer!

Husband: She's the one who's up there and she's trying to place me up there.

F: (to husband) Yah. You've got to answer. (to Beverly) You have to know what I feel.

B: Well he doesn't usually answer. Did you want him out of character? (much laughter)

F: So, you are a clobberer.

B: You need an ashtray.

F: "I need an ashtray." (Fritz holds up his ashtray) She knows what *I* need. (laughter)

B: Oh, no—you have one. (laughter)

F: Now *I* get stage fright. (laughter) I always have difficulties in dealing with "Jewish mothers." (laughter)

B: Don't you like "Jewish mothers"?

F: Oh, I love them. Especially their matzo-ball soup. (laughter)

B: I'm not a gastronomical Jewish mother, just a Jewish mother. (chuckles) I don't like gefilte fish either. I guess I'm a pretty obvious Jewish mother. Well that's not bad to be. That's all right. Matter of fact, that's good to be.

F: What are your hands doing?

B: Well, my thumbnails are pulling at each other.

F: What are they doing to each other?

B: Just playing. I do this often. See, I don't smoke, so what else are you gonna do with your hands. It doesn't look good to suck your thumbs.

F: That's also the Jewish mother. She has reasons for everything. (laughter)

B: (jokingly) And if I don't have one I'll make one up. (chuckles) The ordered universe. What's wrong with being a Jewish mother?

F: Did I say there's something wrong with a Jewish mother? I only say *I* have difficulties in dealing with them.

There is a famous story of a man who was such an excellent swordsman that he could hit even a raindrop, and when it was raining he used his sword instead of an umbrella. (laughter) Now there are also intellectual and behavioristic swordsmen, who in answer to every question, statement, or whatever, hit it back. So whatever you do, immediately you are castrated or knocked out with some kind of reply—playing stupid or poor-me or whatever the games are. She's perfect.

B: I never realized that.

F: You see? Again the sword. Playing stupid. I want once more to restate what I said earlier. Maturation is the transcendence from environmental support to self-support. The neurotic, instead of mobilizing his own resources, puts all his energy into manipulating the environment for support. And what you do is again and again manipulate me, you manipulate your husband, you manipulate everybody to come to the rescue of the "damsel in distress."

B: How did I manipulate you?

F: You see, again. This question, for instance. This is very important for maturation—change your questions to statements. Every question is a hook, and I would say that the majority of your questions are inventions to torture yourself and torture others. But if you change the question to a statement, you open up a lot of your background. This is one of the best means to develop a good intelligence. So change your question to a statement.

B: Well, th—that implies that, ah, there's a fault to me. Didn't you intend it so? . . .

F: Put Fritz in that chair and ask him that question.

B: Don't you like Jewish mothers? Did you have one that you didn't like?

F: Well, I like them. They're just a very difficult lot to deal with.

B: Well, what makes them so difficult?

F: Well, they're very dogmatic and very opinionated and inflexible and the box that they construct for themselves to grow in is a little narrower than many. They're less easy to therapize.

B: Does everybody have to be subject to your therapy?

F: No. (laughter)

B: (to Fritz) Did you ever switch chairs like this with yourself?

F: (laughing) Oh yes—*Oh!* Even *I* get sucked in! (laughter)

B: You said you had problems with Jewish mothers. (laughter)

Husband: Do you understand now why I didn't answer? (laughter and applause)

F: That's right, because you see how a Jewish mother doesn't say "You shouldn't smoke so much." She says, "You need an ashtray." (laughter) Okeh. Thank you.

Fritz would not pander to weakness. One recurrent theme of his was that "a question is the hook of a demand." Refusing to answer most questions, he insisted, instead, that they be rephrased as the statements that they usually were. In the process, the rephraser retook his power and began to appreciate his question as a disguised and inauthentic way of making a comment.

Fritz saw his role as a skillful frustrator, helping the patient to find his own support instead of looking toward and manipulating the environment for support, or, as he more colloquially put it, "to wipe his own ass." It was through his gruffness and unhelpfulness that many of those who worked with him came to realize their own ·self-sufficiency.

"He was a wisely cruel man at times," recalled Alan Watts, philosopher, Orientalist, and fellow Esalen guru. "I remember one evening when there was a woman from the neighborhood who was in extreme distress because of her son's troubles. She was very drunk. I was sitting with her and talking to her and I turned to Fritz and explained the situation. He looked at her with almost complete contempt and turned away.

"But he was wisely, in this sense, harsh at times. Because he had no false compassion. He wouldn't be put upon. He understood the principle that false compassion is bad for the people to whom you give it. It does them no service. It simply increases their dependency and doesn't set them free. And so, for that reason, many people considered him a harsh man."

Arthur Ceppos, his publisher and friend, who saw Fritz evolve from analyst to legend, saw his clinical skills in this way: "I think that Fritz's greatest contribution was his horror at how ridiculous man permits himself to become; and by becoming aware of how ridiculous he is, he can emerge into an identity that is no longer ridiculous, but is relatively free. This is the whole secret behind Fritz's hot seat. He would show people how they made fools of themselves."

And what about his contempt for needy people who would take the hot seat wanting to do no more than suck his teat? "Well," continued Ceppos, "this is connected with the dignity thing. He felt that a human being should be dignified and that they shouldn't try to suckle somebody else's tit that way. Oh, a woman's tit? That's a different thing. This is for his own pleasure."

Fritz's work was constantly marked by his simultaneous attempt to illuminate and destroy people's characters, so as to open them up and enable them to react to life, to go with life's flow instead of being locked in to stereo-typed one-note roles—be they moralists, optimists, cry-babies, nice guys, or grouches. Just as consistent was his unwillingness to endure pretense. Some people would take his hot seat to work on real problems. Others seemed to invent problems just to get close to him. With this sec-ond group he invariably reacted harshly, giving them just enough rope so as to expose both the phoniness of their complaints and the degree of their dependency—their de-sire to suckle some magic nourishment from him.

The only authentic non-problem-oriented occupation of the hot seat I know of occurred a few weeks before Fritz died. He was giving a four-day workshop for The Associ-ates for Human Resources, a growth center in Concord, Massachusetts. It was the last complete program he was to conduct.

On the third morning, Lee Geltman, a bright young psychologist who looked and talked like a young Ted Ken-nedy, walked up to the hot seat and sat down. He looked at Fritz; Fritz looked at him. Fritz nodded; Lee nodded. Both men turned to face their audience. As the silence continued there were periodic demands from people in the group that Lee should say something or return to his seat. He did nothing of the kind. He didn't even answer.

Finally, one, then two members of the group, express-ing the frustrations of many who desired to see a more dra-matic and engaging show, stood up and threatened to drag Lee from the seat. I arose, positioned myself in front of Lee, and told them that they'd have to get rid of me before they removed him. I understood how Lee felt. I had watched Fritz work on several occasions by then, wanted to experience his hot seat, yet never had because I knew I had no dilemmas to work with. And here was Lee, expres-sing that same sentiment, in a direct, responsible, dig-nified, and honest way.

Fritz was amused and accepting of the entire situation.

Certain repetitive criticisms of Fritz as a clinician bear

examining, for they describe, with some accuracy, I believe, both the man and his style: that "he simply was indulgent, giving in to what was convenient"; that "he had no patience for the daily, ongoing work of psychotherapy and so evolved the workshop technique, where he could be on stage all the time, help you get to the core of your difficulty very fast, but left you hanging as to what you were going to do about it"; that "he used the brief workshop as a way of maintaining his own uninvolvement"; and that "he was competitive with other men; was a lot easier, therapeutically, on needy women than he was on needy men—particularly if the woman was young and attractive."

And yet, all these criticisms contain aspects that are positive, for Fritz set a standard that others might well adopt. His "indulgence" can be seen as a shameless commitment to do that which pleased *him*, not *others*. His impatience with "the long arduous task of psychotherapy" might be related to his teaching people that they actually have their own answers. That's what his "take-home-a-Fritz-doll-to-advise-you" idea was about.

The most telling critique of Fritz's work came from Will Schutz.

"I don't like all those labels he used: 'You are a Tragedy Queen. . . . You are a Bear Trapper.' It's like calling a kid clumsy. You give people labels which then pin them. It's a lot like diagnosis in psychotherapy. 'You are a Paranoid Schizophrenic.' It dehumanizes and puts you into a category. It also makes it seem that you are like all the others in that category."

Fritz did have a way with phrase-making. Without doubt, this descriptive name-calling can make it harder to change, for if you are that way, you'll never overcome it unless you can learn to accept it, unless you can laugh at it. If you have a horrible label applied to certain ways of relating, you can't accept where you are at and then go on to other things. Instead, you go underground and figure out another way to hide your attitude.

The polar and often conflicting elements in Fritz's life and work have left their mark upon the psychology that he promulgated. Gestalt Therapy thus contains its own contradictions. Some of these are inherent in any therapeutic school, while others create a richness and despair unique to Gestalt Therapy. The major Gestalt paradox centers on its insistence that you tune in to your own inner truth and follow it wherever it leads you. It is the same message that Emerson proclaimed, and, in contradistinction to other thinking within our society, it reflects a polarity similar to that which existed between Taoism and Confucianism in ancient China.

Those in accord with Lao Tse assumed that nature knew best and that people, freed from rules and conventions, would more naturally achieve a harmonious integration with the world and with each other. Confucious and his followers presumed the opposite: that a body of laws, rules, and social etiquette were necessary to govern men's intereactions and produce a better society.

Where the ambiguity arises is that Gestalt, for all its Taoist and Emersonian allegiance, contains within it its own set of "shoulds," its own unwritten but ever-present prescriptions.

Some detractors, who considered Fritz Perls to be a man with few or no values, have misjudged him. He valued highly such notions as "follow your impulses, not your thoughts," "favor your Underdog, not your Topdog." And he had his own set of *shoulds*. People *should* be free and impulsive like him; they *shouldn't* be uptight or defensive; and they *should* be willing to go into and explore whatever their craziness consists of. Another contradiction in the Gestalt movement involves the issue of accredited versus nonaccredited therapists; the credentialed opposed to the lay therapists. This issue arose directly from the split within Fritz himself regarding respectability and bohemianism.

Fritz aspired first to be a professor at Yale, later at Columbia, and finally at Georgia State University. He wound up teaching, instead, at unaccredited human potential centers such as Esalen, Chicago's Oasis, and The Associates for Human Resources in Concord, Massachusetts.

The larger professional recognition Fritz always sought eluded him until the very end of his life. Along the way, he made do with what was available, picking up uncredentialed converts in droves. The result has caused both an unevenness and excitement in the Gestalt school. Many free spirits who may have spent a weekend with Fritz or read his books have, with impunity, billed themselves as Gestalt therapists. On the other hand, Gestalt has allowed any number of terribly creative and innovative people to become excellent practicing therapists in spite of not having had more formal training. California's Harry Sloan, a former dentist, and New York's Ilana Rubenfeld, a former conductor, are, like Chicago's Diane Berghoff Reifler, among the most capable Gestalt therapists I have witnessed. Each follows the Gestalt essentials of working with projections and the awareness continuum and of fostering emotional experiences. Yet, each works in his or her inimitable style.

This question of style was Fritz's final legacy to Gestalt Therapy. In spite of his believing in unique therapists working with unique individuals, many Gestaltists have imprinted him whole, setting up a situation best described by Abe Levitsky: "Scorn was a weapon he used, and, unfortunately, I feel that scorn has been incorporated by many Gestalt therapists and been perpetuated. But that has nothing to do with Gestalt Therapy. It simply had to do with Fritz's irascability, where his style is imitated instead of his message.

"He had a favorite story about analysis that applies to him as well. There was an American teacup manufacturer who designed a particular teacup, but it would have been too expensive to have it manufactured here in the States. So he sent it to Japan to have it mass-produced. In transit, the handle was broken. The Japanese, being perfect imitators, mass-produced it with the handle being broken in just that particular way. Well, according to Fritz, Freud had a phobia about facing people, so he solved the problem by having his patients look at the wall. And ever since, psychoanalysts have been copying that broken teacup handle in just that kind of way.

"I suppose that any great leader makes his mark on people in all kinds of ways, both the pluses and the minuses. And some of Fritz's minuses have also rubbed off on a lot of Gestalt therapists."

Fritz's liabilities, real as they were, seem unimportant when placed on a ledger alongside of his assets. In a way, these very shortcomings are what gave the man character, drama, and humanness. Imperfections, boldly accepted, are the truest acceptance of the human condition. "If Fritz can live with, and be unashamed of his warts," many have silently concluded, "then I needn't pretend that mine aren't there nor need I get caught up in the never-ending struggle to be perfect."

This shameless willingness to be more than a projection screen and to share himself as he was, including his ugliness, accounted for his greater beauty. That, along with his willingness to teach by example.

He taught courage by holding to his convictions and, with sufficient skill and tenacity, finally getting a hostile and indifferent psychiatric world to give him a fair and important hearing.

He taught people that it was all right to put *their* needs first, because he would invariably put *his* desires first. He permitted, by his example, honest self-interest and self-expression, as opposed to unhappy martyrdom, false compassion, or tortured retroflected accusations of selfishness.

All of us, if we could write the script for our own lives, would invariably create ourselves as perfect beings. Failing to achieve this ideal state we are left with three choices. We can berate ourselves for falling short of our goal, we can pretend to be better than we are, or we can honestly be ourselves.

It is to Fritz's credit that he stood for the last alternative. There was no disparity between his life and his message. Freud might preach the power of sexuality and aggression, but in his personal life he was relatively asexual and controlled. Harry Stack Sullivan would stress the importance of interpersonal relationships, but his were impoverished. Eastern holy men and Catholic clergy might eulogize a life of poverty and deprivation. But many of them live in glittering religious retreats and never want for anything. An American president can extol the virtues of law and order, yet be more corrupt than the average criminal.

Fritz taught that you should be who you are: "You do your thing and I'll do mine." And he lived that way.

He was, for me, a perfect animal—not in a low but in a high sense. He could be nasty or funny, crude or kind, lewd or loving, cheap or extravagant, *and he didn't bother to hide any of it.* He encompassed as broad a range of emotions and responses as anyone I have ever met, the "negative" as well as the "positive" ones.

Fritz wanted to be the world's first "real man." Irma Shepherd, as chairman of the Psychotherapy Committee, Georgia State University, had offered Fritz a three-month visiting professorship there in 1970. He looked forward to going, to demonstrating both his skills and the full force and many faces of his persona.

"This spring I will go and be on the campus of Georgia State College and show them what a psychiatrist and a man can be."

Death cancelled the demonstration.

Suggested Reading

Fagan, Joen, and Shepherd, Irma L., eds. *Gestalt Therapy Now*. Palo Alto: Science and Behavior Books, 1970.

Freud, Sigmund. *Basic Writings of Sigmund Freud*. New York: Modern Library.

Fromm, Erich. *Escape from Freedom*. New York: Holt, Rinehart & Winston, 1941.

Goldstein, Kurt. *Human Nature in the Light of Psychopathology*. New York: Schocken Books, 1963.

Goodman, Paul. *Growing Up Absurd*. New York: Random House, 1960.

Gunther, Bernard. *Sense Relaxation: Below Your Mind*. New York: Macmillan, 1968.

Horney, Karen. *New Ways in Psychoanalysis*. New York: Norton, 1939.

Jones, Ernest. *The Life and Works of Sigmund Freud*. 3 vols. New York: Basic Books, 1953.

Kohler, Wolfgang. *Gestalt Psychology*. New York: Liveright, 1970.

Laing, R. D. *The Politics of Experience*. New York: Pantheon, 1967.

Latner, Joel. *The Gestalt Therapy Book*. New York: Julian Press, 1973.

Lederman, Janet. *Anger and the Rocking Chair: Gestalt Awareness with Children*. New York: McGraw-Hill, 1969.

Lewin, Kurt. *Dynamic Theory of Personality*. New York: McGraw-Hill, 1935.

Lin Yutang. *The Wisdom of of Laotse*. New York: Random House, 1948.

Lowen, Alexander. *Betrayal of the Body.* New York: Macmillan, 1966.

Perls, Frederick S. *Ego, Hunger and Aggression.* London: George Allen and Unwin, 1947. New York: Random House, 1969.

―――. *Gestalt Therapy Verbatim.* Moab, Utah: Real People Press, 1969.

――. *In and Out the Garbage Pail.* Moab, Utah: Real People Press, 1969.

Perls, Frederick S., Hefferline, Ralph, and Goodman, Paul. *Gestalt Therapy.* New York: Brunner/Mazel, 1973.

Perls, Fritz. *The Gestalt Approach and Eyewitness to Therapy.* Palo Alto: Science and Behavior Books, 1973.

Polster, Erving, and Polster, Miriam. *Gestalt Therapy Integrated.* New York: Brunner/Mazel, 1973.

Ram Dass. *Be Here Now.* San Cristobal, N.M.: Lama Foundation, 1971.

Reich, Wilhelm. *Character Analysis.* Translated by Vincent R. Carfagno. New York: Farrar, Straus & Giroux, 1972.

Schutz, William C. *Joy: Expanding Human Awareness.* New York: Grove Press, 1967.

Shepard, Martin. *A Psychiatrist's Head.* New York: Peter H. Wyden, 1972.

Stevens, Barry. *Don't Push the River.* Moab, Utah: Real People Press, 1970.

Stevens, John O. *Awareness: Exploring, Experimenting, Experiencing.* Moab, Utah: Real People Press, 1971.

Thompson, Clara M., and Mullahy, Patrick. *Psychoanalysis: Evolution and Development.* New York: Grove Press, 1957.

Watts, Alan. *Psychotherapy East and West.* New York: Pantheon, 1961.

Index